The Otherworld Awaits You

This uniquely Celtic tarot system was born from the meditations of a High Priestess as she sat upon a green Irish hilltop. With its blend of traditional tarot and faery imagery, the *Faery Wicca Tarot* is a unique tool for divination and Otherworld journeying. Each card represents an aspect of human relationships: with self, others, the planet, or with spirit. When you are ready to weave the lessons of all the cards together, your spiritual journey into the Land of Faery will begin.

Clarity, wisdom and a heart-stirring Irish beauty are captured within the rich symbology of the *Faery Wicca Tarot*. Meditate upon these cards to unlock the knowledge of the Otherworld. Surrender to spirit and prepare to be reborn in the living shamanic tradition of Faery Wicca.

About the Author

Kisma K. Stepanich was born July 4, 1958, in Santa Ana, California. She is a traditionally Initiated Ollamh (elder priestess) of the Irish Faery-Faith Tradition, and a priestess-Hierophant and Dame Commander of the Noble Order of Tara, in the Fellowship of Isis, Clonegal Castle, Enniscorthy, Ireland. She has authored five other books, including the popular series, *Faery Wicca, Book One* and *Faery Wicca, Book Two*.

Visit Kisma's website at: http://www.faerywicca.com.

For information on her world-wide organization, The Faery-Faith Network, send a self-addressed, stamped envelope to:

The Faery-Faith Network
849 Almar Avenue, Suite C-268
Santa Cruz, CA 95060

How to Write to the Author

If you wish to contact the author or would like more information about this book, please write to the author in care of Llewellyn Worldwide and we will forward your request. Both the author and the publisher appreciate hearing from you and learning of your enjoyment of this book and how it has helped you. Llewellyn Worldwide cannot guarantee that every letter written to the author can be answered, but all will be forwarded. Please write to:

Kisma K. Stepanich
c/o Llewellyn Worldwide
P.O. Box 64383, Dept. K696-3
St. Paul, MN 55164-0383, U.S.A.

Please enclose a self-addressed, stamped envelope for reply, or $1.00 to cover costs. If outside U.S.A., enclose international postal reply coupon.

The Ancient Oral Tradition of Ireland

FAERY WICCA
TAROT

Kisma K. Stepanich

illustrated by Renée Christine Yates

1998
Llewellyn Publications
St. Paul, Minnesota 55164-0383

FIRST EDITION
First Printing, 1998

Cover design by Anne Marie Garrison
Cover art by Renée Christine Yates
Card illustrations by Renée Christine Yates
Book editing and layout by Astrid Sandell

Library of Congress Cataloging-in-Publication Data
Stepanich, Kisma K.
    Faery wicca tarot / Kisma K. Stepanich ; illustrated by Renee
Christine Yates. — 1st ed.
       p.   cm.
    "The ancient oral tradition of Ireland."
    Includes bibliographical references and index.
    ISBN 1-56718-696-3 (pbk.)
    1. Tarot. I. Title.
  BF1879.T2S745   1998
  133.3'2424—dc21   97-52373
                                            CIP

Publisher's Note:
Llewellyn Worldwide does not participate in, endorse, or have any authority or responsibility concerning private business transactions between our authors and the public.
    All mail addressed to the author is forwarded but the publisher cannot, unless specifically instructed by the author, give out an address or phone number.

Llewellyn Publications
A Division of Llewellyn Worldwide, Ltd.
P.O. Box 64383, Dept. K696-3, St. Paul, MN 55164-0383

Printed in U.S.A.

Other Books by Kisma K. Stepanich

Faery Wicca, Book One: Theory and Magick: A Book of Shadows and Light
Faery Wicca, Book Two: The Shamanic Practices of the Cunning Arts
Sister Moon Lodge: The Power and Mystery of Menstruation
The Gaia Tradition: Celebrating the Earth in Her Seasons
An Act of Woman Power (Whitford Press, a division of Schiffer
   Publishing, Ltd., 1989)

Forthcoming

The Last Matriarch (fiction)

Dedication

For the Darling of my Life—
My son,
Tristan Shane.
Goddess and God bless you
and keep you safe from harm!

Acknowledgments

Faery Wicca Tarot was made possible by the following people, for whom I am eternally grateful. May you know the depth of my gratitude, and trust that I cherish you all dearly.

Renée Yates, whose gracious Spirit allowed little self to step aside and become my inspired hand! Thank you so much for making my vision a reality. May all your dreams come true.

Sandi Sauer, whose endless devotion to Goddess, and dedication to this project added the special touches to the book's pages in the form of figures! And to the dearest friend I have ever had!

Debbie and Hal, and our midnight club that use to meet at the first stroke of the witching hour beneath the Jesus picture in the hallway when mom and dad went out on the town—you are part of this vision.

Evellyn Brown, Yancey Malloy, and Mary Greer, all of whom have taught and shared with me their tarot wisdoms.

The Honorable Olivia Robertson, my most cherished teacher.

All the students and graduates of my Spiritual School of Tarot.

Mom and dad, especially you dad, for always wanting to know when it was going to be published, and for being open to all my psychic inclinations as a little girl. This one's for our Gypsy blood dad!

Mr. Carl Llewellyn Weschcke, *El Presidente*, and Nancy Mostad of Llewellyn. Thank you both for believing in and supporting this project. A warm blessing and thanks to my editor, Astrid Sandell, as well as art director Lynne Menturweck and Senior Graphic Designer Anne Marie Garrison.

Jack, my heart-trobe, who tolerated all the late hours I spent at the computer away from you and our lovely son—I couldn't have done it without you, honey.

Contents

Part One
The Faery Ring
The Element Cards 7

Part Two
The Mists of Dūn na m-Barc:
The helper Cards 135

Part Three
The Land of Faery:
The Ancient Ones Cards

Part Four
Integration

Tables

Diagrams and Spreads

Introduction

In an age so distant that the age is unknown, the world was inhabited by gods, and the lands and oceans were divided amongst them. One tiny piece of land, a very rich and magickal piece of land, became known as Eire, and was ruled by a goddess named Brigid and three gods of Dana: Brian and Iuchar and Iucharba—the three druids from whom the Tuatha De Danann are named.

In Irish mythology, the Tuatha De Danann are the gods and goddesses of ancient Ireland. They arrived on the Emerald Isle on the first day of May. "In this wise they came, in dark clouds. They landed on the mountains of Commaicne Rein in Connachta, and they brought a darkness over the sun for three days and three nights."[1]

In the Irish Faery Tradition it is believed the De Dananns came from the OtherWorld, the Heavenly Realm. There were four cities where they acquired knowledge and science, prophecy and magic, until they were expert in the arts of pagan cunning. The four cities are: Falais, Gorias, Findias, and Muirias.

From Falais was brought the Lia Fail, which is in Temair, and which used to utter a cry under every king that should take Ireland. From Gorias was brought the spear which Lugh had; battle would never go against him who had it in hand. In his travels, Lugh journeyed into the fire, taking up proprietorship in the southern cross of Ireland. Eventually, his spear was passed to the Dagda, and removed from this world, to be kept under the protection of the gods in the UnderWorld, until such a time when it could be returned to the Plains, into the worthy hands of a wielder of enlightenment.

From Findias was brought the sword of Nuadu: no man could escape from it; when it was drawn from its battle-scabbard, there was no resisting it. In his travels, Nuadu journeyed into the eastern light, where he took up providence as a Commander of the Noble Order of Tara, where, ever since, he has fought in earnest to keep the sword of victory sheathed: "For the unhappy knight who cannot sheathe the Sword lives in perpetual warfare and so the fruits of victory are destroyed."[2]

From Muirias was brought the cauldron of the Dagda; no company would go from it dissatisfied. Today, this cauldron is commonly referred to as the Holy Grail.

Each of the four cities of the Heavenly Realm had a sage: Morfesa, who was in Falais, Esrus in Gorias, Usicias in Findias, and Semias in Muirias. These are the four poets from whom the Tuatha De Danann acquired their knowledge and science, wizardry, and magick. In Ireland this knowledge and science, wizardry, and magick evolved into the Bardic College.

The *Faery Wicca Tarot* cards are based on the De Dananns' ancient Bardic system of understanding the universe (i.e., the OtherWorld, Land of Faery, and the UnderWorld), which today might be considered the shamanic tradition or roots of the Irish Faery-Faith, a pre-Christian, pre-Celtic spiritual tradition. The cards contain a unique system that nicely blends traditional tarot images with the mystical symbology of modern Faery Wicca. I make this ancient wisdom accessible by integrating the Tuatha De Danann shamanic skills or teachings of the pagan cunning arts with meditative practices, bringing forth the knowledge of the Four Great Cities of the OtherWorld into the light of our everyday modern living.

While to read tarot cards one need not be a psychic, there are important times when deeper meaning is required by the reader. Such insights are gleaned through intuition—the Spiritual Intelligence of the Gods. Bringing such insights through requires the art of the psychic, an art easily attained through use of the *Faery Wicca Tarot*; for each card contains a Bardic teaching designed to awaken greater psychic perception.

The Faery-Faith Theory

There are three distinct realms or dimensions in which the *Faery Wicca Tarot* cards are placed. The first realm, casually referred to as the OtherWorld, is the Heavenly Realm. This is the realm from where the Tuatha De Danann originated. It is above our universe, of which our world or universe often reflects bits and pieces.

The second realm is the Plains—this world, and to Faery-Faith practitioners it is specifically thought of as Eiré: Ireland (i.e., the heart center of our planet). In this realm the De Danann once dwelled, and at such a time a thin veil of mist shrouded the earth. This was a magickal mist, a doorway through which the gods could easily slip into their magickal or alternate reality, and one in which we humans would often magickally find ourselves from time to time. In the Plains dwell the astral elements and elementals, dragons and wizards, sorcerers and priestesses of the gods, but as humankind developed and began to separate itself from the gods and magick, the Plains and all its magickal creatures began to recede farther into the mists. In time the gods frowned upon our world and removed themselves from it by closing the doorway and moving into yet another realm of existence—the third realm or the UnderWorld.

In the UnderWorld is found a glimpse of the ancient primal land to which our planet is aligned and which the earth can be a reflection of, if humankind were to remain sensitive and open to the natural world. But most importantly in the UnderWorld now dwell the Tuatha De Danann, or the remaining few who have chosen to retain a connection to earth's creatures with hope of assisting our continual evolutionary process, of which we are only a fragment.

The wisdom of the Ancestors is also housed in the UnderWorld; this containing the memory of the Bardic College to which the *Faery Wicca Tarot* is aligned.

This three-tiered universe is best illustrated on the Tree of Trees diagram (figure 1, page 4). Each card has a placement on the great tree in one of five places: the tree top, the branches, the center of the trunk, the roots, or the jewels of the UnderWorld, located at the root tips.

The Tree of Tree rests on the crown of Dūn na m-Barc—the Holy Mountain; which we must first climb in order to reach the great tree. Each face of the mountain is connected to an element suit, and each suit's lesson is presented in its Ace through 10 cards.

The crown of the Holy Mountain is connected to the Helper Cards of each suit—more commonly known as the court cards. The Helper Cards connect us to the Tree of Trees through which we enter the realm of the Ancient Ones cards (the trump cards), and to which all cards in the deck are connected. While this system may at first appear

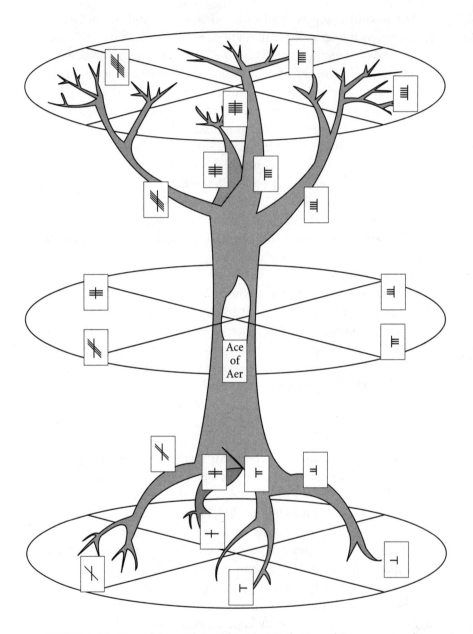

FIGURE 1. *The Tree of Trees. Ohgam placement on the Tree of Trees corresponding to the Otherworld or Heavenly Realm (top circle), the Plains (traditionally thought of as Eiré, the middle circle), and the Underworld. (lower circle).*

complicated, it is relatively simple, as will be elucidated in each section of this book, particularly in Part 3.

Faery Wicca Tarot is divided into four groupings of cards, totaling 83 cards—five of which are specific to this deck. All cards are based on the Irish Faery Tradition. The four groupings are as follows:

The 40 Element Cards: composed of the four suits: Domhan (earth), Aer (air), Tine (fire), and Uisce (water), or traditionally known as pentacles, swords, wands, and cups, respectively.

The 16 Helper Cards: composed of each suit's Ainnir (maiden), Ridire (knight), Ard Rí (High King), and Banríon (High Queen) cards, traditionally known as the court cards.

The 22 Ancient Ones cards: traditionally known as the major arcana cards, the trump cards, or the greater secrets.

The One Power Card: known as the Tree of Life card, which is classified as an Ancient Ones card, and is unique to this deck.

The Four Gift of Faery Cards: the Crane Bag, the Apple Branch, the Hazel Wand, and the Holy Stone, which are unique to this deck.

Creation of the Cards

The inspiration for designing and creating the *Faery Wicca Tarot* deck came directly from the Mother God of the Tuatha De Danann—Dana. She appeared to me early one morning as I sat in a stone circle a-top the Witches' Hill in Loughcrew, Co. Kells, Ireland, in July of 1994. I was shown very clearly that each of the four element suits were to be oriented to the Four Great Cities of the OtherWorld, and I was shown the design for the Tree of Life Power card, upon which all the cards would be located. Each of the Four Gifts of Faery cards, each a sacred object to be received by the Faery while making the Spirit Walk, were fantastically clear, almost materializing before my eyes.

The design of each card was received during meditation, after which I drew a penciled mock-up of the image. This drawing, containing complete detail, was given to illustrator Renée Yates, who would then pencil a first draft. After review, if all looked well, I gave her the go-ahead to draft the card in pen. This draft I scrutinized, making sure that all necessary symbols and other details were in place. After one final look-over, Renée was given the green light to paint the card, adding her unique talent of bringing the illustration to life.

This process took two years of uninterrupted time to complete. Dana's blessing is upon these cards! I hope you enjoy the magickal world of the Tuatha De Danann through the *Faery Wicca Tarot*.

Part One
The Faery Ring:
The Element Cards

Tuatha De Danann

LXII.

1. The Tuatha De Danann of the rich treasures,
   Where got they learning?
   They reached sound wisdom
   In druidry. . . .

4. Four cities-rightful fame—
   they took in a course with great strength;
   pleasantly would they wage a combat
   for learning, for true knowledge.

5. Falias, and clean Gorias,
   Findias, Muirias of great acts of valour;
   a rough instructor of their outbursts (were)
   the names of the lofty cities.

6. Morfhis and Erus lofty
   Usicias, Semias continually rough;
   before a calling of mentions of their palace
   the names of the sages of every free palace.

7. Morfhis the poet (in) Falias itself,
   Esrus in Gorias good as to disposition,
   Semias in Muirias, a fortress of sword-points,
   Uscias the white poet (in) Findias.

8. Four gifts with them from yonder
   had the nobles of the Tuatha De Danann;
   a sword, a stone, a cauldron of bondmaids,
   a spear of the fate of lofty champions.

9. Lia Fail from Falias yonder,
   which used to cry under the kings of Ireland;
   the sword of Lugh's hand which came
   from Gorias, choice, very hard.

10. From Findias far over sea
    was brought the spear of Lug who was not insignificant:
    from Muirias, a huge great treasure,
    the cauldron of The Dagda of lofty deeds. . . .

—Lebor Gabala Erenn
Vol. XLI, Part IV, Section VII

Dūn na m-barc: The holy Mountain

The teachings found in the Element Cards—the minor arcana, Ace to 10—focus on the lessons experienced in mundane or everyday life. These lessons are presented as a "spirit walk." As the spirit walk begins, we are standing at the foot of Dūn na m-Barc, the Holy Mountain. Each face of the mountain is connected to an aspect of ancestral wisdom and spiritual evolution that the Tuatha De Danann learned in the Four Great Cities of the OtherWorld.

In Irish mythology Dūn na m-Barc—translated as The Fortress of the Ships—in Corco Buibne is the location where Cessair's ark on her Ararat landed preceding the actual advent of Noah's Flood.

We begin our spirit walk by climbing the Holy Mountain one step at a time, learning to explore the four elements of our lives: mind, ego, emotions, and body. In the east we enter the landscape of the mind and meet the first holy element: Aer. The sword—Nuada's dividing sword, or the Sword of Illumination—is a sacred talisman of the Faery-Faith, as well as the key to Gorias, the first great city.

The suit of Aer represents the mind and the attitudes we hold in life. Emphasis is placed on learning to balance this masculine energy by centering it and to begin "feeling" with the mind. The ancestral wisdom of Aer reminds us that life experiences, whether of a supportive or problematic nature, happen in pairs. If we can experience happiness, somewhere in our lives we will experience sadness; love-hate, success-failure, birth-death, gain-loss. By understanding this basic nature of life, then we learn how not to "lose our heads" to any given situation, but remain calm and centered.

The suit of Aer is identified by the Feather, representing the weighing of mind and heart.

The second face of the Holy Mountain is the lesson of Tine (Fire). Here we enter the landscape of ego and willpower. The second talisman encountered, the wand—symbolic of Lamhfada's spear—is the key to the second great city, Findias. The suit of Tine represents willpower and ego, or little self; it places emphasis on the masks we wear and how we use our power. This suit teaches the ancestral wisdom of awareness of our control issues, learning how to find balance between ego and Sacred Self, warning against using excessive control, and warning against surrendering our personal power.

The suit of Tine is represented by the symbol of the Candle, the inner radiant light of Spirit within each of us.

On the west face of the Holy Mountain we enter the landscape of the heart, connecting with the lesson of Uisce (water). The cauldron—the In Dagda Mor's cauldron of plenty—is the talisman key to the third great city, Muirias. Uisce represents the emotional body, the feminine element directed toward the heart center and relationships. The ancestral wisdom taught here is to learn to "think" with the heart, to achieve emotional balance, and to move into sacred relationship with self first, then with others.

The suit of Uisce is represented by the Chalice—the Holy Grail—which is the symbol for the feminine principle in life, or the heart and soul of creation.

Lastly, the fourth side of the Holy Mountain is the suit of Domhan (earth), the landscape of instinct—the body, containing the coin, or "faery gold." In this landscape we find entrance into the fourth great city—Falias. The suit of Domhan embraces the lessons of the three other Elements by merging them in the ancestral wisdom of cycles. Here we learn the natural law of giving and receiving, moving into a mode of abundance, one based on nature rather than extreme materialism. Through the natural laws of this physical realm, issues surrounding prosperity and poverty consciousness are explored; respect toward nature and our natural resources are emphasized. We are reminded to get back in touch with the primal land.

Although this would traditionally be the suit connected to the Lia Fail talisman—the Stone of Destiny—I have reserved the Stone for use in the Ancient Ones cards, which will be explained in depth with the Athair Dia Dagda card.

The suit of Domhan is represented by the Bone of Peace, reminding us that immortality is ours if we can get past our clinging need to the material world.

The Wheel of the Year

To understand the Holy Mountain better, let us look at it as if it were a wheel connected to the seasonal year. In figure 2 (page 11), we see a circle divided into four parts. Each part is connected to one of the cardinal directions: east, south, north, or west. Each Element suit has a place on this wheel connecting it to a cardinal point of energy.

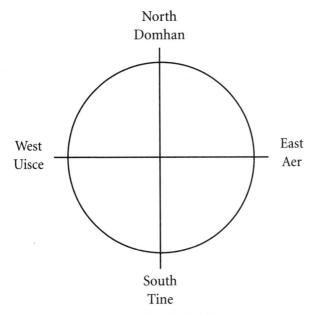

FIGURE 2. *The Wheel of the Year.*

In the east we have the element suit of Aer; in the south we have the Element suit of Tine; in the west we have the Element suit of Uisce, and in the north we have the Element suit of Domhan.

Correspondences

On the next page is a basic Table of Correspondences for Element Cards that can be memorized and applied to each suit. Correspondences are very helpful because they give additional material to draw from when giving a reading. For example, if you wanted to know when an event might take place, the Ace of each suit could be used to determine the season—Aer Ace would be spring, Tine Ace would be summer, Uisce Ace would be autumn, and Domhan Ace would be winter.

A predominance of Tine cards in a reading could give an indication as to something happening around midday, with Aer cards indicating early morning, Uisce cards indicating evening, and Domhan cards indicating night.

Correspondences add depth to a reading. They become food for the mind, prompting deeper psychic attunement.

Table of Correspondences: The Element Cards

QUARTER	ELEMENT	SEASON	TIME OF DAY/NIGHT	GENDER	ENERGY	COLOR	SUIT
east	air	spring	dawn	masculine	mental	yellow (white or green)	Aer (swords, feather)
south	fire	summer	midday	masculine supported by feminine	ego, desire, willpower	red (orange)	Tine (wands, candle)
west	water	autumn	twilight	feminine	emotional	blue (purple, gray, or black)	Uisce (cauldrons) (chalice)
north	earth	winter	midnight	feminine supported by masculine	physical	green (white, brown, or black)	Domhan (pentacles) (bone)

The Elements and Gender

The Element Cards contain the lesser secrets of the Tuatha De Danann. These secrets represent the physical world of action, human consciousness, or the consciousness of the lunar sphere.

As already discussed, each suit is connected with an element, and it is the element that plays a very important role in looking at the gender of the suit.

In the east, the suit of Aer (the element of air) is masculine, and in the west the suit of Uisce (the element of water) is feminine. Here we find the duality of the Element Cards, the extremes. In the south the suit of Tine (the element of fire) is considered to be masculine supported by feminine, while in the north the suit of Domhan (the element of earth) is feminine supported by masculine. With these two suits we have a sense of polarity and balance.

While the gender qualities of the Element Cards are significant, it is very important that we remember the four suits are the signs of the elements and that it is the elements that are the most important factor as we look at the individual suits. In ancient times the four elements represented the only possible means of disposing the physical body when the time to vacate it and to move on occurred. The ancients believed that the four elements consumed our physical bodies by taking them back into an elemental state. It is the four elements that congeal and produce the physical body; we begin to remember that it is out of the four elements we come and it is back into the four elements we go, which is the foundation of the philosophy of the minor arcana.

The only way to learn to live this life is to willingly experience challenges. Spirit challenges our weaknesses so they can be turned into strengths. This is the most basic teaching found in the Element Cards.

The Energy Value of Each Card

Traditionally, there are 56 minor arcana cards—the Ace through Ten, plus the four Helper Cards. Esoterically, 56 was known as the god number, the masculine energy, the active energy, and the force of the creation principle.

The 56 is the vibration of the natal number of the Celtic sun god, who was known as the son of Tara, the Earth Mother. His aura shot out fourteen feet in all directions from his head (the rays went out evenly into the four directions).

When the fourteen minor cards of each Element suit (Ace through Ten and the Helper Cards) are laid out in each of the cardinal directions—east, south, west, and north—we see the design of the Celtic Cross, which also represents the energy vibration of the number 56. Thus, the number of the solar god becomes grounded into the earth plain.

The design of the minor arcana, the lesser secrets, the 56 vibration, the male number, then becomes representative of the phallic or the fertilization gods, activating the masculine principle of the life force both here in the physical world of action and within the conscious mind.

It is important to take into consideration that each card in each suit represents a particular aspect of human consciousness or experience. In each of the Element suits, the Ones (Aces) contain many of the same properties, the Twos are similar, as are the Threes, and so on, through to the Tens.

When the 56 concept of energy vibration is applied to the Element Suits it is represented through the numerological vibration of each card's number first and foremost, then through each card's astrological affiliation.

Numerology

The science of numerology is based on harmonious vibration. Understanding numerology is to find the inner harmony that will enable each of us to vibrate at an equal pace with the vibration of our planet Earth.

The world travels at a rapid rate. Scientists have noted that the vibration of the Earth increases at the rate of one hour a week, which means our inner vibrations will also continually shift.

We are all affected by the vibrations that govern the universe, for we are all a part of it. As a part of the whole we are affected by every change in the universal rate of vibration—and the rate changes every time a different number appears in year, month, or day—or in the case of tarot, with every card.

The universal vibration is like a stage set for a play. We may read the whole play, but we memorize only the lines in our own role. Numerology helps us to work with these natural vibrations rather than against them.

When the science of numerology is applied to the tarot cards, the number that governs the card gives deeper insight into the hidden meaning of the card and can be used as an additional correspondence—an important action for our role in the play.

The following is an easy reference for the basic constructive value of the numbers One through Nine.

One: Creation, originality, independence, courage, progress, ambition, positiveness, will power, leadership, pioneering, activity, force, raw energy.

Two: Love, service, gentleness, harmony, adaptability, charm, diplomacy, friendliness, rhythm, music, receptivity, cooperation, consideration for others, will, purpose, initial understanding.

Three: Artistic expression, joy of living, freedom from worry, optimism, inspiration, talent, imagination, good taste, sociability, friendliness, kindness, conception, beginning manifestation.

Four: Practicality, service, patience, exactitude, organization, application, devotion, patriotism, conservatism, pragmatism, dignity, economy, trust, worthiness, endurance, loyalty, production, mastery.

Five: Freedom, progress, versatility, understanding, variety, adaptability, mental curiosity, life experience, cleverness, unattachment, sociability, change, discord, travel, adventure, companionability, surrender, release.

Six: Love, harmony, home, responsibility, adjustment, musical talent, sympathy, understanding, domesticity, guardianship, stability, poise, protection, healing, firmness, balance, idealism, conscientiousness, justice, burden-fearing, service to All, solution, exaltation, seeing.

Seven: Mental analysis, technicality, introspection, peace, poise, scientific research, spirituality, faith, trust, stoicism, refinement, wisdom, silence, "theories and fundamentals," feeling, deepening, mystery.

Eight: Power, authority, success, material freedom, judgment, discrimination, executive ability, organization, leadership, management, practicality, thoroughness, dependability, self-reliance, control, the power to succeed, repose, consideration, retreat, ripening.

Nine: Universal love, sisterhood, brotherhood, charity, compassion, the Higher Law, artistic genius, selfless service, philanthropy, humanitarianism, magnetism, sympathy, understanding, romance, generosity, breadth of viewpoint, understanding before or beyond words, strengthening.

Each number's "key words" can be applied to the meaning of a tarot card when the number of the card seems to stand out prominently to you, which would then have a significant interpretation in the spread.

The application of numerology to the Element suits can be taken a step further. Figure 3 presents the science of numerology in mathematical symbols and graph form. The mathematical or geometrical symbols tell the story of how numbers evolve, whereas the graph expresses the energy movement of numerology.

Geometric Evolution of Energy

Aces are the number 1; they are a starting point, the beginning, a sharp point, a sharp focus. They have no specific identify at the starting point other than being representative of the raw energy of each Element suit. Raw energy is neither good nor bad, positive nor negative—it's simply the beginning point. The suit element guides the raw power of its ace. The application of the raw energy will depend on the surrounding cards in a spread.

The ace divides; it becomes polarized as the 2, it's moving out from itself, developing on a conceptual level, on an idea level. The 2 becomes dimensional as the 3, and it is now getting ready to be birthed.

The 4 is the square; it brings stability and manifestation, representing developing boundaries. This energy moves into 5, which is shifting, changing, releasing, possibly destroying itself so that as it builds into the 6 it restabilizes itself.

As 6, the energy becomes connected to solution, possibly seeing them. The 6 is a numerical vibration of regrowth. Moving into the 7, the energy becomes more complex. It deepens and could be developing the solutions that were provided in the 6. Most importantly, 7 frees as it goes up into 8, where there is further development, more growth.

However, the energy is also connected to the qualities of response or ripening and possibly the hint of retreat.

The 9 moves into the highest point of every development, moving into possibly the strengthening of the full understanding of the development.

The energy of the 10 is a new plane or a threshold, it's a new level of experience, it's the 1 or Ace taking us back to the beginning. A 10 is a reflection of the ace at a new level of experience. As above, so below. The 10 and Ace are reflections of each other.

To enhance this picture, the meaning of the numbers can be outlined as follows:

1. raw power
2. will, purpose, initial understanding
3. conception, manifestation
4. production, mastery, clinging to achievement
5. surrender, release, destruction
6. solution, exaltation, seeing
7. feeling, deepening, mystery
8. repose, consideration, retreat, ripening
9. understanding before or beyond words, strengthening
10. processing, moving to a new level.

Linear Energy Movement

Looking at the numbers 1 through 10 as a linear graph experience provides understanding into the movement of each number's energy (see figure 3, page 18). There is also a series of symbols that illustrate this growth and development as the movement of numerological energy evolves.

At the 1, something begins. At the 2, it grows in intensity. At the 3, it grows stronger still. At the 4, it reaches its initial peak. At the 5, problems arise. At the 6, the problem is solved. At the 7, there is a deepening. At the 8, real learning that will have lasting results begins. At the 9, the major messages and mysteries of the particular suit or issue at hand have been processed and understood. At the 10, there is an arrival at a new level or new way of knowing.

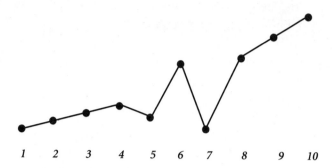

1. ● Starting point (raw energy)
2. — Becomes polarized (will, initial action or purpose)
3. △ Becomes dimensional (conception, beginning
        manifestation)
4. □ Stability (full manifestation, boundaries)
5. ✩ Movement of energy (shifting, changing, release,
        destruction) (space)
6. ✧ Restabilization (solutions, regrowth, seeing it) (time)
7. ⌂ Becomes complex (depending, freeing, developing
        the solutions)(being here)
8   ✺ Grows again, further develops (response, ripening, retreat)
        (consciousness)
9. ✳ Highest point of development (understanding, strengthening)
        (sense something outside of self—bliss)
10. ◉ New plane or threshold (new level of experience)

FIGURE 3. *Graph of Energy Movement and Mathematical Symbols.*

The theoretical meaning of numbers 1 through 10 is uniform in
every tarot deck.

Astrology

Because astrological significance in Celtic mythology was more closely
attached to the ogham moon months than to zodiacal signs, the astrological system that one could apply to the Element cards would be the
standard astrological affiliations generated through the Golden Dawn
system of tarot. These are based on the ogham affiliations with each
suit, as presented in the Table of Zodiacal Assignment on page 19.

Table of Zodiacal Assignment: The Element Cards
(Excluding Aces)

ELEMENT CARD	ZODIAC SIGN	DAYS OF YEAR ATTRIBUTED TO THE DECANS
Aer Cards		
Two of Aer	Libra	September 23–October 2
Three of Aer	Libra	October 3–12
Four of Aer	Libra	October 13–22
Five of Aer	Aquarius	January 20–29
Six of Aer	Aquarius	January 30–February 8
Seven of Aer	Aquarius	January February 9–18
Eight of Aer	Gemini	May 21–31
Nine of Aer	Gemini	June 1–10
Ten of Aer	Gemini	June 11–20
Tine Cards		
Two of Tine	Aries	March 21–30
Three of Tine	Aries	March 31–April 10
Four of Tine	Aries	April 11–20
Five of Tine	Leo	July 21–August 1
Six of Tine	Leo	August 2–11
Seven of Tine	Leo	August 12–22
Eight of Tine	Sagittarius	November 23–December 2
Nine of Tine	Sagittarius	December 3–12
Ten of Tine	Sagittarius	December 13–21
Uisce Cards		
Two of Uisce	Cancer	June 21–July 1
Three of Uisce	Cancer	July 2–11
Four of Uisce	Cancer	July 12–21
Five of Uisce	Scorpio	October 23–November 1
Six of Uisce	Scorpio	November 2–12
Seven of Uisce	Scorpio	November 13–22
Eight of Uisce	Pisces	February 19–28
Nine of Uisce	Pisces	March 1–10
Ten of Uisce	Pisces	March 11–20
Domhan Cards		
Two of Domhan	Capricorn	December 22–30
Three of Domhan	Capricorn	December 31–January 9
Four of Domhan	Capricorn	January 10–19
Five of Domhan	Taurus	April 21–30
Six of Domhan	Taurus	May 1–10
Seven of Domhan	Taurus	May 11–20
Eight of Domhan	Virgo	August 23–September 1
Nine of Domhan	Virgo	September 2–11
Ten of Domhan	Virgo	September 12–22

Ogham

The most commonly acknowledged form of the Irish ogham is called
the Beth-Luis-Nion alphabet, which takes its name from the series of
sacred trees whose initials are the sequence of its letters. The ogham was
used in Ireland some centuries before the introduction of the Roman
alphabet, for there are several hundred known ancient ogham inscriptions on rock faces, stones, crosses, portable artifacts, and manuscripts.
R. A. S. Macalister, a chief druid, published 385 known inscriptions
from the British Isles in the early 1940s. Interestingly, 82 percent were
found in Ireland, while the majority of the others were in Scotland and
Wales, and the remaining in England and mainland Europe.

The symbols of the ogham are arranged along a line called the *druim*
or principal ridge. All characters of the ogham are in contact with the
druim, and are inscribed either above, below, or through the druim.

The ogham was intended for inscription upon upright, or vertical,
pillar stones, or wood slats and posts, and were written from below to
above. The markings equivalent to letters were notches cut across, or
strokes made upon, one of the faces of the angle.

Originally, there were only twenty characters, but today the ogham
number twenty-five—fifteen consonants, five vowels, and five diph-
thong—and are arranged in five basic divisions, each with five characters (figure 4, page 21).

For the most part, since ogham was used only by the Bards and
Druids and not the common people, the ogham appear in only one
Element suit: Domhan (Earth). An ogham inscription is found in the
border of the suit, on the Bone of Peace. However, the Helper cards
and Ancient Ones cards contain ogham. Rather than interpret the
ogham inscriptions, when found in the *Faery Wicca Tarot* cards, I
leave it to the reader to do so if that level of intimacy is desired with
the cards.[1]

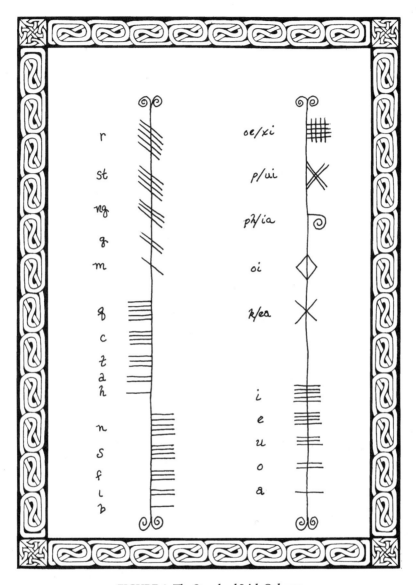

FIGURE 4. *The Standard Irish Oghams.*
Beth-Luis-Nion Alphabet.

Gaelic Alphabet of the Bards

In esoteric studies, the most enthralling information for the novice is magickal alphabets once used to encode the teachings of the Mysteries. Such items are indeed codes, not only used as a secret language to communicate information between adepts, but also to empower working tools and spellcrafts, as well as for divination.

The *Faery Wicca Tarot* is encoded with the secret language of the Bards as represented through several ancient Gaelic and Irish alphabets, as well as sacred symbols and ogham.

Throughout the Element Cards the secret language of the Bards can be seen. Deeper meditation on this language will bridge an attunement to the spiritual vibration of the Faery lesson depicted beneath the surface of the card illustration (figure 5, page 23).

Rather than transcribe the Bardic alphabets where found in the *Faery Wicca Tarot*, I leave it to the reader to do so, if that level of intimacy is desired with the cards.

Celtic Symbolism

The art of understanding magickal and sacred symbolism has always fascinated humankind. Symbols represent an image that links us to higher levels of subjective intuitive experience, as well as to our immediate conscious awareness. Symbols are the midway point between what is outside ourselves and what is deeply etched within.

Through symbolism we can see the soul awakening to the realization of true purpose, leading us to a higher level of spiritual evolution. In symbolism, everything has some meaning and a purpose. The study of symbols allows one to experience the symbol as the gateway to deeper thinking and living. We become aware that we have transcended the personality and touched deeply on our soul quality. When this happens, we then recognize that it is through the self that we make inner contact with the OtherWorld on a level beyond reason or intellect. We become part of the whole, and recognize that the whole is also part of us.

Although symbols have no power of their own, they exert the influence for what they do represent. The powerful symbol is one that attracts beneficent energies for the growth and stimulation of the person working in it.

FIGURE 5. *Gaelic Alphabet Chart.*
Line 1 is the variant letters of the Gaelic alphabet.
Lines 2 and 3 are the Late Celtic magickal alphabets.
Lines 4 and 5 are the Medieval Irish alphabets.

Most symbols will appear in the cards of the Element suit of Aer (air), showing the connection symbols have with the mind or mental body.

The following is a basic summary of the most common symbols found in the Element Cards.

Celtic Cross: This symbolizes the four roads of the four corners of the earth, as well as the meetings of these roads at a central point to form a cross, which indicates the center of the world body. The center of the cross represents the place where all forces come together. The Celtic Cross is also symbolic for the sun and male gods.

Lozenge: This represents the Great Mother Goddess from whose womb we were given birth, and in whose womb still rest the countless unborn. Also symbolic of fertility, stability, and multiplication.

Knot Work Designs: These are considered the Thread of Life. The interlaced knot work patterns, with their unbroken lines, symbolize the process of eternal spiritual evolution.

Spirals: Spirals are the most sacred of all the symbols. Single spirals are the cosmic symbol for the natural form of growth, a symbol of eternal life. Double spirals remind us of the flow and movement of the cosmos. The whorls are continuous creation and dissolution of the world. The triple spiral represents the Triple Goddess; the phases of the moon; and the wheel of life—birth, death, and rebirth.

Labyrinths or Key Patterns: These are spirals in straight lines (see spirals). When connected, they become a processional path leading through a complex maze to the sacred omphalos at the center.

Portcullis: These are the doors leading to the inner sphere that were often adorned with a key pattern lattice archway. The willingness to pass through the threshold was the first step every initiate took at one time. This was a journey through progressive levels of experience, physical, mental, and spiritual, until the vortex at the center was reached—as conveyed by the key pattern labyrinth design of the lattice archway above the door.

Zoomorphic Ornaments: These ornaments represent the shapeshifting attribute common among the Ancient Ones. As symbols they show us that nothing is as it first appears.

Sun Dials and Quartered Circles: These symbols represent the solar year, either depicted by the eight energy shifts or the four seasons, which indicates that everything has its time and place in the natural scheme of life.

The Dragon's Eye

Figure 6 (below) presents a basic layout that can be used when studying each of the four Element suits.

The Dragon's Eye study layout reflects the influences or story line of each suit, showing how each card builds from one to the next, as well as placing emphasis on how the energy builds, how the vibration of the number builds, and how each group has a complete story.

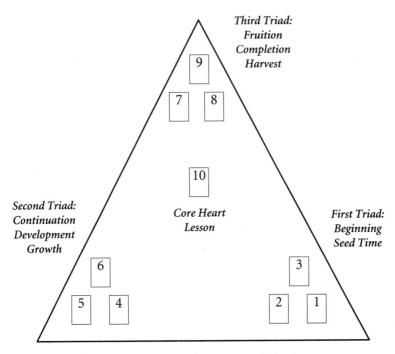

FIGURE 6. *Dragon's Eye Layout for Study.*

Triad One contains the Ace, 2, and 3 cards. It represents the beginning or seed time, the planting, the beginning of each suit.

Triad Two, containing the 4, 5, and 6 cards, represents continuation or development and might be considered the growth phase.

Triad Three, containing the 7, 8, and 9 cards, is the fruition or harvest phase; the completion phase.

The Core is where the 10 card is placed, representing the heart or lesson of each suit.

Each triad shows how the Ace of each suit can be experienced, while the 10 provides the understanding of what the experience implies. The Ace is the pureness of the suit, the seed or beginning point. Ideally it's what we want to get and, interestingly enough, it's what each suit begins with. In order to understand the Ace one must be willing to go through the experience of the lesson of the suit. Realistically, one cannot understand the lesson until they get to the 10, which is the concept or experience of the suit.

In apprenticeship, one of the things that a novice might commonly hear a teacher say is "whatever you think you know now, whatever you think it is now, fine. But wait until a year from now when you come back to this position with a full cycle of experience, because what you knew then will be totally different than what you think you now know."

The Four Great Cities of the Tuatha De Danann

The system of Tarot is ideally a system designed for self-transformation. As already reviewed, each side of the Holy Mountain pertains to our basic life. We learn the lessons of each Element suit and deal with what's learned from our perspective of life, from "being there." In essence, each suit represents an aspect of human relationship, whether with self, others, the planet, or Spirit.

Mundane Living

The Aer cards, which are traditionally connected to the sword, are a suit that has gotten a bum rap because they are presented as the more negative cards of the lesser secrets. This suit contains messages of danger, warning, frustration, sorrow, depression, death, accidents, hostile forces, and setbacks. Yet, the Aer cards contain a very important teaching, which is why they are the first suit dealt with in this book.

While they provide what we might call our "wake-up call," when an Aer card comes up it's because we're telling ourselves to snap out of it. You are reminded that there is a choice, and that you can either choose to experience the negative aspect of the card or look at options and make changes, thereby moving into a different direction.

The Tine cards deal with the basic understanding of power and willpower, ego, politics, and aspects of commerce. The Tines represent conflicts, personality conflicts, successes and failures, winning or losing. Basically, the Tines represent the games of life, the face we show to the world—the mask we wear, our pretenses, attitudes that we sometimes use to cover our own sense of insecurity or fear. The suit of Uisce, which is Water, deals with the heart, emotions, love, and good feelings. Yet, sometimes Uisces will also highlight imbalance within our emotions—where we're sinking, where we're wallowing in self-pity. They also deal with relationships with self and relationships with other people—from familiar relationships to romance to work relationships—children, romance, sex, love, marriage, and so on.

The Domhan cards, representing Earth, move into the physical, the possession aspect of life—money, inheritances, real estate, gifts, giving and receiving cycle, as well as our stinginess and our sharing ability. They help us to understand whether we function in abundance or scarcity consciousness.

Little Self and Sacred Self

We come to understand who we are by studying each Element suit separately.

The Aer Cards

Aer cards are in the east; they represent the element of air, the masculine energy, and the season of spring. The color is yellow and white predominantly yellow, the dawn, and the mental body.

When using the Dragon's Eye study layout to study Aer, this suit will teach little self how to deal with the mental body, about mind, about attitude, about point of view.

"I think, therefore I am," Descartes was known to say, which is about all we know of the mind—that as long as the mind is consciously thinking, we exist. When the mind no longer consciously thinks, we do not exist. The Aer cards immediately communicate to us that if you are brain dead, you're not here. Your physical body can be here, your heart can be pumping, all of your other organs can be working, but if your brain is dead, you're gone.

Traditionally the swords show frustration, paranoia, fear, and sorrow in life amplified in seven of the ten cards in this suit. They communicate a fact to us that we rarely stop to think about that when we over-intellectualize, we create drama. When we get so stuck in the mind that all we do is think, then we're going to get deeper and deeper into the melodramas that our minds create. Thinking and intellect are a great mode of operation—out of that process we've had wonderful advancements within our history. Through the mind, through conceptualizing, through theory, and through research, we dig and dig to try to pull things in to our awareness so that we can prove or disprove. This makes the suit of the mind a very important aspect of life.

Through the mind cards of the tarot, we learn to understand the mental body, how we think, and that thoughts dictate attitude, attitude dictates actions, and actions dictate life. Even though the mental body might be considered a non-active energy, it's very much an action or a force since it is a mechanization.

Twin Flames are located within the body—a female flame and a male flame. The male flame is considered the intellect, the mental body. So when referring to our masculine energy, we're basically referring to the intellect, to the mental body, to rational mind, the conscious mind. Yet, in this there is a paradox; whenever the mental body or intellect is being referred to, the subconscious mind is also being referred to. Subconscious and conscious are parts of the mind, which in turn is part of the mental body, which is of the masculine gender. We can't get into the subconscious mind unless we are willing to marry our male flame with our twin female flame. When we're working with the subconscious, then our twin flames are working together.

The Tine Cards

Tine, Fire, ego, willpower, masculine supported by feminine, red, midday, south, Wands, and Ego versus Spirit.

Tine teaches us how to deal with the ego, personal will, and power. In a very general perspective, Tine pertains to power, because the suit deals with ego, as well as with the aspects of life that might be politically or commercially oriented, such as livelihood, career, work, the face that we show the outside world, conflict, success or failure, winning or losing, and the games of life. The emphasis is placed on whether we are balanced within our power, or whether we give it away or exert it over others.

The Uisce Cards

The water cards and the cups are a metaphor for the all-embracing, all-surrounding essence of love. Love, like water, takes the shape of the vessel that contains it. It is infinitely flexible, however, it can never be squeezed or compressed or coerced. Any attempt to do so might mean that the tighter you try to hold on to the water, especially in your hand, only makes it disappear. As we have to hold the water, we have to hold the love gently so it remains with its life-giving virtue. The Cups teach the lesson of psychic return, the nostalgic or inner pilgrimage. Jung said that emotional progress toward maturity depends in part on a symbolic return to the children's land to reactivate hidden memories. The lesson of Uisce is about getting in touch with the fundamental passage or matters of the fundamental passage of the heart, the mystery of love which is self-love. This passage or journey must start with self-love; if you don't love self, how can you expect anybody else to truly love you, and how can you expect to be able to love another individual?

Within the heart remains the faded memory of all love experiences we've had; each love relationship teaches us to know and identify love more and more perfectly; to learn from our mistakes; to recognize the type of person who is worthy of our love; to know the qualities we require and deserve in relationship. In learning these things about self, wrong choices are eliminated, as are bad relationships, and such a pattern is then broken.

The Domhan Cards

The Domhan cards are in the north. They represent pentacles, Earth, the Feminine supported by Masculine, the physical body, winter, green, and midnight.

First of all, in a very general way, the Domhan cards pertain to physical matter: property or possessions, money, real estate, inheritances or gifts, and our ability to have balance in the give and take process—understanding the giving and receiving of the natural law. Understanding the natural law is to know that there is an increase in wealth—it may not be in physical or material, but spiritual—it all depends on where values are placed. In traditional esoteric schools, we talk about the beauty way, existing and living in the beauty way. When you find the beauty in life—when you really move with the give and take, the ebb and the flow of life—then you create abundance around you and it's the abundance that serves you in a very balanced way. It doesn't create imbalance. This is what the whole suit of Domhan is all about—balance. Domhan teaches us that we don't have to give anything up to be spiritual. Domhan Cards are perhaps the most powerful of the Element suits because they're the culmination of all the suits.

In summary, when we think in terms of the individual lessons in life, we can think in terms of always starting with our attitude in any given situation, clarifying your attitude about the situation, then focusing on your will power or desire. What's going on with your ego? What do you think you deserve?

When ego engages and takes charge, it's because ego thinks it deserves something it's not getting. When this happens, emotions flare. We then want to evaluate our emotional state, what we are dealing with and how we are reacting—remember that emotions are a reaction. Then look at your physical state, at the balance or the culmination of mind, ego, and emotions, and how they have combined or integrated in physical life.

Aer, Tine, and Uisce deal with internal processes, while Domhan represents those internal processes in the physical realm. Domhan represents how well the lessons of Aer, Tine, and Uisce have been assimilated. Domhan, as the holism of life, reveals the connection we have with Sacred Self, which reflects our ability to find Spirit, to connect with Spirit, and become a spiritual being in the physical world, in a balanced and harmonious way.

Doorways into the Four Great Cities

Each suit of the Element Cards is connected to one of the four Other-World cities where the Tuatha De Danann acquired their magick, which later became the foundational wisdom taught in the Bardic College, as well as the traditional teachings of our modern Faery Wicca.

The suit of Aer is connected to the eastern city Gorias. Tine is connected to the southern city Findias. Uisce is connected to the western city Muirias, and Domhan is connected to Falias, the northern city.

Gorias is the city of east. The Sword of Enlightenment—Nuada's Sword—is the key to this Great City. The Element Cards of Aer represent the teachings of the eastern city located in the OtherWorld realm known as the Heavenly Realm. However, Gorias can be accessed through the province of Leinster located in the Plains realm.

Leinster is considered the first spoke on the Champion's Wheel. Here, the warrior begins to learn their connection to the earthly realm, thus entering a partnership with other life-forms of this planet. Through training, they receive the mental stimulation required for enlightenment.

Working with the Sword talismans teaches the warrior to cut through the veils of ignorance caused by the separation between internal female and male energies known as the Twin Flames. The female energy of the body is the Emotional Body, the house of intuition. The male energy of the body is the Mental Body, the house of mental discernment. To marry these two bodies together produces the ability to "think with the heart" and "feel with the mind."

Gorias wisdom unlocks the secret to union with Sacred Self through achieving balance with the conscious and unconscious minds.

Findias is the southern city. The Gae Bulga—or Lugh's Spear—is the sacred talisman or key to the teachings of Findias. The city of the south is also located in the Heavenly Realm, and its mirror reflection is the province of Munster, located in the Plains.

Munster is the province of feelings and passion. Here the champion spirit begins to understand the balance of life energies that must include the feminine aspect of nature; for this is the realm of goddess and inner power. Through training the warrior learns control as they undergo each experience, each season of growth.

Working with the Spear or Wand talisman teaches the wisdom of solar power: strength, passion, will. It awakens the ego, forcing little self to realize its place in the Divine Plan. How one maintains their sense of personal power becomes vitally important, for even the most fierce warrior must learn the art of softness.

Findias wisdom unlocks the soul, leading Sacred Self into the Spiral Dance. Spirit surfaces from the Solar Realm (subconscious mind) into the Lunar Realm (conscious mind), and the marriage of the Twin Flames occurs.

Muirias is the western city. The Dagda's Cauldron—the Undry—is the key into this Great City. This Heavenly Realm City is connected to the province of Connacht in the Plains. Here the warrior spirit learns to integrate the partnership of knowledge and wisdom, moving into a phase of ego-death that births Eldership. This is the realm of the inner mystery, of the artisan—the Draoi.

Working with the Undry teaches qualities of abundance and balance. Here, through creative imagination, divine prophecy is implemented and the art of seership is refined. The Cauldron becomes that of Inspiration, containing within it the mystic Cup of Truth.

Muirias wisdom moves the conscious and subconscious realms together, into the realm of intuition, spiritual intelligence, and creative imagination. Here, one is prepared for rebirth.

Falias is the northern city. Lia Fail, the Stone of Destiny, represents the physical manifestation, or creation. In the Plains, the Heavenly Realm city Falias is reflected in the northern province of Ulster.

Ulster is the formal gateway or doorway through which the warrior enters the Great Circle, both as a novice and as an adepti. This is the seat of wise counsel, of the elder to the high king and queen of Eire. Here the Path of Five Law is learned.

Using the Lia Fail as a talisman or key into the teachings of Falias, the champion is shown that one must be willing to marry the land, or the goddess of the land, in order to truly serve her kings and queens. Only then can one become accepted into the Land of Faery.

Falias wisdom guides the champion into the Fifth Spoke of the Champion's Wheel, which is found in the fifth province of the Plains: Meath, wherein the Champion has learned to surrender to Spirit and dwell in the center of peace.

The Element Cards of Aer

ACE THROUGH TEN
Power of Swords Teach Me To Feel With My Mind

Ace of Aer

SWORD OF GORIAS

Classical Tarot Meaning

Raw power of the mind; freedom from restraint as a new lightness or kind of salvation. Cut through the veils of ignorance: the first step is setting the right attitude. What you think you know now will be different at the end of the journey; keep an open mind. Constructive or destructive powers, depending on how the information is used. Fate.

Card Description and Faery Wicca Tarot Meaning

Journey to Gorias

I am standing on top of a hill, somewhat like the Witches' Hill at Loughcrew, in Ireland. It is both sunset and sunrise simultaneously. I begin by walking down the path to the opening of the stone circle, then moving deosil around the outside of it, in just the same way that I made the pilgrimage around all sacred sites I visited when in Ireland . . . . And as was common when arriving someplace very important to the entire spiritual journey, the Badb's feather stuck straight up in the earth, directly in my path.

When I return to the opening of the stone circle, I stand for a moment, looking over the stones beyond, to the eastern sky, where the silver new crescent moon is rising in an ageless pale rose sky.

I sit down on the pathway and focus on the Gaelic rune and spiral inscribed on the interior stone framed by the opening to the circle.

"POWER."

Spiral. Solar Disc. Dragon's Eye in the Heavens.

The spiral lifts from the stone and attaches itself to my forehead, between my eyebrows. Third eye. Spiral is the symbol for the third eye chakra, the symbol that communicates to us the spiraling motion of the chakra itself.

This is how we feel with the mind—through psychic perception, intuition. So simple. How long have I been working with this concept—"Learn to feel with the mind"—and here it is, plain as . . . light?

Lifting above the stone circle, looking down on it, I realize that the three rings of stones also form the spiral, the chakra: the outer ring, with a golden walkway between it and the second, inner ring; the second ring, with a silver walkway between it and the final and third inner ring; and, the third ring, leading to the grassy rath in the center, and stuck in the earth in the top center of the rath rests the Sword of Gorias, the Sword of Illumination.

With each breath the sword moves in and out of my third eye. Breathing in, and effortlessly piercing my intelligence with clarity and illumination. Breathing out, and effortlessly withdrawing to its place of origination—Breath of Origination!

It is all making so much sense!

The Sword of Gorias slices through the veils of ignorance (hence, the mist circling the stone circle), effortlessly moving through the clouding of our own intelligence to bring the paradigm shift required to move deeper into the intuitive natures of our intelligence. This is not a sword of war and killing, but of enlightenment, raw power that is the untapped, unused power of our soul.

Once more I am sitting before the opening to the stone circle. The golden path draws my attention to it. Yes, to take the first step into the spiral, into the power, would be that of warmth; for the golden color is suddenly so warm, and overhead, the early morning sun sends forth his warm, golden rays to highlight the path even more, and with those warm, golden rays comes this message:

Come into the spiral.
Don't be afraid of the power.
Don't be afraid to enter the spiral
that leads to the Sword of Illumination.
Feel with the mind.
That's the only way to progress.

Two of Aer

THE PATH OF DISCERNMENT

Classical Tarot Meaning

Two forces against one another, perhaps to cancel each other out. There is another option to be considered. Karmic balance, also balance in the moral issues of life: a reminder that every action produces a reaction—what goes around comes around, do unto others as you would have them do unto you, as ye sow, so shall ye reap.

Card Description and Faery Wicca Tarot Meaning

Journey to Gorias — continued

Illusion. As I stand, ready to enter the spiral of light, I find that I am farther from it than first realized, and that I must willingly walk the path. The center is always farther away than at first realized. The path is the way of dedication and experience.

As I start down the path I am greeted by two additional pathways: a pathway that leads to the left, and a pathway that leads to the right. Distractions?

I turn and face the left pathway. Looking down it, all I can see is a shadowy darkness. This darkness begins not more than five feet down the path. Obscurity, confusion, uncertainty. I look down to the ground and there lies a sword, its tip stained with blood. Just like a sacred athame that draws blood, this sword is not an ally but an enemy. This sword is not a Sword of Illumination, but a sword of war, of hatred and of evil. To follow the point of this sword would mean to enter a labyrinth of deception and destruction, and possibly even death. This path of distraction is tainted with negativity.

I turn and face the right pathway. How beautiful this pathway is, sparkling with beautiful color. The sparkling color swarms into a brilliant light, again obscuring my sight not more than five feet down the path. I cannot see beyond all this sparkling light. As I look down, a sword also lies on the ground before the path, but this one points to a beautiful glittering crown. How tempting to reach down and touch the crown and examine all the gems embedded in its golden filigree. But I catch my breath, realizing that to travel this path is to travel a path soiled in materialistic pursuits, that the only reward is that of receiving the crown. What is a crown but an ego stroke? Would I follow the path of ego so quickly?

No, I turn and face the original path. Off in the distance the stone circle rises, and just like the blade of a sword, the path is broad at the base, narrowing at the tip. I know that this path is the hardest path of all to travel, for in its broad beginning, we humans often get so distracted by darkness and ego. That to travel this path one has to be willing to walk in balance, which is never an easy task; that to reach the tip of the path one would make many personal sacrifices along the way to maintain a sense of commitment to the path, as well as direction.

This path is the path of the spiraling light that exists within the mind. This path is the path of personal truth. The willingness to enter into the spiraling of our own mind, no matter how confused or uncertain or clouded that spiraling may at first be, the truth can only be revealed to us through our willingness to spiral through the mists and arrive at the center. Thus, arriving at the center of our own truth, and not the persuading of others—not being caught in the distraction of someone's covert manipulations or overt arguments, no matter how sensible they seem—is a path of discernment.

The path leading to the spiral is indeed the true Sword of Illumination, invisible though it may at first seem.

For this is the path OF personal truth,
and personal truth is the clarity one receives from
*   the Sword of Illumination.*
Know Thy Self.

Three of Aer

WITHOUT FEAR

Classical Tarot Meaning

Natural laws are not always easy to mentally accept. Sorrow and regret. Withdraw into a restricted psychic environment representing endurance of inner pain.

Card Description and Faery Wicca Tarot Meaning

Journey to Gorias – continued

After following the path and arriving at the blade's tip, I stand before the opening that leads into the stone circle. A golden spotlight of early morning Sun flashes over the stone circle, momentarily blinding me. In its wake forms the sign of Spirit, formed out of three SWORDS of Illumination, pointing to the entrance. The Spirit sign is superimposed over a skeleton, which dons the tattered remains of clothing. The skeleton's left arm points that I should enter the stone circle by spiraling to the left, deosil, sunwise.

My mind flickers back to the path of distraction that led to the left, and its ominous message of negativity and death, and I can't help but wonder if I am being misled by this skeleton. But then I understand that to enter into the spiral of the mind we enter in through the left brain, the rational mind, the conscious mind, which would attribute the directional guide now being given.

I study the skull of the skeleton, which is somewhat cartoonish—not real, which at first glance I had thought. This skeleton might very well be a guide, an ally. This skeleton might even be the very bones of my own body lying revealed for my naked eye to see.

To enter the spiral of mind would not be of this physical world, but of the invisible world, which is indicated by the Spirit sign. Only through Spirit do we connect with the Sword of Illumination and receive clarity and inspiration.

The bones of my body. I focus on this thought, closing my eyes, seeking the spiral circle of my third eye. Veiled in swirling mist, I immediately envision the Sword of Illumination moving in and out of the spiral's center with each breath I take. What is it my bones remember about the mind?

The sword moves in and out, in and out, slicing through the mists, effortlessly piercing the third eye without pain or trauma.

To enter the spiral of the mind, to enter into the center of the circle, to enter into the place of power, what is it my bones remember. . . . Then it comes, loud and clear,

Fear.

And with this one word, the mists vanish and a brilliant golden, warm light illuminates my third eye.

How simple. One word is the message that is gained with clarity, not a diatribe—just one simple word. I lift my face to the golden warmth of clarity that fills my third eye. Oh, how delicious it feels (am I feeling with my mind?) As I take a deep breath, the golden brilliance radiates:

To enter into the Spirit of mind,
To enter into the circle of illumination,
To enter into the place of power,
One must have No Fear.

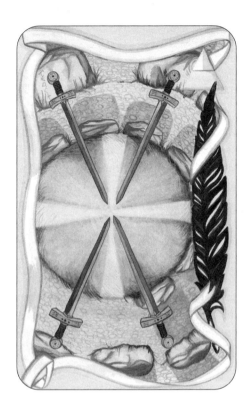

Four of Aer

THE FIRST ATTENTION

Classical Tarot Meaning

Insights generated by seclusion. Prophetic powers invoked in secret. Time to draw a truce. Rest and relaxation required to bring about peace of mind. Meditation would be beneficial at this time.

Card Description and Faery Wicca Tarot Meaning

Journey to Gorias – continued

As I enter the first ring of stones, a transparent map forms before me; it is a map of the mind. Once again I am floating above the Stone Circle, looking down upon the three rings. Four Swords of Illumination appear, pointing into the center of the circle, where a beam of light, rising from the earth, creates an equal arm cross. The cardinal points!

Yes, I understand! When we enter the mind, when we seek illumination, the moment we break through the mists, the moment the Sword of Illumination guides us into the paradigm shift, the four primal elements merge—air and fire and water and earth all merge, creating, for that moment, a perfect balance, a perfect synthesis.

Like the amber eye of an eagle, which sees so far and such detail with clarity, so the synthesis of the elements opens the eagle's eye within.

The tips of the Swords of Illumination lead into an altered state of awareness; one that is extremely heightened. For the mind has many levels of attention and awareness. The outer ring of stones represents the mind's first attention: conscious awareness. When one is able to own the first attention, they can shift their consciousness at will and enter into the second attention.

The second ring of stones might represent this second attention: subconscious awareness. We come to understand our conscious awareness through symbols and archetypes. Such symbols and archetypes guide us ever deeper into the mind, freeing us from bondage until we can shift our awareness and enter into the third attention.

Is the third attention represented by the inner ring of stones, wherein the awareness of the individual is freed from the dictates of the mind and all perception is revealed without limitation? Perhaps.

I catch a glimpse of understanding; when we are free from the physical, the third attention shifts perception beyond the worlds, where a new reality is revealed. This reality is akin to the sorcerer's world, where one learns to dream-awake, bending perception toward a more cognizant one.

The mind is an amazing part of one of our most significant physical organs. Through our willingness to enter into this part of our being, we begin to enter into all realities that are ever present for us to explore and experience, visible and invisible.

Opening to the TEACHing of the Sword of Illumination will guide us through the circles of the mind, pointing us toward the center, to the eagle's eye. As already learned through the first triad of the Aer's Dragon's Eye, having no fear of conscious reality, or personal perception, is the key to moving awareness into the first attention; thus, arriving at a new, sacred "point" of view.

As my vision focuses once more on the image of the Four of Aer, a whispering wafts up from the light:

The true power of the Sword of Illumination
is not in its sharpness,
but in its straightness,
which points to the mark.

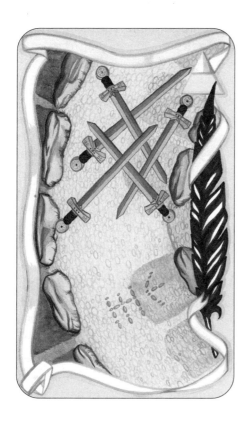

Five of Aer

ALL THAT GLITTERS IS NOT GOLD

Classical Tarot Meaning

Self-abasement, passive endurance, forcible swallowing of pride. Even in the face of death, which arrives in its appointed hour for every living creature, virtue lies in patient endurance and passive courage. Don't fight a no-win battle.

Card Description and Faery Wicca Tarot Meaning

Journey to Gorias – continued

As I move inside the first ring of stones I am engulfed by the sparkling warmth of the golden path. The smooth stones of the first ring are so warm, as if warmed from the heat of the path rather than the sun, for it is still early morning. As I press my cheek against one of the stones I feel an inner strength begin to develop.

Turning back to the path, I continue around. The second ring of stones does not tower over me as the first do, but are only head high. I know that if I stand on my toes I could probably peer over them, yet I know that this is not the way to see beyond; it is too important to feel my way, rather than see. So I restrain myself from looking.

As I move farther down the golden path I become aware that I can see from two directions: I am on the path yet I am floating above the path, looking down. From above it is clear to see that I am ending the first circumference of the Stone Circle, coming back to the entrance. This concerns me, because I have not come upon an entrance into the second ring of stones yet, and I wonder if I have gotten distracted by the warm feeling I am experiencing.

Then as I move down the path, coming around the last curve toward the beginning entrance, I see five swords lying helter-skelter, as if blocking my way, but not really. For if I really want to continue all I have to do is step over them. But I stop and gaze upon them, opening myself to their message.

The Stone Circle of the third eye is a powerful teacher, indeed. I remember the lesson of the four Swords of Illumination and their connection to perception. I have successfully entered the spiraling of my mind, and consciously began moving into the chakra of my third eye. New understanding illuminates my mind.

The first part of the spiral is one that fixes us into conscious attention. The first attention is about self, coming to understand how self thinks, feels, acts. The first ring of stones can put us in touch with the power of the swords to teach us about "ME." After all, the first step taken on any spiritual journey is always in an attempt to understand self better and how self fits into the big scheme of things.

The five Swords of Illumination now blocking my progress contain the message that the time has come to move into a new perception, to change direction and move outside of self. To stay too focused on self would only propel me into a loop in which I would continue to go around and around and be no better off than I was when I first started.

The first attention is helping me to know myself, but self is in no way the center of the Stone Circle. Now is the time to get beyond the big ME.

A glittering off to the right of the swords catches my eye. Turning to it I see—for the first time—an opening into the second ring of stones. The golden walkway turns into a glittering of silver, and with this sight comes a shift in my perception. The new light produced by the silver flashes into my mind:

Staying fixed in the first attention,
staying too focused on the big ME
can blind you faster than the mists.
ME is not and never will be the center,
for it creates self-importance—
an illusive golden image—
a barbarous point of view.

Six of Aer

AS WITHIN,
SO WITHOUT

Classical Tarot Meaning

An anxious time. A passage toward a dark, unknowable future. Every rite of passage is a ride into the unknown. Moving away from danger. Hope. A hint of possible success, though not immediate. Difficulties cannot be avoided, they must be faced and solved before the journey can continue. A short trip; also, a journey by water.

Card Description and Faery Wicca Tarot Meaning

Journey to Gorias – continued

I see the image very clearly before me. I now stand in the second ring of stones. The glittery silver path is beneath my feet. There before me are stationed six swords, points down, forming a walkway through which I must pass if I am to continue the journey.

I close my eyes and see the golden spiral piercing my third eye chakra. As I breathe deeply, the golden hue shifts to silver, and in the center of the spiral a triangle forms. Directly underneath the triangle an inverted triangle forms. The two come together, one point up, one point down, and then they start spinning like the propeller of a plane.

From their spinning a new awareness comes: I am standing between two worlds. One world is that of my conscious perception. I can competently step back into that world of mundania where I could easily survive. The other world, however, is that of a new perception, and to continue the journey I must be willing to enter this new perception, which I know is attached to revelations found within my subconscious.

I open my eyes and focus on the six swords, and muse over why their blades are pointed down—not up or sideways like all the others, but down—and why they form a walkway. Behind the three swords to the left are three symbols: a spiral with three lines above it, an equal arm cross, and the sacred wheel.

The points of the sword blades draw my attention to them once more. The glittering silver spiral superimposes itself over my third eye, and with it comes a piercing of illumination.

To continue the journey toward the second attention, the Swords of Illumination show that one must be willing to descend, to deepen into their subconscious mind, to descend into their soul. To continue the journey means to move in, to move down toward the center.

Without conscious effort, I step between the first two swords and grasp the handles. The movement propels me deeper into the spiral, closer to the second attention.

Stepping forward between the second set of swords, I grasp the left handle, and then the right handle. Instantly, I feel a new sense of balance, of equilibrium.

Making the first step into another sacred point of view is always, at first, disorienting because we are moving into unknown territory. After the first step, rather than rush deeper, it is important to pause and regain an inner sense of balance—to pause and breathe, and gather self into the new perception of unknowing, resting a moment.

A third time I step forward. My left hand closes around the left sword handle. My right hand closes around the right sword handle. The sacred wheel positions itself before me.

The second attention is outside of time and space, it is timelessness, spacelessness. The second attention deals with energy, just as the sacred wheel represents the eight holy energy shifts that annually occur on the earth plane. To enter into the second attention means entering into sacred time, sacred space, and opening to the energy flow.

I cannot, as of yet, let go of the sword handles, I am too connected to an energy flowing up from the earth into me through them. I know that I am so much closer to the center, but I still have a ways to go. I must still find my way TO the second attention, which may or may not be connected to the lesson of the Sword of Illumination. With this thought, a surge of energy flows into my hands, and I feel in my mind:

> *Gorias is not far away—*
> *the center of this cycle of learning.*
> *Learn and become the energy—*
> *feel it in your mind.*
> *As Within—so without.*

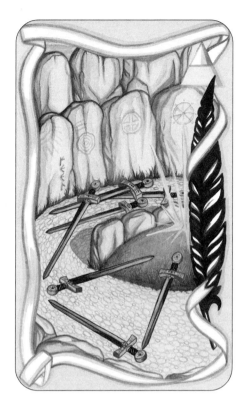

Seven of Aer

SPIRIT TALK

Classical Tarot Meaning

Opposition from relentlessly hostile forces, the source difficult to identify. Traps. Watch your back. A warning card. Difficulties, quarrels and the hampering of movement. Deceit. Betrayal. Trust issues.

Card Description and Faery Wicca Tarot Meaning

Journey to Gorias – continued

After I let go the third set of sword handles (Six of Aer) and move forward into the second ring of stones, I study the different levels of stones: the outer ring, the second ring, the inner ring. I make a full circle and come to the opening of the third ring of stones. I can no longer see the opening that led into the second ring, in which I now stand. It is as if the other two openings have vanished, and the only way to travel is forward.

Four swords are strewn on the ground. They instantly represent outworn and outmoded dogmas, beliefs, thoughts, and ideas; the mental arguments that no longer serve me, but which I would hang myself up on if I held.

Stepping into the world of the subconscious mind, opening to the realm of sacred space and sacred time, it is important to let go of what no longer serves us mentally. Whatever serves us mentally also conditions us emotionally and shows up in our physical world, whether it be a condition in our physical body or a life situation that must be experienced.

Three Swords of Illumination form a triangle,: the symbol of Spirit, pointing into the third ring of stones. To move into the third and final ring, which brings me to the center of the Stone Circle, the center of the Third Eye chakra, I must step inside the triangle—Spirit.

The first Sword of Illumination is like the outer ring of stones, representing the first attention, awakened consciousness. The second Sword of Illumination is like the second ring of stones, representing the second attention, the subconscious realm, while the third Sword of Illumination represents bent perception, the third ring of stones. Entrance here will bring me into the sacred time and space of Spirit, arriving at a new sacred point of view.

To enter and arrive at this new sacred point of view, I must be willing to open to new experiences that will provide me with new thoughts and ideas, nourishing my mental growth, through which I will come to feel the experience of such thoughts and ideas and form new beliefs.

The triangle of swords points to the grassy rath, rising up in the center of the third ring of stones, and from its center, golden white light flares. The grassy rath suddenly represents the nourishment and growth one will acquire when entering into the sacred time and sacred space of Spirit. When stepping onto the grass, one can FEEL the beauty of the grass on the feet, experiencing its nourishment and growth through the golden white light of the paradigm shift within the mind.

The three Swords of Illumination surrounding me makes me think about the light. It becomes clear that the Spirit of this light is truly connected to the Sacred Wheel. At Winter Solstice the new light is given birth, bringing promise of a new cycle of rebirth and growth. This promise carries the light into the season of Spring, at which time the fiery arrow of inspiration is received at Imbolc by those open to it. From the fiery arrow of inspiration comes the illuminated course of action that we will individually focus on for the new cycle of growth. We begin to focus on the light of inspiration, opening to new ideas of what such growth will bring, while designing new plans of action in which to implement such growth. At Vernal Equinox this formulated plan of action is planted into the soil of the mind to be nurtured into manifestation.

The golden white light flares from the center of the grassy rath. In its sparkling light I see a reflection of my own mind, and in that reflection, I FEEL Spirit say:

Don't hesitate now—
With old thoughts, dogmas, ideas,
and beliefs freshly discarded,
step into the sacred,
and become the golden brilliance
of my warmth and illumination.

Eight
of Aer

ILLUMINATION
IS FREE

Classical Tarot Meaning

Loss of faith; inner turmoil. Bad news. Fruitless conflict. Embarrassment. False beliefs. Enforced isolation in retaliation for unkind acts, such as imprisonment might be suffered in retaliation for a crime.

Card Description and Faery Wicca Tarot Meaning
Journey to Gorias – continued

I stand facing the grassy rath. Eight Swords of Illumination circle the top of the rath. A golden spiral glows over the top center of the rath, and the picture gives the illusion that the swords are protecting the spiral. Beyond the rath I see the three rings of stones, the second ring with several symbols: the sun, double spiral, sacred wheel, and cardinal cross.

Focusing back on the swords I wonder why they guard the spiral. Are they guarding it like a fence, keeping me out? In my mind's eye I envision myself squeezing between two of the swords, but the sword blades are sharp and they skin me. Oh yes, I can get to the spiral, but I would do so with tattered clothing and blood letting. That is not the way. I close my eyes.

I envision the silver spiral of my third eye chakra. It becomes clear, and with its image comes the thought: why would the swords protect me from getting to my intuition? And then a new thought arises.

The swords we arrange like fences in our mind are to protect our limited and puny egos from deepening. We think we resurrect fences of protection around our intuition, around our unique abilities, but these fences are more like prison bars keeping us disconnected from such gifts. After we have made the paradigm shift in understanding that we contain the ability to shift our perception and arrive at new levels of attention, we often scare ourselves away from the center connection—that is, connecting WITH our power.

The eight Swords of Illumination simply communicate that we are the ones guilty of binding or keeping ourselves away from the center of our souls by the "protective" boundaries we create. Richard Bach once wrote something to the effect of "Define your limitations and sure enough they're yours." Here that saying was demonstrated before me: the definition of limitations.

I sensed that the swords were illusory and that I could actually run my hand through them. Opening my eyes I stepped onto the grass, but could not bring myself to touch the swords, or even one of them for that matter. No, this site was a holy site and needed special approach. So, I began moving around the swords deosil. With each circuit, my feet created a path in the grass, at first crushing it down under my weight and then slowly wearing the grass away, exposing the soil.

With each circuit I awaited permission to approach the swords and pass through them, entering into their midst and gaining the top of the rath. But then it occurred to me—only I could give myself permission to move beyond the barriers I created for myself. I had two choices: I could either keep walking in circles waiting for outside permission to come, or I could give myself permission and spiral onto the top of the rath, in which case I would easily pass through my own limitations.

I faced the swords thinking I would reach out and pull several free from the earth, but why need I? They weren't real anyway! With a deep, full belly breath I resigned myself to freeing my mind from self-imposed limitations. Stepping forward, I held both arms out in front of me and pushed two swords away like I was parting drapes made out of precious silk. The two swords vanished at my touch and an entrance was instantly created, and with this new access the golden spiral flared WITH brilliant light, and I felt in my mind:

The way to spiritual illumination
is free.
The only boundaries encountered
are within thee.

Nine of Aer

THE SECOND ATTENTION

Classical Tarot Meaning

A cruel fate. Mental or physical suffering (i.e., severe depression). Violent attack. Martyrdom. Isolation from needed help and comfort. Scandal. Misery, hatred, brutal neglect or abandonment. Unreasoning violence. Suicide.

Card Description and Faery Wicca Tarot Meaning

Journey to Gorias – continued

As I pushed through the swords all eight vanished, and with their vanishing I heard a popping sound. Looking to my left I saw a cloaked figure, a deep cowl hood concealing the Being's face from sight. Instinctively, I jumped back. Who or what this Being was eluded me, and I stood there dumb founded, staring, my mouth agape.

The eight swords appeared around the figure, and I had the feeling that in overcoming the limitations of my mind I had succeeded in separating my fears from my mind, and that now as a separate reality, they were safely guarded from entering MY mind again.

No sooner than I felt that this figure was an aspect of my dark side did it raise its right hand and point its fingers toward the grassy rath. The swords were no longer substantial, but had shifted position and clung to the aura of this Being like pins to a magnet.

"I am the Guardian," a masculine voice resonated in my mind. "You have passed the test and are free to continue forward."

From his fingertips shot a beam of white light. I followed its direction, turning back to the rath, and beheld the original Sword of Illumination sticking out of the earth. As the Guardian's beam of light hit the sword it rose swiftly, pulling free from the earth.

The spiral that had been around its base flew to my third eye and, with great effort, and very sluggishly, spun three times deosil before it changed directions. Almost immediately the spiral, now moving widdershins—moonwise—picked up speed and spun at an even greater intensity.

The sensation in my third eye was one of being drawn in, deeper and deeper into my inner consciousness. The paradox of having it first spin sunwise and then moonwise made me realize that I was just now entering the second attention, not earlier as I had intellectually analyzed.

The second attention consisted of the duality. I had only been moving in the conscious world, moving ever forward, moving clockwise, moving along the linear line. Although I had connected with the spiral of the third eye, I had to first spin consciously with it, moving in the most obvious direction: into clarity, understanding, intellectual analysis. That, of course, is the first attention awakened. That was the lesson in learning about self, coming to the big me, so that MY mind could then relax its hold on being in control, and in letting go of my self-imposed limitation of being in control, I could then change direction without effort, moving inward, deeper into the self I don't yet fully know.

With a deep breath I relaxed, letting go of all thoughts, surrendering to the driving force that pulled me inward. Very clearly, I heard the voice of the Guardian:

What you think
with the mind,
you must first feel.
What you feel
comes from a deep well
within you.
This is the paradox—
as within, as without,
all fear must be surrendered
or you will hold self-doubt.
The mind can cripple
the awakening soul —
The mind is an enemy
to the budding Spirit.

Ten of Aer

ONWARD TO GORIAS

Classical Tarot Meaning

As the Ten, this card has a double meaning. It can mean ruin, desolation, pain, the worst of afflictions, endings; as well as a new birth of hope, a paradigm shift fully integrated, right attitude, and new awareness. The winter is always darkest before it turns into spring.

Card Description and Faery Wicca Tarot Meaning

Journey to Gorias – continued

The Sword of Illumination hung suspended above the rath. A blast of white light rose from the earth beneath it. Behind me came a loud thud, and I looked back to the Being, who was no longer there. On the ground lay his discarded cloak, pinned to the earth by ten Swords of Illumination. Turning back to the rath I beheld a most profound sight: an opening into the earth.

I leapt to the top of the rath and peered down into the opening. Golden steps led down into the earth, while all the while a soft white light glowed from some source below. I could not tell how far the golden steps led because the light swallowed them within its brilliance.

Suddenly I knew that if I were to follow the steps down into this opening, I would be stepping into my inner MIND, moving deeper into my own soul.

I stood upon the first step, and felt the warmth of the white light swallow my feet and ankles. I looked around the Stone Circle and saw its full message in all its simplicity. The symbols of my subconscious were everywhere. Had I only known all along that moving into the second attention was the simple act of meditating on these personal symbols, I would have communed with my soul long ago.

But we always think there is more. We want to believe that the way to Spirit is so complicated. I laughed. What was it I was so fond of saying: "Keep it basic. For in simplicity is the foundation." My foundation had circled me all along.

I looked down into the light and, with a huge smile on my face, began my descent, moving down the steps, down into the light, into my soul. I knew that upon my resurgence into this circle of stones, I would not be the same person. As I stepped beneath the surface of the rath, my body completely within the opening, the steps slid out from beneath me and I was gently floating down.

The white light softly swallowed me, embracing me into its brilliance, into its clarity. It moved through me and around me, the light spread in all directions. In that pristine moment, I felt my mind understand the lesson of the Sword of Gorias:

I have stepped into illumination,
And I AM FREE.

The key to the Great City of Gorias had been fit into the keyhole, and I was now beginning a new journey. Behind me lay the discarded struggles and strife of my own mental battles. I was no longer bound to them, they were no longer a burden, because I had come to know that I was not them, nor were they me, and that though they had existed within me all I had to do was change them and release what was no longer useful and perceive a new form of belief.

With the Great City of Gorias before me, waiting to be explored and experienced, I open to the powers of Air, my intellect, my clarity, and I am filled with the magick of illumination. The attic of my mind was being swept out, tidied up. The window shutters had been opened to let the illumination in, and the glass panes raised so clarity could breeze through the space. With that breeze came this enticing invitation from somewhere beyond:

The journey leads ever on,
turn not to the past,
remember what you will
but leave the treaded path behind
it serves you not to retread
that which has already been passed.
Onward, onward,
onward, onwar. . .
onwa. . . onw. . .
on. . . o. . . .

The Element Cards of Tine

Ace of Tine

WAND OF FINDIAS

Classical Tarot Meaning

The raw power of personal power. The fiery dragon of sexual desire, (i.e., the "sacred fire"). Aspirations, contests, enlightenment. Constructive power or the power to oppress and destroy. The power to control significant or even fearful forces. The gut reaction.

Card Description and Faery Wicca Tarot Meaning
Journey to Findias

I am in a beautiful landscape with gentle rolling hills, trees scattered alone or in small groups. The sky is washed in a peaceful rose hue, and a full moon rests just above the horizon. This is a strange landscape, for no matter which direction I turn and face, the full moon is always there, yet I am always facing south. My stomach feels as if it has butterflies in it, and I wrap my arms around my midriff.

As I look down, I see that I am standing on a dirt path and I begin to move down it. Soon I am moving up a small hill and as I arrive on top I am greeted by two amazing trees, one standing on either side of the path.

The tree to the right is in flames, a mixture of oranges, reds and white—an eerie but beautiful sight. The tree to the left has a strong trunk and leafy boughs that shimmer in the light breeze. On this tree's trunk is a word carved in ancient runes, but I can make out the word easily, and as if on cue, a giant WAND materializes between the two trees. It is as long as I am tall. In fact, it appears to be more of a staff than a wand—but a wand it is, and I can't help but think the wielder of this wand must be a giant.

Beyond the two trees and wand the pathway continues to wind up yet another hill and it seems to end or pass through a circle of slender trees.

My focus is drawn back to the wand. As I gaze upon it, I am so drawn to it that I suddenly desire to touch it more than I've desired to touch anything else. I step forward, and as I do the flames on the tree to the right shoot across the path and ignite the tree to the left. I am flabbergasted, for now the tree on the left is in flames while the tree to the right has a trunk of brown and green leafy boughs. But more than that, with this exchange, the sky overhead is now a midday sky filled with hot sunlight. The sunlight washes over me, beading my upper lip with sweat, and from the ground an amazing heat rises. I feel as if this world is suddenly a world of pure fire.

I gaze upon the wand, standing boldly between the two trees that beckon me to step forward again. And then I realize that this wand is a symbol of courage; to move forward into this landscape I must have the courage to feel the heat of this raw power of fire.

Hesitantly, I step forward. As I do, flames shoot across the path and the right tree is again the flaming tree and the left tree has returned to its original state. I laugh at the change in the sky—back to a rosy red, with full moon and cool breeze that instantly relieves the tension that had been building. With this change I feel the butterflies tickle my stomach and I hug my midriff again.

The flaming tree cracks and pops, as if speaking to me. Flames leap into the air and flicker. The power of fire is forceful and unpredictable, yet I know that if I observe the fire's pattern I will be able to ascertain the right time to pass between the two trees. Sure enough, the trees juxtapose their images and I begin counting. When they have returned full circle, I don't even hesitate but race forward, passing effortlessly between the two.

I reach for the Wand of Courage, but it has disappeared! My heart is thumping in my chest, and behind me the trees switch and I hear the racing of the flames cross the path and in their passing my heart seems to beat out this message:

The courage to feel the fire
Is felt in the stomach—
The seat of willpower and
The house of all desire.
Power is both gentle and forceful.

Two of Tine

THE PATH OF POWER

Classical Tarot Meaning

How will you use your power? The energy of this card is the creative principle of the universe, which implies that a partnership of powers is at hand: sun-moon, male-female, thought-action, one that is a combination of different individual capacities. Alliance is necessary if anything is to be truly accomplished and each partner must be reconciled to the different qualities of the other.

Card Description and Faery Wicca Tarot Meaning

Journey to Findias – continued

The moment I pass through the two trees an amazing thing happens: I find myself standing back between them, as if I am on film and the film has been reversed and is moving in slow motion. On either side of me two wands appear, guarding me from the flashing fire like castle sentries. The tree on the right is half flames and half trunk and green leafy boughs. The tree on the left is half trunk and green leafy boughs and half flames.

Neither is moving—they are still as stone, frozen in motion. The landscape before me has the gentle, rose-hued sky and full moon, while the landscape behind me is washed with the powerful heat of the midday sun. The words *force* and *gentleness* race through my mind.

The path winds up the hill before me, and the circle of slender trees now look so much closer than before. I can see a radiating glow coming from their center and I long to find out what causes the glow.

It's as if my longing, my desire, pulls my attention back to the wand sentries. I automatically reach out with my hands, resting them against the sides of the wands. They are not wood as I thought, but have a smoothness beyond description, and feel neither hot nor cold, nor even warm, but tingling as if radiating with the glow that is inside the circle of trees.

Closing my eyes, I push my hands against the wands and feel so very protected. I feel somehow in balance. With this thought a rush of heat rises from the ground beneath my feet through me. POWER, I am being filled with the power of an unknown source; it certainly isn't mine, and I am not sure it is coming from the wands either.

I begin to understand the meaning of the wands—they are symbols of power, communicating a very simple factor about the different qualities of invoked or evoked power. These qualities of power are found in the fire of life that also runs through our veins and gives us our creativity. This power is alchemical.

The power of this alchemy had already been demonstrated through the trees reversing their image with every pause of each exhalation. The sentries of this fantastic land are now challenging me to connect with my own fire, making me consciously aware that the pause of my out-breath is a regular part of mundane living, which places me between the worlds—between creativity and destruction.

Instantly, my stomach becomes filled with that butterfly sensation. My fire naturally lives in the solar plexus center of my body, which is the house of willpower and ego. Am I on a journey to my willpower, my ego? The roaring crackle of the trees' fire comes as the two Wands of Power disappear and I am propelled forward. The passing flames lick at my backside and I hear them hiss:

> How do you wield your power?
> Forcefully or gently?
> Where is your balance found
> in the world of ego?

Three of Tine

THE DANCE OF PARTNERSHIP

Classical Tarot Meaning

The Trinity holds the absolute destiny over all lives, even those of the gods. Destiny unfolding. Powers of creation with regards to invention, commercial enterprises and grand fortune. However, this card also implies rewards or punishments in the karmic sense.

Card Description and Faery Wicca Tarot Meaning

Journey to Findias – continued

The path leads unobstructed to the circle of slender trees rising on the crest of the hill. I begin moving down it, and as I take three steps, three Wands of Courage materialize before me. I am overwhelmed with the desire to dance around them and so I weave in and out, circling around each and moving on to the next to repeat the pattern.

I am exhilarated, and in my dancing I find that I am pulling threads from the Web of Life into my dancing; they appear as brightly colored ribbons that I weave around each pole as if dancing the May Pole at Beltaine. Each time I complete the circuit and reach for another ribbon, the others that have already been woven become ghosts and I move through them with my new ribbon without disturbing their placement.

Around and around I dance and weave the ribbons and I am aware that the three wands and ribbons begin to create the Spirit symbol. I am so very happy that I am finding the Spirit of this land, that I can feel my smile so intense that my cheeks begin to ache.

In that moment, I become aware that I feel very balanced and connected to the courage power of the landscape and wands; it feels as if I am weaving some type of partnership between the wands and the land. I feel this partnership inside me and outside me.

My dancing abruptly ends and I want nothing more than to sit inside the ribboned Spirit symbol I have created. I find myself instantly sitting inside, the ribbons' ghosts allowing glimpses of their colors. I stare at the wand before me, the other two behind on either side of me, like the sentries between the two guardian trees.

"Wand of Courage," I whisper, "TEACH me." Closing my eyes, I open to the Spirit lesson I know is being conveyed. I think back to the lesson learned when traveling in the landscape of Air. That is where the Spirit symbol first revealed itself to me, and now I am sitting within it in the landscape of Fire.

The Sword of Illumination had taught me to feel with my mind and how to shift into the second attention, thus arriving at a new sacred point of view. Perception shifts when we learn how to enter sacred time and sacred space, which is accomplished by attuning oneself to the eight energy shifts of the Wheel of the Year.

Ah, it made sense. Here I was, dancing the three vibration of the first triad of this landscape and I'd felt as if I was dancing the May Pole at Beltaine! Yes, that was it: the landscape of Fire I know to be connected to the season of summer, and the first major energy shift occurs at the Great Festival of La Baal Tinne on May 1, when the May Pole dance is performed. This act is focused on reconnecting the energies of Father Sky (the masculine) with Mother Earth (the feminine) and bringing that "partnership" of energy into your own center.

As I danced I felt this partnership being created!

I opened my eyes and lay back inside the Spirit symbol. The rose-hued sky washed overhead. Again I felt the butterflies stir in my stomach, but this time I didn't hug my midriff, instead I allowed them their dance, and I wasn't surprised when their fluttering moved up into my heart.

My heart! I sat up and looked to the Wand of Courage. Yes, I was dancing the dance of reconnecting my ego (which resided in my solar plexus) with my Spirit (which resided in my heart) and I was doing this through my willpower, my desire to feel the balance, feel the polarities alive within me, which was the reason for the desire to dance the Spirit of Fire awake.

I jumped to my feet and looked to the circle of trees. Somehow I feel that the circle of trees represents the heart, and that I have successfully conjured Spirit but now through my willpower, through courage I must connect with the heart of the land of Fire. A rush of heat came up from the ground, rising through my body like the Kundalini and I hear the voice of the Fire Spirit crackle:

The power of courage
is only the first step in the dance—
The second step
is dancing ego to Spirit—
This is a very hard step indeed,
for it takes action of heart
to achieve success.

Four of Tine

THE MARRIAGE OF THE TWIN FLAMES

Classical Tarot Meaning

Four corner posts of the earth, signifying a home place, security, and the sacred marriage. Success, the reward of effort, the first establishment of a secure position in the world. Initial security is of a provisional nature, with much knowledge still to be acquired, and many future challenges to be met.

Card Description and Faery Wicca Tarot Meaning

Journey to Findias – continued

Forming a partnership with ego and Spirit, the path leads ME, in just one breath, to the circle of trees, where three wands appear, forming an archway under which I am to pass.

I can see inside the circle of trees, and there, in the middle of the space, dances a huge bonfire. For one moment my heart misses a beat—for this bonfire is not contained in a pit, but seems to devour the land from which it rises.

A jolt of surprise ripples through my belly, as a cloaked figure appears out of nowhere. I do not know who this person or Being may be, and can't help but wonder if it is the same Being who appeared to me in the Landscape of Gorias.

Two letters appear over the flames in mid-air, flames themselves. I know this word, and as I speak it aloud the Wand of Courage reappears in the flames.

Suddenly I understand that the Wand is symbolic for Spirit made manifest. Only through true belief does such an occurrence transpire. The roaring bonfire becomes representative of my own Spirit Flames now awakened in my heart.

If I were to surrender all to the flames, I would become the guardian of the Wand of Courage, a mediator for the Gods.

A shudder moves the material of the cloak. I focus intently on this Being. Why did such a thought cause the Being to visibly shudder? Then, interestingly enough, I realize it was I who shuddered at the thought, for it provoked fear in my heart. To have such power becomes a threat to my inner security, yet is also the greatest temptation to throw myself into the flames: to become One With The Gods! To be immortal! Who would not desire such power?

I am frozen and close my eyes. The popping and crackling of the bonfire sings its power to me:

The next step is
recognizing your position—
your Divine Relationship with Spirit,
In this there is great courage,
A gift of comfort
And a true marriage
Between the inner Twin Flames.

Five of Tine

ONE WITH THE NOBLE ORDER

Classical Tarot Meaning

A time of trial and difficulty. An inability to stand up to hostile powers. A sense of powerlessness. Earlier security collapses into acute insecurity. This impasse may, however, serve a higher goal not immediately apparent, no matter how agonizing it may feel at the moment. Conflict around you.

Card Description and Faery Wicca Tarot Meaning

Journey to Findias – continued

As I open my eyes I see that the wand archway has collapsed; only one remains standing, while two lie on the path as if blocking the entrance to the sacred grove.

Slowly, the cloaked figure raises a fifth wand. This movement changes the intensity of the bonfire, the flames subside somewhat, and the tips curl into themselves rather than reach upward.

A far-off sound comes in bits and pieces—horse hooves pounding the earth and the creaking and clanking of a chariot. The wind begins to stir the fire and the flames dance wildly.

Then I hear the voice of a woman, "I am Anand." The word *Anand* vibrates through my midriff. Anand? Who is this Faery?

I look to the cloaked figure, who stands still as a statue. Then slowly, the wand in hand is lowered, barring any attempt to touch the Wand of Courage.

"The fear of power corrupting your heart is a major breakthrough. Realize the irreparable damage corrupt power yields. TO be one with the Gods, to become immortal, is to become humble." The voice is masculine.

"Move into the center of the flames. Be consumed by Spirit. Such purification will align you to true intent. Desire modes will be as dust in the wind, as the ashes of your old self, your little self, is transmutated into cinder."

My teeth click together as I think of the flames eating my flesh, for flashes of the Burning Times spring to life and my heart breaks with a "Why?"

The voice of Anand seems to scream now into my ear: *"That is why you must become as pure as fire—in memory of them!"*

Now the vibration of the pounding horse hooves ripple through my body, and I throw my arms apart, which have been hugging my midriff. A blast of heat scorches my skin, and I hear:

Time to dance with the Faery again—
In and out of seasons and years,
Becoming One with the radiant light
Of the full power of your
Inner soul's delight.

Fear not the Dance of the Heart,
More true than the ego's flight,
For in the end, when the tune dies still,
The Ancient Ones will hold your Love
With them in the Hollow Hill.

Six of Tine

THE POWER OF THE HEART

Classical Tarot Meaning

Resurrection followed the sacrifice. Glory, victory, and triumph. A personal or a vicarious experience of adulation and fame, a sense of victory with all adversaries conquered and all blockages overcome. But the triumph is finite, it will eventually come to an end. Glory will shift to some different meaning, perhaps less glorious and more perilous.

Card Description and Faery Wicca Tarot Meaning

Journey to Findias – continued

I am learning to surrender to the Will of Spirit and to become the Champion of the Noble Order of the Divine Plan of Deity.

There the wands align—the changing reality of the Five, under directorship of the One, whose hooded cloak has fallen back. Long, gray hair curls down his back. He is a Fay of the OtherWorld, the guide, the guardian, the Wise One—all three.

The Draoi Gebann, who holds the Wand of Courage to direct the energy flow of the Ancient Ones, now lifts his wand, and all the others align. His role is that of the enlightened one. Enlightenment: the result of becoming purified by fire.

My heart center floods open as I MERGE with the greatest desire to become an instrument of power, to become a Wand of Courage, and conquer all obstacles set in my way. To become the victor!

Stand Strong.
Speak Strong.
Dance Strong.
Act Strong.
Rest Strong.
See Strong.
Play Strong.
Work Strong.
Love Strong.
Believe Strong.
Powerful Anand!

Seven of Tine

THE CHAMPION'S WHEEL

Classical Tarot Meaning

After achieving glory, we must hold it against challengers. While high ambitions are honorable, beware that they don't consume you. This card warns against the challenges of high ambition, always vulnerable to threats from both parties above—who are watching your progress—and below you—who want your position. Possession of power is always envied by those as yet ignorant of its risks; but the possession of power can be held only by sustained effort, skill, and courage.

Card Description and Faery Wicca Tarot Meaning

Journey to Findias – continued

As I become aware of the Spark of Divine Will, I become as the Warrior, but not the enraged, battle-frenzied warrior who is out of control, and thus a hazard to the Ancient Ones, but the warrior who is the Champion, dignified, controlled, centered in Spirit.

"There are five spokes on the Wheel of Champions," the Wise One communicates telepathically as he holds his wand against the tip of the Wand of Courage, to which five more wands are attached. "You must become all five spokes to be the Champion."

I focus on the Wand of Courage, how it rises from the center of the flames. How clear it seems. While this wand represents the spine upon which our internal energy rises and falls, it also represents the Spindle of Necessity, the trunk of the Great Tree of Life. Each of the five wands holds the position of energy connected to the five provinces of the blessed isle of Erin.

The Champion of Leinster is a warrior for Mother Earth. I must defend her safety and the safety of all life forms on her great body. I defend her—with no compromise, thus becoming a knight or dame in the Noble Order of Tara.

The Champion of Munster is as the Bard, Amorgen, master of magickal verse, poetry, and song. I know the Three Noble Strains, which every great master of the harp should command. I know how to conjure the natural energies of the sidhe. I become the lover-spouse of Erie once more.

The Champion of Connaught is the Celtic Artisan, whose magickal crafts include weaving, sculpting, ogham, healing, and divination. The Sacred Druid Grove of Dana is my home, and I know the mystery and power of the mistletoe berry and the *fé*.

The Champion of Ulster is the wise counsel to the High King and Queen of Eire. I am the Draoi, whose counsel governs even the Lia Fail. I direct the rituals and seasonal ceremonies. I know the Five Paths of Law, which govern the cosmos. My magick is made manifest.

The Champion of Meath is a companion to the Tuatha De Danann, co-walker in their realms. All other positions of the Champion are surrendered to the others for this one, as I dwell in the center of peace.

To pass the Ordeal of Fire, one receives the blessing from the solar gods and goddesses of Ireland, thus becoming the guardian of the OtherWorld Spear of Lugh!

The landscape of Findias begins to quake. The Champion's Wheel begins to spin round and round, as the Wise One continues to channel energy through his wand into the Spindle of Necessity—into my spine.

A jolt of energy races up my spine—warm, tingling heat, pulsing through my body. A band of sweat beads my upper brow. "Receive

Now! Become the Champion," the fires hisses and crackles. "You must do so willingly, though. You must desire it. Your EGO must be strong enough to withstand the challenge, and your Spirit must be aligned with destiny."

I reach my hand out to touch the Spear of Lugh. Just one touch is all that is needed to feed the fire and become One with the Power.

To touch the Spear of Lugh,
You become the power of alchemy,
The wielder of creativity or destruction.
Only the Champion knows how to channel such power
Effectively and with balance.

Eight of Tine

THE GOLDEN RING

Classical Tarot Meaning

An important journey, changes of scene, motion, and progress implied, but all could be ruined by over-eagerness, over-confidence, or excessive activity. Warning: pride goeth before a fall. Energy flowing. Situations can change very quickly. Development. Time speeds by.

Card Description and Faery Wicca Tarot Meaning

Journey to Findias – continued

The Spear of Lugh is as a lightning bolt and the moment my fingers touch the Wand of Courage, the world changes.

The bonfire roars with thunder, as a flash of enlightenment, so brilliant, wipes out all vision. Eight wands align, as a blast of energy comes from the end of each into the center of the fire.

An opening appears in the earth and is now ringed by the flames; it emits such a brilliant light that it is impossible to soon make out the earth opening.

A vacuum of air pulls at me, tugging my body closer and closer to the earth hole.

"Come into the center of peace," the flames hiss and crackle, as my body is pulled off the ground, and I feel myself spinning into the flames.

"Which Spoke of the Champion's Wheel do you claim for yourself now?" asks a distant voice. The flames reach out to lick my skin.

I am so amazed. The flames are not searing, not furiously hot, but cool to the touch!

The Ordeal of Fire is not the searing, hurting trauma so often expected, but a cool and refreshing experience.

"You must walk through the Plain of Cold Fire to get to the Center of Peace. This can only happen when one knows the Cup of Truth."

Power is all consuming, it so easily pulls us in misguided directions. We can so easily become corrupt WITH power when little self desires power, and, as the Gnostics say, "Absolute power corrupts absolutely."

To have true power
One is centered in the Golden Ring.
Yet, true power is an illusion,
For such power is corrupt.
True power is Shared Power.

Nine of Tine

FORTRESS OF
SACRED SELF

Classical Tarot Meaning

You can build your castle, but it may become a fortress. This applies to an element of the unconscious, hidden deep in the mind, closed away and dark to everyday perception. Fortresses can also be thought of as prisons, housing savage, uncontrollable characters. However, fortress also implies a barrier, but every barrier has two sides: it keeps things out and it keeps things in. No position of defense can be held forever.

Card Description and Faery Wicca Tarot Meaning
Journey to Findias – continued

I am in an underground cavern, a room of sorts. The light is very dark, shadowy. As I turn around I see a wall that isn't really a wall, yet it has an oak-plank door set among green pillars, which are actually the handles of giant wands set upright like columns.

At the top of the wand columns are what appear to be an island, grass, rocks, water, and trees peeking thorough a layer of mist. There seems to be no route for accessing the island, and then I wonder if it lies behind the oak door.

I study the door. On it appears a word written in an ancient Irish alphabet—a magickal alphabet once used only in the Bardic College. I instantly know the word; its meaning brings a smile to my face, for almost naturally, I understand the lesson of Findias, of the Wand of Courage, which is what I have become.

A peaceful and vibrant light shines out a keyhole positioned under the doorknob . . . ah, yes . . . the light of SACRED mystery . . . the mystery of shared power . . . shared resources . . . the power of Findias . . . the reflection of our world!

To return to the primal land, one must share their power, their energy, their resources, their truth and love, by trusting Spirit, by allowing little self the opportunity to become a fortress, guarding the kingdom of peace. This way, little self is transformed by the light of peace delivered by the enlightenment of Lugh's Spear. The jolt of thunder caused by this bolt of lightning is felt within the midriff, the solar plexus. It forces one to swallow hard and hold fast to the contents of their stomach.

When all is calm once more, the person becomes a Champion and is asked what type of Champion they wish to be at this time. Finding one's true place in life in the present is indeed a Gift of Courage; for when this position is known the Champion must become the Wand of Courage and wield their power to become the full expression of their position.

The talisman of Findias
The Wand of Courage
Will open the door
To who the True You is
At any given point in time—
But to use such power
You must be willing
To become that which you are
And thus return to the Sacred Self.

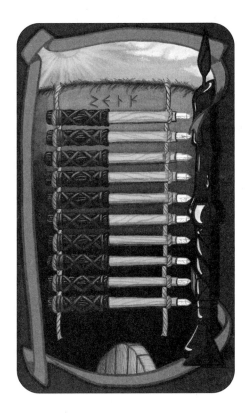

Ten of Tine

STAIRWAY TO
PARADISE

Classical Tarot Meaning

Supreme power, triumphant, unchallengeable. Taking full responsibility. Moving away. A burden. Ten of wands expresses meaning similar to the Gnostic view: a triumph of tyranny, misuse of power, selfish authority demolishing its opposition, excessive pressure, punishment of ambition. Oppression of this magnitude could only generate resentment or mutiny. Misuse of power encourages egocentrism. The oppressed can only suffer, hope, and wait.

Card Description and Faery Wicca Tarot Meaning
Journey to Findias – continued

The oak door has been unlocked and swings open. Inside is a small chamber, containing a ladder hanging down from above.

Above there is an opening and overhead shines a beautiful sun in a blue sky. The sun is descending and casts the first hint of sunset into the surrounding clouds.

To climb the ladder out of what now seems a dark pit means to become mySELF, to begin really living—no more false illusions, no more masks, no more fear. I can leave such things behind in this grave and rise into a new day just like a phoenix reborn.

I have received a great awareness journeying through the Land of Falias: it is about personal power, becoming it while at the same time linking it with the power of Spirit so that it becomes shared power. But the lesson is more than this. I have learned to become a Champion, someone who strives to become what they desire to be and to accomplish such goals, but most importantly, knowing that to be a True Champion, a holy knight, means one must take full responsibility for their actions and learn to be grounded and balanced in the center of peace.

As I reach up and grab the first wand of the ladder, I hoist myself up and hear the faint thunder of horse hooves pounding the earth, and the far away creaking of chariot wheels. On the breeze, a warm breeze of summer, I smell the smoke of power, and hear a gentle laughter:

"Welcome Home."

The Element Cards of Uisce

Ace of Uisce

THE CAULDRON OF MUIRIAS

Classical Tarot Meaning

Birth; beginnings; fruitfulness; pleasures; home; nourishment; satisfaction; caring. Ace of Uisce enhances all other cards. In a difficult situation it means that any trouble is easier to bear with the help of Love. New love.

Card Description and Faery Wicca Tarot Meaning

Journey to Muírias

A cool breeze ruffles my hair. The ground is moist beneath my feet. Lush grass covers gentle rolling hills. Cutting through the hills winds a flowing stream; its water is iridescent, reflecting the rainbow colors of the sunset.

I stand on the stream bank and follow its flow with my eyes, calmly flowing on its course into the sea.

Waves rise and fall where the two bodies of water meet. I close my eyes and breathe in the ocean air—saline and moist. The "caw" of a seagull brings my attention to the sky, where I see a waning crescent moon.

But how can this be? The old moon is rising in the west, not the east! How can it be just above the setting sun—this is an impossibility!

In a twinkling, as if in the space between two soft lights, a crystal castle rises from the sea. There, on a dais, before the castle entrance threshold shines a huge golden CAULDRON. From its belly rises a soft, bubbling light in a glow of rose and muted purple.

This cauldron dwarfs the crystal castle, and appears to be the heart of the castle.

The beating of my own heart matches the crashing rhythm of the waves, ebb and flow . . . ebb and flow . . . ebb and flow. Closing my eyes, I place my hand on my chest, listening, feeling, the inner rhythm of life, matching and mingling it with the outer rhythm of life.

I am lulled into a trance as if Faery Struck. I am no longer solid, but as the water in an Undine Dance, flowing to and from the belly of the cauldron.

Come to me—
Return to me—
Regenerate—
Recycle—
Rebirth—
Flow from me—
Go from me—
Re-entry—
Regrowth.

Two of Uisce

THE TWISTED TREE

Classical Tarot Meaning

A unified concept of Love (the Ace) becomes a duality; active partnership. Trust; sympathy; consummation of desires; vows; promises; engagements; proposal of marriage; intimate friendships.

Card Description and Faery Wicca Tarot Meaning

Journey to Muírias – continued

As effervescent as the froth on waves, I shapeshift into a creature of the OtherWorld. I am of the primal land, and recognize the sweet beauty its mystical image conjures in the minds of mortals: it is a daydream landscape of romantic impressions, the language of the heart, the face of Soul.

On the crest of a small knoll, two trees twine together as if they are long-lost lovers feeling the embrace of the other after being apart for years. The twisted tree is alive with the primitive POWER of the earth—feeling, sensation, raw emotion, polarizing into something beyond itself.

Two golden cauldrons sit side by side on the bank of the rainbow stream, flowing calmly to the sea. All is perfect bliss and happiness. The ecstatic breath of love. The force of Love.

I am neither human nor inhuman in this land. I am neither land nor non-land in this daydream. I am the emotion of union. The first cauldron has divided and doubled itself—it is abundance, but more than just in the sense of the word. It is in relationship with itself, the self and the inner self made manifest; the sweet extension of the self. As such, the self in relationship with the extension of self generates a total of ideal love; it represents the allusiveness of love, which is neither tangible nor intangible—all or nothing.

Love exists in the land, yet it is the land that implies it is something more than what it seems, something greater than itself.

A sigh, light and airy, flows from my lips—a breath, a dewdrop, a gentle shift in the sands. The lapping spring water, the rainbow water, darkens the embankment, caressing the soil, imprinting its auric energy as a word, an impression in the land. I know this mystic truth, inside and outside. I am this impression:

Nature . . . pure and simple,
Is the exalted power—
The mystic center of the Ancient Spiral—
The calm center in the belly—
A point of beginning and ending—
Peace.

Three of Uisce

THE THREE CAULDRONS OF INSPIRATION

Classical Tarot Meaning

"May She, who is before all things, the incomprehensible and indescribable Grace, fill you within and increase in you Her knowledge." Feminine qualities: sympathy, sensitivity, responsiveness, loving kindness, good will, intelligence (intuition). Codes of honor; contracts and agreements. Celebrations; fruition, joy, satisfaction, solace, fulfillment of hopes. The card of healing. In a relationship reading this card can signify conception (i.e., child).

Card Description and Faery Wicca Tarot Meaning

Journey to Muirias – continued

A lullaby swirls on the eddy of the stream, baked by a sloshing sound. Enchantment is here. The vibrations and harmonies weave together and create. Aois Dana (inspired poet) appears from the Other-

World—co-walkers, four of whom are the cup-bearers who guard and dispense the Holy Waters found in the Cauldron of Inspiration only to the truthful of heart.

The two cauldrons have now become three cauldrons. One of the Fay moves close to the cauldrons, while two of the cup-bearers hover near.

"These are the Three Cauldrons of Amorgen," he says, enchanting me. "Mysterious elements, embedded with warming, votary, and knowledge. Has your soul been warmed?"

The warmth in my belly is the house of my soul. I have sat in the heat, the source of my poetic art.

A second Fay moves forward, behind her the other two cup-bearers hover.

"And what is the position of your Cauldron of Vocation? SHOW us."

When I practiced Bardic and poetic skills, the side was prominent in reception, and then I attained upright as I became the master of knowledge and learned art.

The two joined hands, speaking in unison, while the four cup-bearers gathered behind.

"There are two chief divisions of joy by which joy can overthrow the third cauldron."

I sing of the Cauldron of Knowledge whence the law of each art is dispensed which gives boundless treasure, which magnifies each artist in general and gives each person its gift.

Divine Joy and Human Joy can overthrow the Cauldron of Knowledge. I am human and know joy in one of four divisions: the force of sexuality; the joy of health; the joy of attaining poetic privilege after long study; joy at the approach of . . . .

"Imbas," the two fays chant. "Amassed by the nine hazels of fair fruitfulness in the Well Segais of the sidhe, which hurtles upstream along the Boyne in a ram's head bore, swifter than a three-year-old at the racetrack, in the middle of June each seventh year."

My mind is swirling with such information. The rainbow stream seems to glow brighter and brighter. The fays and cup-bearers come closer. The crashing of waves thunders in my ears:

Look deep into the waters.
The cauldron of vocation sings
with insights of grace,
with measures of knowledge,
with streams of inspiration;
an estuary of wisdom,
a confluence of knowledge,
a stream of dignity. . . .

In my mystic center I see the Three Cauldrons of Inspiration: one in my belly, the second in my heart, the third in my brain. They all stand upright, surrounded by the rainbow stream . . . .

Insights of grace—
Measures of knowledge—
Streams of inspiration—
An estuary of wisdom.

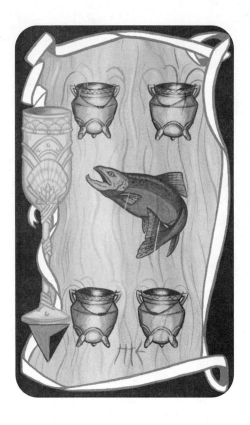

Four of Uisce

SALMON OF KNOWLEDGE

Classical Tarot Meaning

Following the fulfillment of love in the first triad of the Dragon's Eye, a new cycle is initiated with a sense of decline, or regression of happiness (i.e., the after the honeymoon phase, when love becomes an everyday part of life). Hints of new insights. Search heart for answer. Water can teach us trust and can quench our spiritual thirst.

Card Description and Faery Wicca Tarot Meaning
Journey to Muirias – continued

One of the Faery has become my companion. She beckons me to gaze into the rainbow stream. I am Sinend, gazing into Connla's Well, with the nine hazels of inspiration falling into its water, then eaten by the salmon of knowledge swimming there. As the salmon swallow the nuts their bodies become speckled with purple spots.

As the mist clears and my sight is restored, I see salmon swimming upstream from the sea. I spot one fish in particular that twists sideways as it passes between four golden cauldrons. The cauldrons, though under water, have water flowing from their bellies, as if they are the source of the stream, thus the source of the sea as well, and all waters for that matter.

My eye locks on the eye of the salmon. We stare at the other with great intensity. For one second I am the salmon, opening and closing my mouth—water filling my gills—an inner knowing so clear and present.

As if the mind of the salmon is within ME, I hear his thoughts; I suddenly know the truth of my own heart!

The Cauldron of the Heart
Gives and is replenished,
Promotes and is enlarged,
Nourishes and is given life,
Ennobles and is exalted,
Requests and is filled with answers,
Sings and is filled with song!

Five of Uisce

PERFECT TRUST

Classical Tarot Meaning

Turning away from old ties, looking forward to new interests; something comes to an end; hiatus of regret; alienation; poverty; frustration; loss of pleasure; a marriage without real love; abandonment; "this too shall pass."

Card Description and Faery Wicca Tarot Meaning

Journey to Muirias – continued

My heart fills with harmony, abundance, and beauty, and I am encouraged by the Faery Companion to catch my wisdom, knowledge, and omniscience. Without hesitation, I plunge my hands into the water and feel them close around a slippery and scaly body.

I lift the salmon out of the water and from its mouth spews five cauldrons that tumble in the air about his body before falling to my feet.

As the cauldrons tumble about the salmon's body—in what seems the blink of the eye—I feel an opening grow larger and larger within my heart.

"Do you know the knowledge and qualities of the water?" I hear the salmon ask.

Yes, I am realizing these things now—in this moment—as the salmon's body wiggles in my hands:

Love . . .

I want to shout, but only think, and the salmon grows larger.

"Purity . . ." I whisper, and the salmon grows even larger.

"Fertility. . ." I say, and the salmon is gigantic, my hands no longer fit around it. HOW will I be able to hold on?

The salmon begins to twist, and I fear that I will lose my knowledge and wisdom and omniscience, but the Faery Companion places her hands about mine—her hands are those of a giant. As she does so, the salmon jerks me off the ground.

A haze of rainbow colors fill my vision, swirling and spiraling around me. The sound of water crashes against my ears, and a bubbling gurgling sound brings these words up from the depths of my heart and mind:

Utilize my gifts of water!
Trust the words that rise from deep within—
All the answers lie beneath the surface of your
Cauldron of the Heart.
Learn to trust—
And your spiritual thirst will be quenched!

Six of Uisce

POETIC INSPIRATION

Classical Tarot Meaning

Following the failure of love associated with the five of Uisce, there is a return to the early love experience; reunion; faded memory; vital energy of love refreshed; psychic return; nostalgic inner pilgrimage; mother's love; soul-mate.

Card Description and Faery Wicca Tarot Meaning

Journey to Muirias – continued

The concept of bliss is one that we all desire. Aligning with the flow and moving forward, deeper and deeper into the ocean of the psyche, is such a refreshing experience.

This is freedom—the journey into wisdom and knowledge; freedom from self-condemnation.

I still hold the salmon in my hands. I am flowing through the rainbow stream into the sea. My three cauldrons are aligned and their reflections show the reality—the truth of what is inside my heart.

Each cauldron is an accumulation of water; each enriched by diligence, fermented by inspiration, overturned by joy—an enduring power whose protection never ebbs.

As if from a trickle to a vast body of water, my inner cauldrons move me inTO sacred relationship with self, preparing me for sacred relationship with my Patron Moon Goddess. As if this inner knowing is backed by a wave of inspiration, I hear the far-off cry of a Bard singing to me not to forget where I am, where I have been:

The three forges wherein I was enclosed
Brought me delight of mind;
That I cannot revisit these three forges
Wears away my mind's treasury.

I reflect on my three cauldrons and their reflections, each set creating the forges that the Bards sing of, becoming a Bardic School. Each forge is representative of a house in learning, to which his words refer. The house of memorizing is the first. Oh well, I know this house in my spiritual training.

The second is the house of reclining. This forge is well known to those seeking inspiration and prophetic artistic gifts. Many times I have reclined in this house, while the third—the house of the critic, where the exposition of poetry is learned—is the school room I have known all my life, for:

I am the daughter of poetry,
Poetry, daughter of reflection,
Reflection, daughter of meditation,
Meditation, daughter of lore,
Lore, daughter of research,
Research, daughter of great knowledge,
Great Knowledge, daughter of intelligence,
Intelligence, daughter of understanding,
Understanding, daughter of wisdom,
Wisdom, daughter of the three gods of Dana!

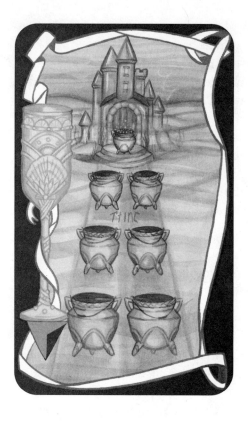

Seven of Uisce

BAPTISM OF WATER

Classical Tarot Meaning

Pragmatic thought; the rich depths of unconscious mind tapped by dreams and archetypal imagery; source of inspiration, feminine spirit; ambivalent attitude toward mystical experiences and inspirational dreams; true vision; poetic sensibility; talent; fantasy; illusion; unrealistic attitude; wishful thinking.

Card Description and Faery Wicca Tarot Meaning
Journey to Muirias – continued

The most beautiful crystal castle ever seen, the vision of dreams, appears before me, as if on cue after the recitation of poetic inspiration. The city of Muirias rises there—its threshold blocked by the Cauldron of bubbling water and fading light—the Undry—Cauldron of Abundance.

If I move between the three sets of cauldrons, the three forges of sacred relationships, up to the cauldron on the dais, I know that I will understand the vision of my dreams. I will know and understand the deep messages of the OtherWorld as they echo through my cauldrons of inspiration into my conscious mind.

Dare I dip my hands into the water of purity? Dare I receive the blessing of Brigid's fire and water? If I receive the baptism of such holy water, I must be willing to see the reality and let go of all self-induced illusion. The fantasy—the self-deceit—will be cleansed and I will be freed to step into the truth of my personal power. I THINK, therefore, I am.

I circle around the cauldron three times. I dip my hands in the water and anoint my heart with the holy water in the act of purification, for I long to be free.

Instantly, a choir of voices fills my ears and I hear the most beautiful song in all the world, its words rising up from the cauldron on bubbles of fading light:

A small wave for your form
A small wave for your voice
A small wave for your generosity
A small wave for your appetite
A small wave for your wealth
A small wave for your life
A small wave for your health
Seven waves of grace upon you.
Waves of the Giver of Health.

Eight of Uisce

ALCHEMICAL FUSION

Classical Tarot Meaning

Turning away from what is no longer useful; severing links with the past; a passage into a new phase of life; alone one must be willing to climb their holy mountain to find their sacred self.

Card Description and Faery Wicca Tarot Meaning

Journey to Muirias – continued

This act of baptism has magickally caused the door to the castle to open, and there stands my Faery Companion, WITH outstretched hand. She beckons me to take hold.

As I rise to my feet, I am acutely aware of the two pillars of cauldrons that I must pass between.

To my left is one column of four cauldrons, stacked one on top the other. They are illuminated by an unearthly light that shines on them from the castle through the open door. But the column of four cauldrons to my right is dark and shadowy, disappearing into the dark void that suddenly encroaches upon the exterior of the castle.

To pass between the columns feels as if I must pass between my subconscious and conscious minds—to enter into the third attention which the lesson of Aer taught.

Passing between them will allow me to grasp the hand of the Faery Companion and be taken into the realm of Muirias, like an alternate reality.

These two columns will give me the gifts or blessings of alchemical fusion. In this realm I am like the water that will flow between the worlds, and by the breath of the Faery Companion I will be heated. As I become heated I will become the primary function of my mistress, Brigid, Goddess of Inspiration.

This is a solitary task one must do if they wish to deepen spiritually.

From the belly of the cauldron
flows the gifts of dispensation—
Open now to find the way
Between your head and heart.

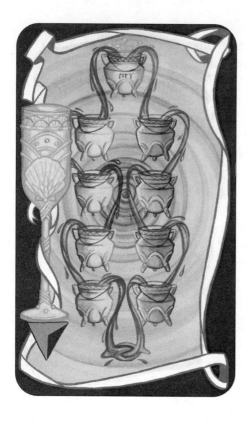

Nine of Uisce

THE GIFTS

Classical Tarot Meaning

Karma; full expression of love; happiness; sexuality and sensuality with kindness, good will, contentment, fruitfulness; physical health; emotional stability; wish comes true; be careful what you wish for, it just might come true.

Card Description and Faery Wicca Tarot Meaning

Journey to Muírías – continued

The nine cauldrons are alive and active. Moving between the two columns initiates this reality. The fusion has taken place and the two columns are now inseparable. They stand together as a platform supporting the Cauldron filled with bubbling water and fading light.

In this structure, the Cauldron of Inspiration spills forth its waters into two streams. The stream to the right represents the holy waters, while the stream to the left is the sacred life blood. These two streams flow down, filling the other cauldrons.

There is an ancient poem that is remembered in the flow of the two streams:

The cauldron of vocation
gives and is replenished,
promotes and is enlarged,
nourishes and is given lire,
ennobles and is exalted,
requests and is filled with answers,
sings and is filled with song,
preserves and is made strong,
arranges and receives arrangements,
maintains and is maintained.
Good is the well of measure,
Good is the abode of speech,
Good is the confluence of power:
it builds up strength.
It is greater than any domain,
It is better than any inheritance.
It numbers us among the wise,
And we depart from the ignorant.

These are the nine gifts of the Cauldron of Vocation. This vessel of the heart is active within all who are aware of their creative resources; it gives out in the physical world and is replenished by the inner world.

A great lesson is taught here: the practice of one's art is not to empty oneself, but to be filled again. There is no diminution in either quality or quantity of the personal gift.

The water spirals behind the pedestal of cauldrons. I am sucked into it, sucked into the Cauldron of Vocation within me.

"By the nine gifts of the cauldron," I hear in the swirling of the water. "The poet becomes a mediator for the people who seek them out."

This brings a new understanding: the Cauldron of Inspiration is the Holy Grail, which contains all the blessings and wishes come true in life! And in the split second between thought and realization, a ripple of the spiral carries me into the center of the Well of Connla, and the nine hazels drop one by one before me, and I hear:

Which hazel do you receive:
Poetry—Reflection—Meditation—
Lore—Research—Great Knowledge—
Intelligence—Understanding—
Wisdom?

Ten of Uisce

THE GODDESS' COVENANT

Classical Tarot Meaning

Attainment; harmonious love; security; peace; salvation from greatest fears of loneliness or abandonment; realization of dream; good marriage, lasting many years; a lifetime of contentment; true family.

Card Description and Faery Wicca Tarot Meaning

Journey to Muirias – continued

At last I have been admitted to the land of Muirias inside the crystal castle. The land is lush and green. Shamrocks lace the grass. A twisted tree stands before me, and rising beyond it are green hills.

Upon the hills sit ten cauldrons overflowing with rainbows. Above them hovers my Faery Companion.

As I gaze upon this surreal scene, a luscious warmth flushes my cheeks a crimson red. I am truly home, for this green and fertile landscape is none other than that contained within my HEART!

The Holy Grail within me is very full, filled with joy and love, truth and abundance, knowledge and wisdom. All these things can only be found within. Once found, they flow outward into one's life, creating an outward world filled with such things.

My beautiful Faery Companion has shown me the simple truth, which the Goddess has always spoken to us:

For if that which you seek—
You find not within your heart—
You will never find it without!

The double rainbow is Her covenant, Her confirmation that heart is aligned with the purity of water, thus evoking the blessing of Her gifts into our lives!

For behold—
I have been with you
From the beginning,
And I am that
Which is attained
At the end of All desire!

The Element Cards of Domhan

ACE THROUGH TEN

Power of Pentacles Show Me the Cycle of Spiritual Balance

Ace of Domhan

EARTHLIGHT

Classical Tarot Meaning

Star of Knowledge; reward of knowledge; a revelation of the mystery of life emanating from woman and the earth; fertility; abundance; creation and giving; the birth of material wealth; symbol of beginning; new job; opportunity in the worldly sense; new source of income; stable foundation for future building.

Card Description and Faery Wicca Tarot Meaning
Journey to Falias

A black moon sits in a charcoal sky. This landscape is ominous. Chills shiver up my spine. Dare I enter it? For that matter, how can I? The path is blocked by thick and dangerous looking thorn bushes. I see no way to pass through, no matter whether I search to the right of the path or to the left. The path simply ends.

I look down and realize I am standing on a golden stone slab that is flat and engraved with a pentagram. From this angle, the pentacle is upright, its top point indicating that forward movement would be required to continue my journey.

I step back, allowing the full star to come into view, and as I do I feel strong, as if a POWER radiates from it to me.

"Master of the elemental world" is a thought that seems to come from it to my mind. Telepathy—empathy. Do I know the deeper meaning of the five-pointed star?

While it represents the four elements—earth, air, fire, and water—and the synthesis of them, symbolized by the fifth part, representing ether or spirit, there is a more powerful meaning to this symbol. I sense that such knowledge is the key to finding one's way to the Lia Fal—Stone of Destiny.

Unlike the other three Cities, the De Danann treasure for the City of Falias is nowhere to be seen.

I am suddenly filled with sorrow. Again I step onto the golden slab. A renewed sense of strength fills my heart, mind, and body.

"Welcome to the land of Ancestors!" says someone, yet I see no one.

"Step upon the primal land and feel the sorrow, the residue of mourning and grieving attached to the ancestors. Humans will experience loss and that is natural—just as it is natural and healthy to grieve such loss—but to stay fixed in such grieving risks loss of balance and thus loss of vision.

"Look down at the pentagram, it teaches you about the Life-Death-Life cycle, a peaceful heart, and a compassionate spirit."

This knowing flowed up through my feet, as if the pentagram slab radiated a soft power of energy—an earthlight that comes up from the core of Mother Earth, yet spirals beyond, into a source of unknown power.

I am standing on a starting point; the full experience obscured from my knowing, just like the path obscured by thorn bushes.

In this moment I am reconnecting with the land of our ancestors, my native land. In doing so, I am receiving the wisdom of their experiences, which can help me on my journey in this world, but only if I am willing to use this information wisely; only if I am willing to learn from someone else's life.

Then I know that the wisdom of the ancestors reunites us with our spiritual foundation.

The chatter of song birds fills the air. I am elated. Their singing is a call from the OtherWorld, urging me forward:

To pass through the thorn bush is to risk harm—
Oh this you fear.
But to pass through the thorn bush is to cross the boundary
between your reality and the OtherWorld.
Learn to trust with strong faith.
The OtherWorld does not lie or deceive.

Two of Domhan

CYCLES

Classical Tarot Meaning

A card of contrasting light and dark, yang and yin; the presence of the infinity sign suggests an appeal to the Earth for salvation; life is a cycle of perpetual change; gain where there is loss and vice versa; difficulty where there was ease, growth, alterations, new directions, new ideas; hints that opposites are illusions; all things are ultimately different forms of the same thing; knowledge of this sort is seeker's reward; gift of hope; major decision at hand.

Card Description and Faery Wicca Tarot Meaning

Journey to Falias – continued

Earth qualities are endurance, stability, and abundance. The primal land connected to Falias is the land of the ancestors, containing the knowledge OF the earth. This I know and understand.

There is a challenge taking place: a challenge to remember that beyond the boundary of our reality we must live according to the rules of the OtherWorld.

What exists in our realm is reflected in the OtherWorld, but not as a mirror reflection but as an opposite, for example, night here is day there, gold here is silver there, etc.

I gasp as the thorn hedge shapeshifts into a silver net. Now the golden pentagram slab hangs in the air, and it glows with a brilliant light. This light snakes down and around another pentagram, cast in silver. The brilliant light forms a lemniscate—infinity sign—around and between the two disks.

As above—so below.
Life moves in cycles.
Giving and receiving.
The ebb and flow—
Moon and Sun,
Goddess and God.
As above—so below.
Use your imagination.

Three of Domhan

SPIRAL OF LIFE

Classical Tarot Meaning

Commercial success through effort and training; work undertaken or performed with others; a joint effort or partnership; skilled labor; crafts.

Card Description and Faery Wicca Tarot Meaning
Journey to Falias – continued

A new sense of confidence and trust overcomes me as I realize the OtherWorld is connected to the imagination, creation, the Will of Goddess and God, and that new possibilities will arise through the selfless action of simply letting go.

My creative imagination is spiritual intelligence, and when coupled with this world and the Other creates a trinity that is powerful. Each corner of the trinity reflects a different quality of the same thing, just as the Triple Goddess reflects different aspects of Great Goddess.

Likewise, the two PENTACLES disks have multiplied into three: a gold one, a silver one, and a bronze one. Their union has created a spiral opening into the earth. A white light shines up from the earth's core, illuminating what appear to be eight black spokes attached to the center of the spiral. I see the symbol of the Wheel of the Year, each spoke one of the High Holidays, while the three disks become the symbol of the Gods: the silver for Goddess, the bronze for God, the gold for Dana.

What then does the earthlight represent? I bend over and peer down into the hole, trying to catch a glimpse of anything. Suddenly, I lose my footing and fall head first down the hole! The light spirals around me.

Down, down, down, I fall into infinity and as I fall weightlessly into the earthlight, I hear a song:

We come from the stars,
We come from the stars,
Shining down to the earth.

Four of Domhan

THE ENTRANCE

Classical Tarot Meaning

Warns against the danger of working only for material gains; miserliness; greed is ultimately barren; accumulated wealth must be protected, but in the process of protecting it, the miser becomes its prisoner and its slave; selfishness, suspicion, mistrust; inability to let go of anything or to delegate responsibility; blockages of thought and action naturally follows to excessive devotion to piling up material wealth and the provisions for guarding them; there is a need for boundaries in your life.

Card Description and Faery Wicca Tarot Meaning

Journey to Falias – continued

I gently touch ground and find myself before the entrance to a cave. But this entrance is unlike all other cave entrances—this one shines forth the same white light that rose from the center of the earth.

Could it be that I now stand in Earth's heart? I glance around blinking my vision into focus. A beautiful St. John's Wort plant is in full bloom—the yellow flowers hold the sun's rays in their color. As I gaze upon the blooms, I am imbued with their solar power and my mind clears.

I look back to the cave entrance and spot the stone inscribed with spirals and diamonds. Dragon's eyes stare at me and for one moment I am looking at the sun's refracting light in the sky.

I rub my eyes. Am I seeing correctly? Four pentagrams are inscribed on the entrance standing stones, a portcullis design is inscribed in the lintel stone and over this is a word. I know this place where I stand— it is my inner world fully realized and enlightened.

The four pentagrams are SHOWing me that I am close to the truth of the five-pointed star. I have mastered my mind, conquered my ego, achieved emotional balance, and can move between one physical place to another, whether of this world or another. In fact, I have arrived at a most important threshold—one which is solidly balanced, but to enter requires the willingness to relax my hold on what we know and understand as the manifest world.

The design of the portcullis shows me that I must follow the thread of the Weaver Goddess from one end of the thread, at one opening, through to the other end of the thread, at another opening. Only then will I have really danced the Spiral Dance and fully lived.

I am mesmerized by the white light as it shines even more brilliantly from the cave mouth. An image begins to form in this light, but I can't quite see who or what it is. Then a blast of brilliant light sends me spinning and I hear:

Do you dare to know
to will
to keep silent?

Five of Domhan

The Lozenge

Classical Tarot Meaning

Known as the beggars card, it implies hard times, poverty, loss or lack of comfort. Survival cannot be found from institutions or organizations. Indifference from friends and family. Discouragement. Things are not as bad as they seem; there is always choice, always something one can do to change the situation.

Card Description and Faery Wicca Tarot Meaning

Journey to Falias – continued

Blackness.

Wait, this is all about ME! Me and my relationship to values and physical possessions. What is it I am really willing to pay any price for? Is there anything?

What do physical possessions really mean to me? How much importance do I place on money? Do I believe in abundance? Or do I live in poverty? Spiritual poverty is the result of extreme materialism.

The physical realm—earth—is the Great Trickster. "See my jewels," she coyly says. "Enjoy my abundance," she implores. "Dine on my scruples," she entices. "Dress in my finery," she insists. "Lose yourself to materialism," she explodes.

Lose your mind if you dare.
Lose your heart if you dare.
Lose your body if you dare.
Lose your soul if you dare.
And dwell forever in the dark and lonely labyrinth
of wanting more, needing more, searching, always
searching for more, more, more!

Bronze disks flash out at me. They sit across from each other horizontally. I know I will and can balance mind and heart. I can come to balance my male and female energies. These do not belong to anyone else. I do not have to purchase this balance from anyone else—balance is mine internally.

"Balance yourself then," Mother Earth coos.

Two silver pentagrams show themselves. They rest one above the other. Goddess and God forces of the outward energy of life—of nature are free. I don't need to purchase these two primal powers from anyone. All I need to do is open my mind-heart to them and align with them as they flow through me. Moonlight-Sunlight. Winter-Summer. Night-Day. I do this through a peaceful connection with the natural world.

"Polarize yourself then," Mother Earth sings.

A gold pentagram appears in the center of the labyrinth. The four others ideally leading to it. Love. Truth. I hear Mother Earth rejoice:

The natural world of senses
is alive now—
Taste, touch, smell, sight, hearing—
But in the darkest place of dense matter
Your dear soul must learn to trust the instinct of the physical,
For there is where creation is found.

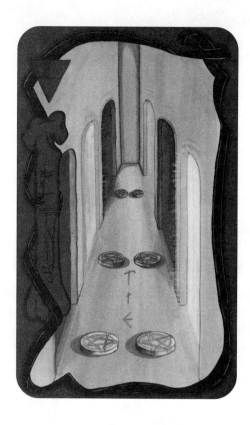

Six of
Domhan

MATERIAL
WEALTH

Classical Tarot Meaning

Charity comes; gifts; material gain; help from someone favored by fortune; charity is never a dependable or secure income. This card warns against excessive expenditure of resources through misplaced generosity; financial increase.

Card Description and Faery Wicca Tarot Meaning

Journey to Falias – continued

The physical world is full of inconsistencies. A long corridor appears. There are six doors: three on either side, creating three groupings of doors.

The first grouping of doors has golden pentagrams on the floor before it. The door to the right shines with a golden light, while its OtherWorld reflection is dark.

I sense this pair of doors is the forge into the Lunar Realm.[2] To enter the door to the right is to live in our physical world with awareness of only our world. The OtherWorld would be dead to one's awareness, lost from sight.

The second grouping of doors has silver pentagrams on the floor before it. The door to the left shines with a silver light, while its OtherWorld reflection is dark.

I sense this pair of doors is the forge into the Solar Realm. To enter the door to the left is to journey into alternate realms of reality, recognizing that our physical world is not quite as all or alive as once perceived.

The third grouping of doors has bronze pentagrams on the floor before it. The door to the right shines with a fiery radiance, while its OtherWorld reflects a dark door.

I sense this pair of doors is the forge into the Stellar Realm. To enter the door to the right is to enter a new circle of Existence, one that is not connected to this world, or the OtherWorld for that matter, but is wholly separate. The door to the left is not even dark, it is a void into infinity.

There is an old cliché: when one door closes, another one opens. This within itself is an inconsistency. For all doors are closed and all doors are open—it's whether we see them open or closed, or see them even at all, that determines their usefulness to us.

In this corridor, many would never even see THE doors because they would be blinded by the appearance of the coins, and their minds would be focused on material wealth. Thus, their hearts would become dead to the lights that shine from inside themselves.

Only balance brings regrowth.
Only heart-body-soul combined
Shows us the way.

Seven of Domhan

BLOCKED DOOR

Classical Tarot Meaning

Inertia, alienation, lost opportunities, laziness. A new vision is required to overcome such deep-seated blockages. Natural abundance is around you, but you fail to see it and recognize how valuable it can be.

Card Description and Faery Wicca Tarot Meaning

Journey to Falias – continued

I stand at a doorway blocked by pieces of wood. A large plank inscribed with six pentagrams guards the opening. On the floor before the opening is the golden pentagram; however, in this position it is inverted.

A wood sign is nailed above the opening. It reads one word in ancient Gaelic. A beautiful golden light shines from the cave. How enticed I feel to tear down the boards and go in, but I sense: Beware! Don't go there. Don't enter the door to the right of the golden pentagram. This desire toward extreme materialism will lock you into the world of the Great Trickster, and you will live in illusion.

What is it the earth teaches us? CYCLES . . . life cycles . . . give and receive. Don't take, take, take, or you are in jeopardy of staying locked in the cave of the UnderWorld of Regret.

The way is barred—
think twice, three times,
as many times as is needed before continuing forward
to heed the messages being given you
from the OtherWorld.
Warnings of danger echo around you.

Eight of Domhan

INITIATION

Classical Tarot Meaning

Inner wisdom. A card of learning or relearning, secret doctrines. The time for an apprenticeship has come. Extension of understanding into new areas; a questing for knowledge; the serenity of true enlightenment. If you've been considering going back to school, do so.

Card Description and Faery Wicca Tarot Meaning

Journey to Falias – continued

I feel as if a battle has been won, for an incredible peace comes over me. I moved down the corridor, away from the golden pentagram, and entered the silver pentagram door to the left. It led down a corridor into an anteroom and a small hallway. I stand before the hallway.

Eight pentagrams frame the hall archway; four on either side. I feel a sense OF balance looking at the symbols.

The floor of the hallway is carpeted in green and black plaid. This is the color of the Faery and the UnderWorld. A green bag sits on the carpet.

The hallway leads to an oak door, which is closed. It has the Tree of Life glyph painted on it. A crescent moon lantern, located above the door, provides the only light in the hallway. But it is more then enough light to see by.

To the left of the door are two symbols. The first has two crescents back to back, forming an *X* and next to this a small *i*—I wonder what they mean. To the right of the door are two more Xs with three *I*s with an *x* through them. Above the first two *I*s is a circle, half is dark and the other half is white.

I sense that these symbols are a code of some sort, giving information to the traveler who stands at the door. And there, painted on the walls and along the floor is a serpent with ruby eyes.

This is the doorway into Falias. I feel excitement radiating through my bones. Something big is about to happen. If I dare to open the door and move into this Great City, I will never be the same.

To cross the threshold of oak is to be initiated into the mysteries; to begin walking my talk and taking full responsibility for all my actions from this day forward.

The green bag comes to mind. I turn to it. Perhaps it is a magickal bag filled with all kinds of magickal tools.

My attention is swept to the serpent. I could have sworn it moved!

Just then the lantern flame flickers. There is a rustling noise, and the sound of coins jingling together.

I am very ready to become an initiate. I am very ready to walk my talk. I am very ready to take full responsibility for all my actions from this day forward. *I am!*

Spiritual integrity
is the necessary ingredient required
for the novice to become an initiate.
Spiritual integrity

reflects the dignity of the soul
the difference between someone still sleeping
and the person who has experienced the awakening.
Spiritual integrity
is the key to finding passage
to the Lia Fal—
Stone of Destiny.

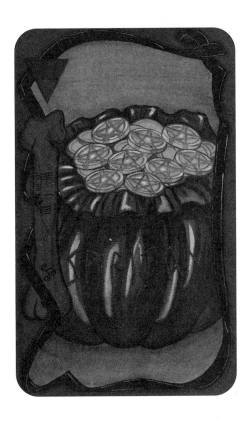

Nine of Domhan

SPIRITUAL WEALTH

Classical Tarot Meaning

Accomplishment in the sense of gestation, productivity, careful cultivation, the establishment and nurture of beauty through learning. Love of nature is another traditional meaning of this card; the gift of mother love. Material well-being and increase of wealth.

Card Description and Faery Wicca Tarot Meaning

Journey to Falias – continued

The lantern flame shoots for a beam of light and it highlights the green bag. I move to the bag. I see a word beaded in red on the outside of the bag. A thrill of excitement runs through my body. Is this what I think it is?

I bend down and untie the drawstrings. At the slightest release in tension, the bag pops open, exposing a bounty of silver pentagram coins. A silver light shines from the center of each coin. The coins contained within the bag seem to be alive, for they shift and clink together as if engaged in a frenetic dance of excitement.

"Faery Gold!" someone whispers in my ear.

I stand and look around. A slithering and hissing jerks my attention to the oak door. The serpent has come to life and has disengaged itself from the wall! Everything appears to be coming to life.

"Why you are in the Land of Faery," hisses the serpent as it coils through my legs. "What did you expect?"

I have no answer to give. I'm not sure what I expected.

"Well, my dear," comes the serpent's hiss. "You have been rewarded for your SPIRITUAL diligence. The Faery deem you worthy of entry into their world. I am to guide you to the Lia Fal, Stone of Destiny. Are you ready?"

Before I can speak, I feel the support of the serpent lift me off the ground. The oak door has been flung open, and I am carried away. As we pass under the threshold of the door, a choir of voices wafts through the air:

Shhh, listen the Queen of Sidhe draws near.
And she beckons you to follow her,
into the Land of Faery for a year and a day.
Beware my dear, follow if you dare,
for your mortal life will be forever changed,
And you will long to dwell with her
forever and a day!

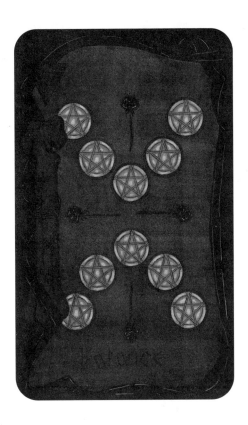

Ten of Domhan

THE SACRED GROVE

Classical Tarot Meaning

Regarded as a preeminent sign of protection. A charm surpassing all power, protection especially in the sense of material advantages. Known as the inheritance card; not only in the form of ancestral properties, but gifts from other people as well, business loans, and cash advances, as well as gambling winnings. A true community is around you. There is protection and support from others.

Card Description and Faery Wicca Tarot Meaning

Journey to Falias — continued

This is the meaning of the teaching of Falias: the sacred grove, the location in which all things, hitherto separate, become connected together. At such a point, all things become clear. The initiation into the mysteries of the Faery is alignment, working within the natural cycles of life, dancing the Wheel of the Year, working the magick of the four seasons, understanding the energy and power of Goddess, and understanding the energy and power of God. The blessing that the initiate receives from the Faery is one very simple thing; yet, it is the hardest thing to achieve in all the world, strive though many may to achieve it, for it is true:

BALANCE.

Spreads for Personal Development Using the Element Cards

The Element Cards can be used alone to give a reading for a variety of areas in life. The primary areas, of course, would deal with everyday living, what is often referred to as mundane life. Mundane life is where we grow, experience, and learn the lessons necessary for our humanistic and spiritual evolution.

Several basic spreads will be covered on the following pages, which can aid in understanding oneself and others mentally, emotionally, physically, as well as understanding desire modes, personal power, and past elements that need to be considered in the present. On occasion, these spreads will give a peek into the future, but for the most part they focus the reader in the Now.

In addition to working with the Element cards only, one can also work with one suit within the Element cards at a time. This is done when deeper understanding into the suit's energy is needed for personal growth.

For example: Aer cards would be used when insight is needed in mental processes; Tine cards would be used to glean understanding into personal power. Likewise, Uisce cards can be used for added insight into one's emotional state, whereas Domhan cards would focus on the physical world, what one is capable of manifesting, as well as when balance is needed.

Reversed Cards

While many systems of tarot and modern cartomancers subscribe to a reversed card meaning, the *Faery Wicca Tarot* does not for three simple reasons.

- Readers are encouraged to begin every reading using all cards in their upright position. This lends to the reading the opportunity for the cards to be reversed by the querent during the shuffling or card selection process. If and when a card is reversed in this process, it provides insight into the energy state of the querent (e.g., confused, chaotic, conflict).

- A reversed card can signify a possibility of event, giving the querent a choice whether to strive to make the event happen, or make necessary changes to avoid the event.

- A reversed card can indicate where an energy blockage is occurring in the querent's life, thereby giving insight into an immediate area of attention. Perhaps the card indicates there is a desire for the area, but it is not ready to manifest.

- Finally, a reversed card can indicate a challenge getting ready to come in and acts as a warning.

The Use of a Significator

When performing readings using only the Element Cards, a significator card can help anchor the energy of the querent in the foundation of the reading.

The significator card will focus the reader on just the querent's life, keeping distracting and miscellaneous information from interrupting the reading.

To find your significator card, refer to the guidelines in Part Two: The Helper Cards, page 140.

In each of the following spreads, the significator card is placed down in the first position, followed by the number one card of the reading, which is placed directly over the significator. The significator card is not read.

Single Spiral—One Card Reading

This one card spread (figure 7) can be used on a daily basis to ascertain the area of focus most important for that day. An Aer card would indicate that the day would highlight mental processes. A Tine card would indicate attention be given to personal power and desire mode. An Uisce card would indicate emotions are going to be important, while a Domhan card shows that your body or physical nature will be highlighted.

The best time to do this daily reading is before starting your day. Focus on the day, ask Goddess or God to show you the area you most need to pay attention to for that day. Shuffle your cards. Draw one card. Interpret it and record your insights in your daily journal. The next day, make note of what actually happened before performing the daily reading.

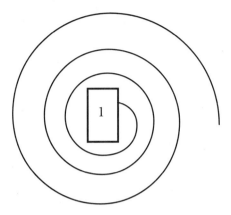

FIGURE 7. *Single Spiral Spread.*

The spread is an excellent way to work with just one suit at a time to attach personal meaning to each card. For example, if you are working with Aer cards you might ask, "What must I contemplate Now?"

If you are working with Tine cards you might ask, "What must I meditate on Now?"

If you are working with Uisce cards, you might ask, "What must I visualize Now?"

If you are working with Domhan cards, you might ask, "What must I create Now?"

Double Spiral—Two Card Reading

As with the first spread, and all of those listed here, all of the Element Cards can be worked with, or only one suit. This two card spread (figure 8, page 132) will provide insight into an immediate situation, and can be worked one of two ways.

Method One

Focus on the one thing from the past that most needs to be taken into consideration. Pull a card and place it in the first position. Then focus on what is likely to occur based on the present. Pull another card and place it in the second position. Interpret the cards individually, and then together.

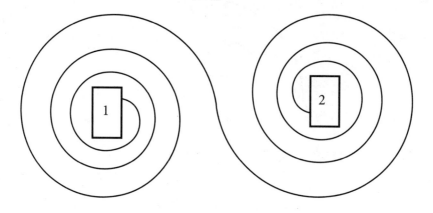

FIGURE 8. *Double Spiral Spread.*

Method Two

Focus on what is beneficial in the situation. Pull a card and place it in the first position. Then focus on what is challenging in the situation. Pull another card and place it in the second position. Interpret the cards individually, and then determine whether they are compatible or supportive of one another, or whether they are incompatible or in conflict.

Triple Spiral—Three Card Reading

This three card reading (figure 9) can be used on a weekly basis to give insight into your personal lesson for the week, or on the major event of the week. This spread can be used in one of two ways:

Method One

Focus on your mental processes, pull a card and place it in the first position. Interpret the card. Focus on your physical body, pull a card and place it in the second position. Interpret the card. Now compare the mind and body cards to determine whether they are compatible or incompatible. Next, focus on your soul, pull a card and place it in the third position. Interpret the card. See if it is the likely result of the combined meaning of the first and second cards, and whether it represents a challenging or beneficial energy. This will give you insight into your lesson for the week.

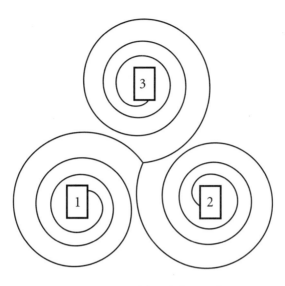

FIGURE 9. *Triple Spiral Spread.*

Method Two

Focus on the past week, allowing the card you pull for the first position to reflect the one thing you must take into consideration for the current week. Pull the card and place it in the first position. Interpret the card. Focus on the current week, asking for the main event for the week to be reflected in the second card. Pull the card and interpret it. See any connection between the first and second cards. Then focus on the following week, allowing the card you pull for the third position to give insight into what you need to take into consideration for next week's main event. Pull the card and place it in the third position. Interpret the card. See if the first and second cards support or challenge this card. This reading gives insight into how you might want to handle the current main event, taking into consideration the near future.

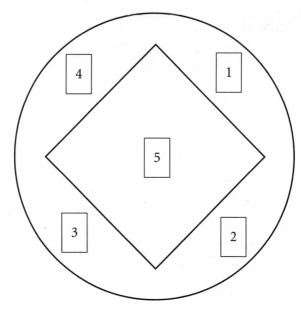

FIGURE 10. *The Lozenge.*

The Lozenge

This five card spread (figure 10, above) provides insight into the lessons being learned by Sacred Self in each of the following areas:

position 1:   attitude
position 2:   ego
position 3:   emotion
position 4:   reality
position 5:   soul

If you have a mental dilemma, then you would work with the Aer cards. If it's an emotional dilemma, work with just the Uisce cards, and so forth.

Learn to work with smaller spreads such as the ones presented above. You'll be surprised at some of the information that you glean from small spreads. While they may look insignificant, they can be more powerful than laying 20 cards down. We want to strive toward being able to give a very extensive and informative reading off of one card, so you will want to get used to working with your cards in a very basic and simple way.

Part Two

The Mists of Dūn na m-Barc:

The helper Cards

Tuatha De Danann

LXII.

1. *The Tuatha De Danann under obscurity. . .*

2. *Nobles yonder of the strong people,*
   people of the withered summit,
   let us relate, in the course in which we are,
   their periods in their kingdom.

3. *A space of seven years of Nuadu noble-stately*
   over the fair-haired company,
   the rule of the man large-breasted, flaxen-maned,
   before his coming into Ireland.

4. *In Mag Tuired, heavy with doom,*
   where fell a champion of the battle,
   from the white defender of the world—
   his arm of princedom was lopped off.

6. *. . . till Lug the spear-slaughterous was made king—*
   the many-crafted who cooled not.

7. *Forty to Lug—it was balanced—*
   ion the kingship over the Palace of Banba;
   he reached no celestial bed of innocence;
   eighty to The Dagda.

9. *Twenty-nine years, I have proclaimed it,*
   over every peace-land of Ireland,
   in the kingdom over Banba enduringly great
   had the grandsons of The Dagda skilled in denseng.

LIII.

10. *Eriu, though it should reach a road-end,*
    Banba, Fotla, and Fea,
    Neman of ingenious vesicles,
    Danann, mother of the gods.

11. *Badb and Macha, greatness of wealth,*
    Morrigu-springs of craftiness,
    sources of bitter fighting
    were the three daughters of Ernmas.

—*Lebor Gabala Erenn*
Vol. XLI, Part IV, Sec. VII

Theory of the Crown of Dūn na m-Barc

Traditionally known as the Court Cards, the *Faery Wicca Tarot* Helper Cards are not just considered to be the cards of people, but are the links to the OtherWorld through the magickal symbols and alphabets used by the Faery to encode the teachings of the Four Great Cities. Here we find Irish Oghams, Celtic Sacred Symbols, and Animal Totems.

The Helper Cards access intuitive guidance and speak directly to inner consciousness. They begin to shift our awareness into the Solar Sphere. They have a dual role of also representing personalities and character traits through each card's assignment as a Ridire (knight), Ainnir (maiden), Ard Rí (High King), or Banríon (High Queen).

In this ancient system. emphasis is placed on Female-Male energy balance, and the Banríon cards are given their rightful place of power opposite the Ard Rí cards. This ancestral wisdom teaches balanced polarity, undoing the manipulated card changes enacted by the dominator societies. The Banríons are returned to the north with respect, and the Ainnirs resume their dignity in the west, as a duality in conjunction with the Ridire cards in the east. This major change in the Helper Cards makes the *Faery Wicca Tarot* an invaluable system of study and divination to all female tarot and psychic readers, as well as to the men who are seeking to achieve a greater sense of balance in their spiritual lives. The return of the Banríons to the north may challenge the established systems of tarot used today, as based on nineteenth-century occultism, but it is in alignment with earth wisdom and all aspects of paganism and Wicca.

Through this ancient secret of balanced polarity, the Helper Cards are able to become the true magickal archetypes they were designed to be: the guides into the OtherWorld of Knowledge and Wisdom.

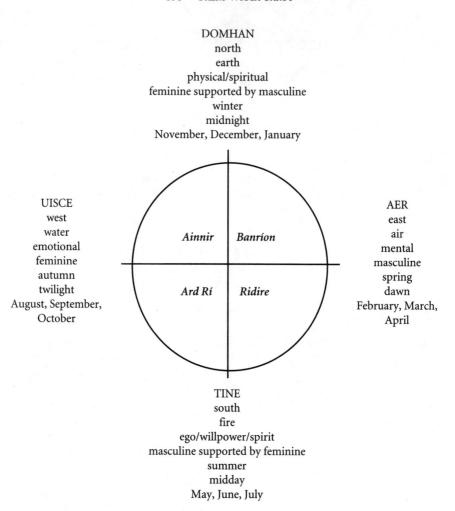

FIGURE 11. *The Properties of the Helper Cards.*

The Wheel of the Year

The Helper Cards have specific placements on figure 11, above. All Ridire cards are placed in the east, and are connected to the element of air. Ridires are representative of the pure masculine energy in various forms of application with regard to the mental processes (e.g., Ridire of Aer is the intellect, Ridire of Tine is an idea put into action, Ridire of Uisce is an ideal or inspiration, the vision quest, while Ridire of Domhan becomes the dream made manifest).

Ard Rí cards are placed in the south, and are connected to the element of fire. Ard Rís are representative of the energy of force or action in various degrees of application with regard to willpower (e.g., Ard Rí of Aer is a force of defense, Ard Rí of Tine is ego in full action, Ard Rí of Uisce is the force of desire, while Ard Rí of Domhan is the power of manifestation).

Ainnir cards are placed in the west, and are connected to the element of water. Ainnirs represent pure feminine energy in various forms of application with regard to the emotional processes (e.g., Ainnir of Aer is the balance between mind and heart, Ainnir of Tine represents the sexual emotion of love, Ainnir of Uisce is pure emotion, while Ainnir of Domhan represents the receptive emotion of fertility).

Lastly, the Banríon cards are placed in the north, and are connected to the element of earth. Banríon cards represent the manifested world and all forms of spirituality.

Duality and Polarity

As stated earlier, the element association given the Ainnir and Banríon cards in the *Faery Wicca Tarot* are different than those assigned by other esoteric and occult systems. The *Faery Wicca Tarot* placements work according to the ancient earth traditions, placing emphasis on female-male energy balance. This ancestral wisdom teaching expresses balanced polarity. By placing the Ainnir cards in the position representing pure female energy, across from the Ridire cards, which represent pure masculine energy, a balanced duality is established, one that does not overpower the other, but rather reflects the other.

The lesson between the Ridire and Ainnir cards is to learn to "think with the heart" and "feel with the mind"—when one is too intellectual, the absence of heart or emotion is at risk, thus creating an imbalance between the duality of masculine and feminine energies in one's psyche. The Ainnir and Ridire cards focus us inwardly.

Likewise, the Ard Rí and Banríon cards create harmonized polarity. The energy of the Ard Rí cards is of a masculine nature but is supported by the feminine energy, whereas the Banríon cards are feminine energy supported by masculine energy. This polarization of energy is essential in maintaining one's sense of connectedness to the outer world, the Goddess and God forces in nature.

Spiritual Guidance

While tarot cards of themselves do not have powers, we can use the Helper Cards to connect us with the Goddess and God archetypes of the Irish Pantheon by contemplating the Faery lore of each card, and by using the card itself as a focal point for meditation.

By meditating on an image of deity, spiritual guidance can be received, as well as deeper insight into the mystery of one's inner self. When we have deeper knowledge of Self, access to the OtherWorld is easier to gain.

The Center—Doorway to the OtherWorld

The Helper cards act as doorways into the OtherWorld. Access to these realms can be gained by focusing on the center of self, known as the heart center—or the Cauldron of Vocation. When one knows what one's mission or goal is in the *now*, then one can more easily move between one web of reality and the next. The Element Cards help us to learn about our true selves via the lessons we are being taught by Spirit Challenges. The Helper Cards help us to align, both inwardly by achieving a greater sense of balance with our internal masculine and feminine energies, as well as outwardly through the polarization of the Goddess-God forces in nature.

We then use the Helper Cards as divine archetypes, striving to embrace these characteristics into our personalities; we become centered in the Now. When we are here now the doorways into the other realms are easier to find, and in the *Faery Wicca Tarot*, the Spirit Cards are linked to both the threshold into the realms and the OtherWorlds.

Relationships and Sub-Relationships

As we've seen above, each Helper Card is assigned a gender-energy:

Ridire cards are masculine.

Ard Rí cards are masculine supported by feminine.

Ainnir cards are feminine.

Banríon cards are feminine supported by masculine.

These gender-energy assignments create relationships between the different classes of Helper Cards. The Table of Relationships (page 141) gives the relationship groupings for the Helper Cards. Within some relationship groupings we see that sub-relationships are formed, as denoted in the Table of Sub-Relationships (page 142).

Table of Relationships: The Helper Cards

SUIT	HELPER CARD	ELEMENT	SUB-ELEMENT	POLARITY	BALANCE	RELATIONSHIP
Aer	Banríon	air	earth	Ard Rí of Uisce	Ainnir of Tine	feminine supported by masculine-masculine
Tine	Banríon	fire	earth	Ard Rí of Domhan a true polarity	Ridire of Uisce a true balance	feminine supported by masculine-masculine-feminine
Uisce	Banríon	water	earth	Ard Rí of Aer	Ridire of Tine	feminine supported by feminine
Domhan	Banríon	earth	earth	Ard Rí of Tine	Ridire of Aer	feminine supported by masculine-feminine-masculine
Aer	Ard Rí	air	fire	Banríon of Uisce	Ainnir of Domhan	masculine supported by feminine-masculine
Tine	Ard Rí	fire	fire	Banríon of Domhan	Ainnir of Uisce	masculine supported by feminine-masculine-feminine
Uisce	Ard Rí	water	fire	Banríon of Aer	Ridire of Domhan	masculine supported by feminine-feminine
Domhan	Ard Rí	earth	fire	Banríon of Tine a true polarity	Ainnir of Aer a true balance	masculine supported by feminine-feminine-masculine

Table of Sub-Relationships: The Helper Cards

Polarity Card	Gender/Energy	Balance Card	Gender/Energy
Ard Rí of Uisce	masculine supported by feminine	Ainnir of Tine	feminine
Ard Rí of Domhan	masculine supported by feminine	Ridire of Uisce	masculine
Ard Rí of Aer	masculine supported by feminine	Ridire of Tine	masculine
Ard Rí of Tine	masculine supported by feminine	Ridire of Aer	masculine
Banríon of Uisce	feminine supported by masculine	Ainnir of Domhan	feminine
Banríon of Domhan	feminine supported by masculine	Ainnir of Uisce	feminine
Banríon of Aer	feminine supported by masculine	Ridire of Domhan	masculine
Banríon of Tine	feminine supported by masculine	Ainnir of Aer	feminine

This information can help illuminate what ingredients—personality, characteristic, energy, etc.—based on the Helper Cards involved, are necessary to bring about a solution, change, or stabilization of a situation in a reading.

Significators

Each Helper Card is connected to an element, which when used to represent a person's sun sign becomes what is known as their significator card. The element assignments are:

Ridire cards are the element of air: Gemini/Libra/Aquarius.

Ainnir cards are the element of water: Cancer/Scorpio/Pisces.

Ard Rí cards are the element of fire: Aries/Leo/Sagittarius.

Banríon cards are the element of earth: Taurus/Virgo/Capricorn.

A significator card is often the first card placed on the table in a reading. It acts as an energy anchor for the querent, thus becoming the foundation of a tarot spread. While the usage of a significator can act as an energy anchor, it does eliminate one card from the deck, which does not allow its natural use in a reading.

Another way to use the significator card is to see if it comes up in a reading, paying particular attention to its position in the spread, as well as to the surrounding cards. This method will allow the reader to observe the area or situation closest to the querent, and in many cases the top priority in need of attention.

Astrology

Specific zodiac signs and dates can be assigned to the Helper Cards. Because astrological significance in Celtic mythology was more closely attached to the ogham moon months than to zodiacal signs. The astrological system that one could apply to the Helper Cards would be the standard astrological affiliations generated through the Golden Dawn system of tarot, as represented in the following Table of Zodiac Signs for Helper Cards on the next page.

Table of Zodiac Signs: The Helper Cards

CARD	DATES	ZODIACAL SIGN
Ridire Cards		
Aer	January 10–19	Capricorn
	January 20–February 8	Aquarius
Tine	July 12–21	Cancer
	July 21–August 11	Leo
Uisce	October 13–22	Libra
	October 23–November 12	Scorpio
Domhan	April 11–20	Aries
	April 21–May 10	Taurus
Ard Rí Cards		
Aer	May 11–20	Taurus
	May 21–June 10	Gemini
Tine	November 13–22	Scorpio
	November 23–December 12	Sagittarius
Uisce	February 9–18	Aquarius
	February 19–March 10	Pisces
Domhan	August 11–22	Leo
	August 23–September 11	Virgo
Banríon Cards		
Aer	September 12–22	Virgo
	September 23–October 12	Libra
Tine	March 11–20	Pisces
	March 21–April 10	Aries
Uisce	June 11–20	Gemini
	June 21–July 11	Cancer
Domhan	December 13–21	Sagittarius
	December 22–January 9	Capricorn
Ainnir Card		
Aer	March 21–April 21	Aries
	April 21–May 20	Taurus
	May 21–June 20	Gemini
Tine	June 21–July 21	Cancer
	July 22–August 22	Leo
	August 23–September 22	Virgo
Uisce	September 23–October 22	Libra
	October 23–November 21	Scorpio
	November 22–December 21	Sagittarius
Domhan	December 22–January 19	Capricorn
	January 20–February 18	Aquarius
	February 19–March 20	Pisces

Characteristics and Personalities

This area of correspondences brings in the humanist depiction for the Helper Cards. Fifty percent of the time the Helper Cards will represent other people. The Table of Characteristics (page 147) will provide deeper insight into the "other" people, whom the cards are representing. Bear in mind that all correspondences will not always apply, though several will in any given case.

Unlike the list of characteristics, personality classifications seem to apply more as a whole than in part. Below is a brief description of the personality traits assigned each card.

Ridire of Aer: A very intellectual young man. The brain. Scholarly. Could be warlike, dominating others.

Ridire of Tine: The athlete. Someone who acts without thinking things clearly through. Mischievous nature. Can never sit still.

Ridire of Uisce: The dreamer. Very gallant. A gentle young man in touch with his feminine qualities. Sensitive. Bringer of ideas and inspiration.

Ridire of Domhan: The hopeless romantic. Someone who stands up for what he believes. The true knight.

Ainnir of Aer: Quick witted, vigilant, active. Has a keen sense of judgment. No nonsense. The "brain." Can be cruel.

Ainnir of Tine: A valuable friend, but dangerous enemy. An enterprising young woman. The ingenue. Sexually charged. High spirited.

Ainnir of Uisce: The artist. Sensitive nature. Loyal nature. Stays close to home until an adult. The fantasizer.

Ainnir of Domhan: Fertility. A young female interested in the arcane. Fearless. Desires to learn. Scholarly pursuits.

Banríon of Aer: The eternal feminine Enigma. An excellent communicator. Can be harsh verbally. Very intelligent. The widow card.

Banríon of Tine: The career-minded woman. Very businesslike. Fiery personality. Powerful. Passionate.

Banríon of Uisce: The psychic's card. A woman of the Other-World. Someone who is involved with the arcane. A priestess of Goddess.

Banríon of Domhan: The wife and mother card. Generous, compassionate, comforting, and supportive. A warm, nurturing personality. Inspires others.

Ard Rí of Aer: A powerful judge. Has godlike authority. The embodiment of discipline and order. Opinionated. Can have a dangerous, inhumane, perverse side.

Ard Rí of Tine: A powerful person of a fiery nature. Energetic, active, hard to control. Very attractive, but can be a womanizer. A man interested in the arcane. Business minded. The salesman.

Ard Rí of Uisce: A man not afraid of emotion. A romantic lover. Can sometimes stifle his feelings when threatened. Very demonstrative with his attention. The writer.

Ard Rí of Domhan: The money man. Happy-go-lucky. Thinks of his relationships as possessions. Takes care of those he loves. Likes to have a good time. A very astute businessman. Successful. Wealthy.

Oghams, Animals, and Symbols

The Helper Cards link us to the OtherWorld through the magickal symbols and alphabets used by the Bards to encode the teachings of their mysteries. Irish Ogham is used both as an alphabet and symbol in the Helper Cards. As shown in the Table of Ogham Correspondences (page 148), the oghams are a rich source of knowledge, Celtic lore, and wisdom. While all the correspondences connected to an ogham may not visually appear on the card in which an ogham appears, the full list of correspondences assigned the ogham can be woven into the deeper meaning of the card.

As depicted in the list, each ogham is associated with an animal. However, additional animals may appear in a given card, in which case the esoteric meaning for the animal will be listed under the heading Oghams and Symbols. Likewise, any Celtic symbols appearing in a card will be covered under the same heading.

Table of Characteristics: The Helper Cards

HELPER CARD	SUIT/ELEMENT	AGE GROUP	CULTURE	HAIR COLOR	EYE COLOR
Ridire	Aer/air	birth–30	Asian	blond	hazel
Ridire	Tine/fire	birth–30	Latino/Indian	red	brown
Ridire	Uisce/water	birth–30	African/Middle Eastern	black	blue
Ridire	Domhan/earth	birth–30	European/Norwegian	brown/white	green
Ainnir	Aer/air	birth–30	Asian	blond	hazel
Ainnir	Tine/fire	birth–30	Latino/Indian	red	brown
Ainnir	Uisce/water	birth–30	African/Middle Eastern	black	blue
Ainnir	Domhan/earth	birth–30	European/Middle Eastern	brown/white	green
Banríon	Aer/air	30–death	Asian	blond	hazel
Banríon	Tine/fire	30–death	Latino/Indian	red	brown
Banríon	Uisce/water	30–death	African/Middle Eastern	black	blue
Banríon	Domhan/earth	30–death	European/Norwegian	brown/white	green
Ard Rí	Aer/air	30–death	Asian	blond	hazel
Ard Rí	Tine/fire	30–death	Latino/Indian	red	brown
Ard Rí	Uisce/water	30–death	African	black	blue
Ard Rí	Domhan/earth	30–death	European/	brown/white	green

Table of Ogham Correspondences

Ogham	Name	Tree	Date	Animal	Bird	Color	Zodiac Sign	Planet
⊥	Beth	birch	Dec. 24–Jan. 20	stag	pheasant	white	Capricorn	Sun
⊥⊥	Luis	rowan	Jan. 21–Feb. 17	green dragon	duck	gray	Aquarius	Uranus
⊥⊥⊥⊥	Nion	ash	Feb. 18–Mar. 17	seahorse	snipe	clear	Aquarius/Pisces	Neptune
⊥⊥⊥	Fearn	alder	Mar. 18–Apr. 14	man	seagull/hawk	blood red	Pisces/Aries	Mars
⊥⊥	Saille	willow	Apr. 15–May 12	eel	hawk	bright	Aries/Taurus	Moon
T	Uath	hawthorn	May 13–Jun 9	bee	night-crow	purple	Taurus/Gemini	Vulcan
TT	Duir	oak	Jun. 10–Jul. 7	white horse	wren	black	Gemini/Cancer	Jupiter
TTT	Tinne	holly	Jul. 8–Aug. 4	unicorn	Starling	gray-green	Cancer/Leo	Earth
TTTT	Coll	hazel	Aug. 5–Sept. 1	salmon	crane	nut-brown	Leo/Virgo	Mercury
⌁	Muin	vine	Sept. 2–29	swan	titmouse	variegated	Virgo/Libra	Venus
⫻	Gort	ivy	Sept. 30–Oct. 27	butterfly	mute swan	blue	Libra/Scorpio	Persephone
⫻⫻	Ngetal	reed	Oct. 28–Nov. 24	white hound	goose	glass-green	Scorpio/Sagittarius	Pluto
⫻⫻⫻	Ruis	elder	Nov. 25–Dec. 22	black horse	rook	red	Sagittarius/Capricorn	Saturn

In the East

Ridire of
Aer

Ruled by Luis

DIARMAID

Meaning

Air of Air; pure mental energy; the masculine force in life; in the springtime of life; young male between birth and age thirty; ideas are easy to achieve; a sense of clarity; intellectual pursuits; ready to fight for ideals; defending one's right of belief.

The magick of the Faery World can become enlightenment if you learn to feel with the mind; intuition is a result of the Faery Eye Ointment, when all that you see shines the glamour of the natural world of beauty.

Card Description

Diarmaid, the lieutenant of Finn Mac Cumhal's fianna, stands beside the most magickal tree in all of Faery lore, the Rowan. He blocks the way, but not with hostility, for although his sword is drawn, he keeps the blade grounded on the earth. He is in exile and protecting the one for whom he has given up everything—the Ainnir Grainne.

Diarmaid was son of Donn, son of Duibhne of the fianna, and his mother was Crochnuit, who was close in blood to Finn. At the time he was born, Donn was banished from the fianna because of some quarrel they had with him, and Angus Og took the child from him to rear him up at Brugh na Boinne (Newgrange). Because of his father's quarrels, eventually the Druid of Cruachan put a geis on Diarmaid that his death would be brought about by a wild boar without bristle or ear or tail, called the Boar of Slieve Guillion, and it was by him Diarmaid came to his death at last.

Diarmaid was known to be a "master and charmer of women," and wore a love-spot on his forehead. This love-spot won him Grainne, who stands in the background roasting wild pig over an open fire.

In his exile he would not cook where he killed his prey, nor eat where he cooked, nor sleep where he ate. In Duvnos Forest, where he stands now, he finally settled. Here he befriended the giant Sharvan the surly, who protected the two lovers, instructing Diarmaid to build a wood cloghan with seven doors. In this way he could see who was approaching in all directions, and easily make their escape in an opposite direction, sight unseen.

Diarmaid wields a blue-hilted sword, a sign of his connection to the element of water, through his love for Grainne. However, he was a Ridire who never sheathed his sword, and so never knew peace.

Oghams and Symbols

Luis is the second ogham character in the B group and is connected to the magickal Rowan tree. The time of Luis extends from January 21 to February 17, the second moon month, ruled by the sign of Aquarius.

The rowan berry is the food of the gods. Luis serves to protect its user against psychic attack and to develop the individual's powers of perception and prediction. Rowan was planted outside the front door of country dwellers to ward off harmful spirits, energies, and on-lays.

The torc around Diarmaid's neck is a symbol of royalty, although he himself is not royal. In this case, it shows that he is cut off from his rational thinking, which got him into this place to begin with.

The love spot on his head indicates his ability to access deep insight and inspiration and then bring such ideas and ideals forth. It also represents the pure male sexual energy.

Other Correspondences

Element: air

Sub-element: air

Element Card Connection: Four of Domhan, Five of Aer, Six of Aer

Helper Card Connection: Ainnir of Aer

Ancient Ones Card Connection: Muirneach Deirdre and Noise, Uisce Coisricthe, and Grain Páiste

Numerology: 14 or 5

Planets: Earth, Venus, Mercury

Energy: mental, in defense

Gender: masculine

how Diarmaid Got his Love Spot

Diarmaid and Conan and Goll and Osgar went one day hunting, and they went so far they could not get home in the evening, and they spent the first part of the night walking through the woods and pulling berries and eating them. And when it was about mid-night they saw a light, and they went towards it, and they found a little house before them, and the light shining from it. They went in then, and they saw an old man there, and he bade them welcome, and he called them all by their names. And they saw no one in the house but the old man and a young girl and a cat. And the old man bade the girl to make food ready for the fianna of Ireland, for there was great hunger on them.

When the food was ready and put on the table, there came a great wether that was fastened up in the back of the house, and he rose up on the table where they were eating, and when they saw that, they looked at one another. "Rise up, Conan," said Goll, "and fasten that wether in the place it was before." Conan rose up and took hold of it, but the wether gave itself a shake that threw Conan under one of its feet. The rest were looking at that, and Goll said: "Let you rise up, Diarmaid, and fasten up the wether." So Diarmaid rose up and took hold of it, but it gave itself a shake the same way as before; and when Diarmaid was down it put one of its feet on him. Goll and Osgar looked at one another then, and shame came on them, a wether to have done so much as that. Osgar got up, but the wether put him down under one of his feet, so that it had now the three men under him. Then Goll rose up and took hold of it and threw it down; but if he did, it rose up again in spite of him, and put Goll under his fourth foot.

"It is a great shame," said the old man then, "the like of that to be done to the fianna of Ireland. And rise up now, cat," he said, "and tie the wether in the place where he was." The cat rose up then and took hold of the wether, and brought it over and tied it in its place at the end of the house.

The men rose up then, but they had no mind to go on eating, for there was shame on them at what the wether had done to them. "You may go on eating," said the old man; "and when you are done I will show you that now you are the bravest men of the world."

So they ate their fill then, and the old man spoke to them, and it is what he said: "Goll," he said, "you are the bravest of all the men of the world, for you have wrestled with the world and you threw it down. The strength of the world is in the wether, but death will come to the world itself; and that is death," he said, showing them the cat.

They were talking together then, and they had their food eaten, and the old man said their beds were ready for them that they could go to sleep. The four of them went then into the one room, and when they were in their beds the young girl came to sleep in the same room with them, and the light of her beauty was shining on the walls like as if it was the light of a candle.

And when Conan saw her he went over to the side of the bed where she was.

Now, it was Youth the young girl was, and when she saw Conan coming to her: "Go back to your bed, Conan," she said; "I belonged to you once, and I will never belong to you again." Conan went back to his bed then, and Osgar had a mind to go over where she was. Then she said to him: "Where are you going?" "I am going over to yourself for a while," said he.

"Go back again, Osgar," she said; "I belonged to you once, and I will never belong to you again."

Then Diarmaid rose up to go to her: "Where are you going Diarmaid?" she said. "I am going over to yourself for a while," said he. "O Diarmaid," she said, "that cannot be; I belonged to you once, and I can never belong to you again; but come over here to me Diarmaid," she said, "and I will put a love-spot on you, that no woman will ever see without giving you her love." So Diarmaid went over to her, and she put her hand on his forehead, and she left the love-spot there, and no woman that ever saw him after that was able to refuse him her love.[1]

Ridire of Tine
Ruled by Tinne

CU CHULAINN

Meaning

Air of Fire; mind in action; male sexual energy in nature; the first light of day; young male between birth and age 30; inspiration is freely channeled and aggressively pursued; a sense of false immortality; driven by ego of glory.

The magick of the Faery World can lead you betwixt and between, but beware the need to fight your way in to where you don't belong; once focused, goals are easy to achieve; learn to maintain your fury; become the aura of Spirit by finding the Fire in the Head instead of in the gut.

Card Description

Upon Magh Muirtheimme, Cu Chulainn stands in his chariot, which is facing us backwards, making it seem as if he is standing on a throne. A residue of battle frenzy halos his head. Cu Chulainn is victorious. In his right hand he holds the famous Gae Bulga, passed down to him by Lamhfada. Trophy heads hang from the sides of the chariot. The two horses are Faery horses: the Grey of Macha and the Black of Sainglui. He is oblivious to his own mortality, which the pillar stone and the presence of the crow foretell.

Cu Chulainn has many interesting characteristics: he has tri-colored hair, seven pupils in each eye, seven toes and seven fingers. On both checks are four moles: yellow, green, blue, and red. He wears a tartan kilt from Alba, showing his connection to the mighty warrior goddesses, Skatha and Aifa, the last of whom was his lover for a year and a day. Aifa bore Cu Chulainn a son named Connla, whose unfortunate death was Cu Chulainn's undoing.

Cu Chulainn is the greatest figure in ancient Irish heroic literature. The storytellers of ancient Ireland never tired of recounting his deed and attributing new exploits to him. His original name, Setanta, appears to go back to remote times, and it is possible that he may be a personage adopted by the Gaels from a still older population.

According to what seems the oldest tradition, Cu Chulainn was the son of the Tuatha De Danann prince Lugh and Dechtire, the sister of King Conchobar of Ulster. Throughout his short but brilliant career, Cu Chulainn reveals his supernatural origin. Even as a child of five years he possesses remarkable strength and skill; when only six he slays the terrible watchdog of Culann the Smith, thereby winning the name "Hound of Culann." at seven he becomes a full-fledged warrior; at seventeen he holds at bay the entire army of Connacht and her allies; and he is only twenty-seven when he meets his death, after refusing the help of the Morrigu, and fighting against overpowering odds.

Oghams and Symbols

Tinne, the holly, is placed as the eighth ogham letter. Tinne rules the eighth moon month, which extends from July 8 to August 4 under the astrological rulership of Cancer and Leo. The eighth month is known as the Spear Month, or the Warrior's Moon.

He wears a jeweled crown to show his royalty. Around his neck hangs a necklace with two important oghams and two symbols hanging from it. The first ogham is a reversed Uinllean. The magickal characteristics of this ogham are hardness and resistance, the solidity of knowledge, and tried-and-tested actions. It refers to the solidity of ancient wisdom, the cultural or physical foundation that must be in place before any constructions can be made, either physically or figuratively.

The second ogham is Koad, which signifies earth but is associated with death; it can be described as the sacred grove, the location where all things, hitherto separate, become connected. At such a point all things become clear.

The first symbol is a triangle, representing the Fire nature of the warrior's will, while the second symbol is the Triple Spiral, the most sacred of all Irish symbols. The Triple Spiral shows the Three Circles of Existence, all interconnected, as well as the triad of Deity. For this symbol to be worn as jewelry shows the wearer to have the unique alignment of mind-body-soul.

Two other significant symbols are portrayed as jewelry. The Celtic Cross broach, symbolizing the four seasons, as well as the 56 vibration of the masculine gender or the God force. The other piece of jewelry is the double-spiral belt buckle representing dual nature.

In the background rises a pillar stone inscribed with ogham. This is the very stone that Cu Chulainn fastens himself to at the time of his death. The Morrigu, in the form of a crow, sits upon it. Her presence foretells his impending doom.

Other Correspondences

Element: fire

Sub-element: air

Element Card Connection: Four of Uisce, Five of Tine, Six of Tine

Helper Card Connection: Ainnir of Tine, Ard Rí of Tine, and Banríon of Aer

Ancient Ones Card Connection: Carbad na an Morrigu Anand, and Bean Sidhe Cailleach

Numerology: 8 and 11 or 2

Planets: Moon, Saturn, Jupiter

Energy: Mental, in action

Gender: Masculine

Cu Chulainn Champion of Erin

A lord of Ulster named Briccriu of the Poisoned Tongue once made a feast to which he bade King Conor and all the heroes of the Red Branch, and because it was always his delight to stir up strife among men or women, he set the heroes contending among themselves as to who was the champion of the land of Erin. At last it was agreed that the championship must lie among three of them, namely, Cu Chulainn, and Conall of the Victories, and Laery the Triumphant. To decide between these three, a demon named The Terrible was summoned from a lake in the depth of which he dwelt. He proposed to the heroes a test of courage. Any one of them, he said, might cut off his head today provided that he, the claimant of the championship, would lay down his own head for the ax tomorrow. Conall and Laery shrank from the test, but Cu Chulainn accepted it, and after reciting a charm over his sword, he cut off the head of the demon, who immediately rose, and taking the bleeding head in one hand and his ax in the other, plunged into the lake.

Next day he reappeared, whole and sound, to claim the fulfillment of the bargain. Cu Chulainn, quailing but resolute, laid his head on the block. "Stretch out your neck, wretch," cried the demon, "'tis too short for me to strike at." Cu Chulainn does as he is bidden. The demon swings his ax thrice over his victim, brings down the butt with a crash on the block, and then bids Cu Chulainn rise unhurt, Champion of Ireland and her boldest man.[2]

Rídíre of Uísce

Ruled by Gort

OENGUS OG

Meaning

Air of Water; mental energy in union with the female energy; the masculine force of creative imagination in life; in the reflection of daylight; young male between birth and age thirty; feeling with the mind; knowing how to dream and seek vision; duality.

The magick of the Faery World is a spell woven through the heart strings of all who seek to enter; love is the golden key; compassion, kindness and loyal chivalry.

Card Description

Oengus Og (Angus the Young), son of the Dagda, sits by his mother Boanna (the river Boyne). He is the Irish god of love. His palace was at Newgrange on the Boyne. Four bright birds that always hovered about his head were supposed to be his kisses taking shape in this lovely form, and at their singing, love came springing up in the hearts of youths and maidens. Two of the birds would continually cry to the young men of Ireland, "Come, come," and two of them would say, "I go, I go." In his youth, he used to be called the Frightener, or the Disturber; for the plough teams of the world, and every sort of cattle that is used by men, would make away in terror before him.

In the Tain, Oengus is represented as a Gaelic Eros, a god of love and beauty, described as "slender and as swift as a wind. His hair swung about his face like golden blossoms. His eyes were mild and dancing and his lips smiled with quiet sweetness. About his head there flew perpetually a ring of singing birds, and when he spoke his voice came sweetly from a center of sweetness."

Here he makes himself known as Infinite Joy and Love. Like his father, he had a gold harp, and when he plays it, his music is so sweet that anyone who hears it will follow.

Oengus is the special deity and friend of beautiful youths and maidens. Dermot of the Love-spot, a follower of Finn Mac Cumhal, and lover of Grania—both Helper Cards—was bred up with Oengus in the palace on the Boyne. Dermot was the typical lover of Irish legend. When he was slain by the wild boar of Ben Bulben, Oengus revives him and carries him off to share his immortality in his Faery palace.

Oghams and Symbols

Gort is the twelfth ogham character and is connected to the ivy. The ivy month extends from September 30 to October 27, and is under the rulership of Libra and Scorpio. Symbolically, ivy is a tree of transformation, starting as a small, weak, herb-like plant, which finally, after centuries of growth, becomes an enormously thick, woody, serpentine tree in its own right.

The cauldron is the Dagda's Undry, the cauldron of plenty, representing a connection to the eternal abundance of the universe and the feminine energy.

The sun appears to be setting, yet is as vibrant as the rising sun. This represents the stillness of conception, when all things can happen in the same moment, the same hour, the same day, just as the Young God was begotten at break of day and born betwixt it and evening.

The swan is the symbol of Oengus' heart, his passions, his companion of the lake, for whom he shapeshifts, taking the form of the swan to be with her for half the year. The swan is the form that the Tuatha

De Danann are known to take when passing betwixt and between this world and their own.

The ivy twining around the tree trunk is connected to Gort, signifying one's ability to bind oneself to the heart's desire.

Other Correspondences

Element: water

Sub-element: air

Element Card Connection: Four of Aer, Five of Uisce, Six of Uisce

Helper Card Connection: Ridire of Aer, Ainnir of Aer, and Banríon of Aer

Ancient Ones Card Connection: Athair Dia Dagda and Grain Páiste

Numerology: 10 or 1

Planets: Jupiter, Mars, and Venus

Energy: mental, in emotion

Gender: masculine, balanced

The Dream of Oengus

Once the God of love felt sick of love for a maiden whom he had seen in a dream. He told the cause of his sickness to his mother Boanna, who searched all Ireland for the maiden, but could not find her. Then the Dagda was called in, but he too was at a loss, till he called to his aid Bōv the Red, king of the Dananns of Munster—the same as in the tale of the Children of Lir, and who was skilled in all mysteries and enchantments. Bōv undertook the search, and after a year had gone by declared that he had found the visionary maiden at a lake called the Lake of the Dragon's Mouth.

Oengus goes to Bōv, and, after being entertained by him three days, is brought to the lake shore, where he sees thrice fifty maidens walking in couples, each couple linked by a chain of gold, but one of them is taller than the rest by a head and shoulders.

"That is she!" cries Oengus. "Tell us by what name she is known." Bōv answers that her name is Caer, daughter of Ethal Anubal, a prince of the Dananns of Connacht. Oengus laments that he is not strong enough to carry her off from her companions, but, on Bōv's advice, betakes himself to Ailell and Maev, the King and Queen of Connacht, for assistance. The Dagda and Oengus then both repair to the palace of Ailell, who feasts them for a week, and then asks the cause of their coming. When it is declared he answers, "We have no authority over Ethal Anubal." They send a message to him, however, asking for the hand of Caer for Oengus, but Ethal refuses to give her up. In the end he is besieged by the combined forces of Ailell and the Dagda, and taken prisoner. When Caer is again demanded of him he declares that he cannot comply, "for she is more powerful than I." He explains that she lives alternately in the form of a maiden and a swan year and year about, "and on the first of November next," he says, "you will see her with a hundred and fifty other swans at the Lake of the Dragon's Mouth."

Oengus goes there at the appointed time, and cries to her, "Oh, come and speak to me!"

"Who calls me?" asks Caer.

Oengus explains who he is, and then finds himself transformed into a swan. This is an indication of consent, and he plunges in to join his love in the lake. After that they fly together to the palace on the Boyne, uttering as they go a music so divine that all hearers are lulled to sleep for three days and nights.[3]

Ridire of Domhan

Ruled by Saille

NAOISE

Meaning

Air of Earth; mental energy manifested; the masculine force of the physical world; in the waning of the youth light; young male between birth and age thirty; reliable, stable, dedicated; a wisdom beyond years; ready to pursue love and life; romanticism.

The magick of the Faery World is the seer's ability to know that emptiness follows false promises; through the substance of matter all things are possible when backed by spiritual inspiration.

Card Description

Naoise, the son of Usna and champion of the Red Branch of Ulster under the high kingship of Conor, stands on the Glen Etive lakeside in solitude. Now, he is ready to return to Ireland and serve his true sovereign once again after being exiled. He is a noble knight, one who takes his vows of chivalry with dignity. His ideals and dreamy romanticism lead him astray. He offers his heart, with loyalty, and then finds himself in conflict, forced to choose between his convictions.

On the bluffs behind him stands Deirdre, the most beautiful maiden in all of Ireland, an obsession of Conor. Naoise and Deirdre are the Irish Romeo and Juliet, and their tale is one of the three sorrows of Irish storytelling.

Oghams and Symbols

Saille is the third peasant tree, and the fourth character of the ogham alphabet. Saille moon month, under the astrological rulership of Aries and Taurus, begins on April 15 and ends on May 12. Saille, the willow tree, is associated with the growth of lunar power and is known as the sacred moon month of the goddess. This ogham is of linking, a watery symbolism that brings itself into harmony with the flow of events, most notably the phases of the moon. The willow is sacred to all death aspects of the Triple Morrigu. The words *witch* and *wicked* are believed to be derived from the same ancient word for *willow*, which also yields *wicker*.

The sword is the magick sword of Manannon, named Fragarach, the Answerer, which can penetrate any armor. The spear is called Yellow Shaft, another gift from the Sea God; it, like the sword, never fails to slay when thrown.

The pillar stone is a holy stone because of the natural hole bored through its top, signifying that fate has already been preordained, and no one can undo it. The tower in the background has the ladder down, showing that it is a time of peace rather than war.

Other Correspondences

Element: earth

Sub-element: air

Element Card Connection: Four of Tine, Five of Domhan, Six of Domhan

Helper Card Connection: Ainnir of Domhan, and Ard Rí of Uisce

Ancient Ones Card Connection: Muirneach Deirdre and Naoise, An Clogás, and Breithiúnas

Numerology: 16 or 7

Planets: Venus, Mercury, Moon

Energy: mental, in slowness

Gender: masculine

The Sons of Usna

Among the lords of Ulster was one named Felim son of Dall, who one day made a great feast for the king. The king came with his Druid Cathbad, Fergus Mac Roy, and many heroes of the Red Branch. While they were enjoying the feast of roasted meat, wheaten cakes, and wine, a messenger from the women's apartments came to tell Felim that his wife had just borne him a daughter. The lords and warriors drank to the health of the newborn infant, and the king asked Cathbad to perform divination in the manner of the Druids to tell what the future had in store for the child.

Cathbad gazed at the stars and drew the child's horoscope. He became quite troubled, and finally said "The infant will be fairest among the women of Erin and shall wed a king. But because of her, death and ruin will come upon the Province of Ulster."

The warriors wanted to put her to death at once, but Conor forbade them. "I will avert the doom," he said, "she shall wed no foreign king, but will be my own wife when she is of age." He took away the child and placed her in the care of his nurse, Levarcam. They named the baby Deirdre, and the nurse was given strict orders to keep the child in a strong dun in the solitude of a great wood. No young man was to see her, or she him, until she was married to the king.

One day, as the marriage of Deirdre and Conor drew near, Deirdre and Levarcam looked over the rampart of their dun. A heavy snow had fallen during the night. In the still, frosty air the trees stood as if made of silver and the green in front of the dun was a sheet of unbroken white, except for the blood of the calf that a scullion had killed for their dinner. As Deirdre looked, a raven flew down from a tree and began to sip the blood.

"Oh, nurse," she cried suddenly, "that is like the man that I would love, not like Conor. His hair like the raven's wing, and in his cheek the hue of blood, and his skin as white as snow." This was not the image of

Conor, and Levarcam, taking pity on the girl, said "You have pictured a man in Conor's household."

"Who is he?" asked the maiden.

"He is Naoise, a champion of the Red Branch," the nurse responded.

Deirdre begged the nurse to bring Naoise to her. Because the old nurse loved the girl, she finally consented. Deirdre implored Naoise to save her from Conor. He resisted, but finally her her pleas and her beauty won him, and he vowed to be hers.

He came secretly one night with his two brothers, Ardan and Ainlé and took Deirdre and Levarcam away. They escaped the king's pursuit and boarded a ship for Scotland, where Naoise entered the service of the King of the Picts. Yet they could not rest, for the king found Deirdre— and would have taken her from the young knight—but they escaped, making their home in the solitude of Glen Etive by the lake. They lived here in the wild wood, hunting, fishing, and seeing no one but each other and their servants.

Years passed and Conor made no sign—but he did not forget, and his spies told him everything that happened with Naoise and Deirdre. At last, judging that Naoise and his brothers would have tired of the solitude, he sent Fergus son of Roy, the closest friend of Naoise, to ask them to return, and to promise them that all would be forgiven.

The news was received joyfully by Naoise and his brothers, but Deirdre foresaw evil and wanted to send Fergus home alone. Noise blamed her for her doubt and suspicion and promised her that they would be under the protection of Fergus, which no king in Ireland would dare to violate. At last, they prepared to go.

When they landed in Ireland, they were met by Baruch, a lord of the Red Branch, whose dun was nearby. He invited Fergus to a feast he had prepared for him that night. Fergus refused, and Baruch said, "you must stay with me tonight, for it is a geis for you to refuse a feast."

Deirdre implored him not to leave them, but Fergus, who was tempted by the feast, fear breaking his geis. He asked his two sons, Illan the Fair and Buino the Red, to take charge of the party in his place.

And so the party came to Emain Macha, and they were lodged in the House of the Red Branch, but Conor did not receive them. After the evening meal, as he sat silently drinking heavily, he sent a messenger to call Levarcam to come before him.

"How are the sons of Usna?" Conor asked her.

"They are well," she said. "You have the three most valorous champions in Ulster in your court. Truly the king who has those three need fear no enemy."

"Is Deirdre well?" he asked.

"She, too, is well," said the nurse, "But she has lived many years in the wild wood, and toil and care have changed her. Little of her beauty now remains, O King."

The king dismissed her, and sat drinking again.

After awhile, he sent his servant, Trendorn, to spy and see if Deirdre had indeed lost her beauty. Looking through a high window, Trendorn saw the Naoise's brothers and the sons of Fergus as they talked, or cleaned their weapons, or prepared for bed. Naoise sat with a chessboard in front of him. Playing chess with him was the fairest woman that Trendorn had ever seen. As he looked in wonder at the noble pair, one caught sight of him and rose with a cry, pointing to the face at the window. Naoise hurled the chess board at the spy, and it struck out his eye. Trendorn hastily descended and informed the king.

Conor went into a rage. He called his men to attack, and in the fight Fergus's sons were killed, but Naoise and his brothers escaped with Deirdre. Conor requested that Cathbad the Druid cast spells upon them so that they might become enemies of the province. He vowed to do them no harm if they were taken alive.

So Cathbad conjured up a lake of slime that seemed to be around the feet of the sons of Usna, they could not tear their feet from it. Naoise picked up Deirdre and put her on his shoulder as they seemed to sink into the slime. The guards and servants of Conor seized and bound them, and brought them before the king. Conor called man after man to come forward and slay the sons of Usna. None would obey him until, at last, Owen son of Duracht and Prince of Ferney came and took the sword of Naoise. With one sweep, he shore off the heads of all three and they died.

Conor took Deirdre with force. For a year, she lived with him in the palace in Emain Macha. During all that time she never smiled. Finally, Conor said, "what is it that you hate most of all on earth, Deirdre?"

She said, "you, and Owen son of Duracht," as Owen stood by.

"Then you will go to Owen for a year," said Conor.

When Deirdre climbed into the chariot behind Owen, she kept her eyes on the ground and would not look at her tormenters.

Taunting her, Conor said, "Deirdre, the sight of you between me and Owen is that of a ewe between two rams."

Deirdre, flinging herself head first from the chariot, dashed her head against a rock. She fell dead.

The country folk buried her next to Naoise, it is said, against the king's order. From their burial sites, two yew trees grew. The treetops, when they were full grown, met each other over the roof of the great church of Armagh. They intertwined, and no one could part them.[4]

In the South

THE ARD RÍ CARDS
High Kings of the Emerald Isle

Ard Rí
of Aer
Ruled by Uath

NUADA OF THE
SILVER HAND

Meaning

Fire of Air; willpower pursued through judgment; the masculine force supported mentally by the feminine force in life; the lightning light of day; storm magick; mature male between age thirty and death; in full rulership; an authority figure; may not be in touch with intuitive side or creative right-brain activity; extreme linear thinking.

The magick of the Faery World beckons; slice through the veils of ego; don't forget the softer side of life; think before reacting; war is not the answer; learn to sheathe the sword.

Card Description

Nuada of the silver hand, the King of the Tuatha De Danann, sits upon his throne on the Hill of Tara. Upon his blond hair rests the crown of his rank, with its crest of the sundial. He is full-bearded to show his maturity. Around his neck is the dragon's torc, another sign of royalty. In his left hand he brandishes his invincible sword, while his right arm, made of silver, rests in his lap.

His throne is made of gold, inlaid with blue stone and edged in silver. It sits on an elaborate blue carpet placed directly upon the plush green grass of Ireland. There are four pillars around the throne, each in the four directions, upon which ogham have been carved. Above and over Nuada, royal blue, sheer cloth canopy.

A rose-tinted dawn sky is clouded, but not with storm clouds, although flashes of lightning spring from them. This is the sky of power, illuminating Nuada's origin: the city of Findias, although in Erin he is guardian of the Leinster Province.

The Oghams and Symbols

Uath is the sixth character of the ogham alphabet, and is the hawthorn tree, which is classified as the fourth peasant tree. The hawthorn is the tree of enforced chastity and takes its name from the month of May, in fact it is sometimes referred to as the May tree. The sixth moon month begins on May 13, which accounts for the medieval habit of riding out on May Morning to pluck flowering hawthorn boughs and dance around the May Pole in anticipation of the sixth month when sexual interchange was looked down upon. The sixth moon month ends on June 9, which places Uath under the astrological rulership of Taurus and Gemini. Huath is the Goddess' tree of sexuality.

In the Irish Brehon Laws, the hawthorn appeared as the *scieth* (harm) and was considered generally an unlucky tree. The ogham's name means terrible, referring to the hag, or destroying aspect, of the Threefold Morrigu, who are the daughters of Nuada.

The red and the half-yellow, half-white triangles symbolize the fire and air qualities of the card, or the stimulation of thought in action.

Other Correspondences

Element: air

Sub-element: fire

Element Card Connection: Seven of Domhan, Eight of Aer, Nine of Aer

Helper Card Connection: Ridire of Uisce, Ard Rí of Tine, and Banríon of Tine

Ancient Ones Card Connection: Athair Dia Dagda, Carbad na an Morrigu, and Crochadóir Amorgen

Numerology: no numerological value, because it is an ogham of the UnderWorld

Planets: Saturn, Jupiter, and Mars

Energy: willpower/ego/spirit, in judgment

Gender: masculine, supported by feminine

Nuada Argetlám

When the Tuatha De Dananns arrived in Erin, Nuada was their great king. The Firbolgs, however, were not impressed with the superiority of the Dananns, and decided to engage them in battle. The battle was joined on the Plain of Moytura in the south of Co. Mayo, near the spot now called Cong. The Firbolgs were led by their king, Mac Erc, and the Dananns by Nuada of the Silver Hand, who got his name from an incident in this battle. His hand, it is said, was cut off in the fight, and one of the skillful artificers who abounded in the ranks of the Dananns made him a new one of silver. By their magical and healing arts the Dananns gained the victory, and the Firbolg king was slain. But a reasonable agreement followed: the Firbolgs were allotted the province of Connacht for their territory, while the Dananns took the rest of Ireland. As late as the seventeenth century the analyst Mac Firbis discovered that many of the inhabitants of Connacht traced their descent to these same Firbolgs. Probably they were a veritable historic race, and the conflict between them and the People of Dana may be a piece of actual history invested with some of the features of a myth.

Nuada of the Silver Hand should now have been ruler of the Dananns, but his mutilation forbade it, for no blemished man might be a king in Ireland. The Dananns therefore chose Bres, who was the son of a Danann woman named Eri, but whose father was unknown, to weight over them instead.

In the meantime, because Nuada had gotten his silver hand through the art of his physician Diancecht, or because, as some versions of the legend say, a still greater healer, Mich, the son of Diancecht, had made the veritable hand grow again to the stump, he was chosen to be king in place of Bres once again.

It was, however, in the Second Battle of Moytura, when the Dananns fought against the Fomors, that the king of the Fomorians, Balor of the Mighty Blows, raged among the gods, slaying their King, Nuada of the Silver Hand, as well as Macha, one of his warlike wives.

Ard Rí
of Tine
Ruled by Uath

LAMHFADA

Meaning

Fire of Fire; exalted willpower; ego in full action; Spirit in battle; the masculine force subordinating the support of the feminine force in life; in the summertime of life; mature male between age thirty and death; a jack-of-all-trades, master of all—slave to none.

The magick of the Faery World equips you with the ability to overcome all odds and adversity; superior strength; listen to Spirit to hear the ancient voice of wisdom.

Card Description

Lamhfada stands in the Great Feast Hall of Tara. Nuada is celebrating his return to the throne by a feast to his people. Lugh is in the process of presenting himself to Nuada as a master of all skills, seeking to be accepted as a champion of the Tuatha De Danann.

He is clothed like a king, with a crown of two pieces of gold chain twisted together, the torc of royalty around his neck, a deep forest green mantle pinned with the broach of seasons, golden bracelets about his wrists, and a golden ornamented belt about his waist. In his hands he holds the Gae Bulga, the bloodthirsty spear, which never misses its mark when thrown.

On the back wall hang weapons and shields, a sign that all who are joined in the banqueting hall are allies. His foot, casually placed on the edge of the golden throne, is a hint of his future kingship. A crow sits on the back of the throne, while a sheathed sword, a sign of peace, and a beautiful shield lean against its front. Before Lamhfada and the throne, a chess board is set up, the game in progress.

The Oghams and Symbols

Ngetal is the thirteenth ogham, and is connected to the reed. According to Bardic tree classification, the reed is the first of the kiln or shrub trees. Ngetal's tree is not a tree, according to modern botanical definitions. However, it appears that the reed was classified as a tree because the scribes of ancient Ireland used the hard, resistant stems of the reed to make pens, and in ancient times, any plant with woody stems, such as a reed or ivy, was called a tree.

The thirteenth ogham's moon month extends from October 28 to November 24, making it the ogham of Samhain, the festival of the dead, marking the beginning of the new year in the Celtic Calendar. Ngetal is thus under the astrological rulership of Scorpio and Sagittarius.

The reed was an ancient symbol of royalty, and was made into scepters. It is the tree arrows that were cut from and shot into every direction as a symbol of sovereignty. The greatest power of Ngetal is as a preserver. As a pen, the reed preserves memory and knowledge; as a rod, it preserves measure; and, as roofing, it preserves the house. Above all else, Ngetal is the ogham of written communication, thereby signifying conscious precision and the maintenance of order in chaos.

The Gae Bulga is magickal spear that never misses its mark when thrown. Upon it are carved symbols: the Triple Spiral, representing the Trinity and Celtic Circles of Existence; the four colored triangles of the elements, symbolizing a unity with the natural world; and a single spiral, representing the continuum of life.

The sheathed sword is a sign of peace. The chess board represents pragmatic intelligence. The crow sitting on the back of the throne on a red cloth symbolizes that death, when called, is only a breath away.

The two red triangles represent the complete presence of either Spirit or, in a worst-case scenario, Ego.

Other Correspondences

Element: fire

Sub-element: fire

Element Card Connection: Seven of Uisce, Eight of Tine, Nine of Tine

Helper Card Connection: Ard Rí of Aer, Ard Rí of Uisce, and Banríon of Tine

Ancient Ones Card Connection: Draoi Gebann, Athair Dia Dagda, Rúndaigne Banba, and Crochadóir Amorgen

Numerology: 1

Planets: Venus, Mercury, and Moon

Energy: willpower/ego/spirit, in action

Gender: masculine, supported by feminine, in extreme

Lugh of the Long hand

Nuada of the Silver Hand was holding a great feast at Temhair after he was back in the kingship. The door was tended by two door-keepers, Gamal, son of Figal, and Camel, son of Riagall. A young man came to the door, where one of them stood, and asked to be taken to the king.

"Who are you?" asked the door-keeper.

"I am Lugh, son of Cian of the Tuatha De Danann, and of Ethlinn, daughter of Balor, King of the Fomor," he answered, "and I am foster-son of Taillte, daughter of the King of the Great Plain, and of Echaid the Rough, son of Duach."

"What are you skilled in?" asked the door-keeper. "No one without an art comes into Temhair."

"Question me," said Lugh. "I am a carpenter."

"We do not want you. We have a carpenter ourselves already, Luchtar, son of Luachaid."

"Then I am a smith."

"We have a smith. Colum Cuaillemech of the Three New Ways."

"Then I am a champion."

"That is no use to us. We have a champion, Ogma, the king's brother."

"Question me again," he said. "I am a harper."

"That is of no use to us. We have a harper ourselves, Abhean, son of Bicelmos. The Men of the Three Gods brought him from the hills."

"I am a poet," Lugh then said, "and a teller of tales."

"That is no use to us. We have a teller of tales, Erc, son of Ethaman."

"And I am a magician."

"We already have plenty of magicians and people of power."

"I am a physician," he said.

"That is no use. Diancecht is our physician."

"Let me be a cup-bearer," he said.

"We have nine cup-bearers ourselves."

"I am a good worker in brass."

"We have a worker in brass ourselves. Credne Cerd."

Then Lugh said, "Go and ask the king if he has anyone who can do all these things. If he does, then I will not ask to come into Temhair."

The door-keeper went to the king and said, "There is a young man at the door whose name should be the Ildánach, the Master of all Arts. All the things the people of your house can do, he can do all of them himself."

"Test him with the chessboards," said Nuada. The chessboards were brought out, and Lugh won every game that was played. Once Nuada was told this, he said, "Let him in. No one like him has ever come to Temhair before."

The door-keeper let him pass. Lugh entered the king's house and sat down in the seat of knowledge. A great flag-stone that could hardly be moved by eighty yoke of oxen stood nearby. Ogma lifted it and hurled it through the house so that it lay outside of Temhair, as a challenge to Lugh. Lugh hurled it back again, so that it lay in the middle of the king's house. Then, he played the harp for them and had them laughing and crying, until he put them asleep at the end with a sleepy tune. When Nuada saw all that Lugh could do, he began to think that by his help the country might get free of the taxes and the tyranny the Formor had put on it. He came down from his throne and put Lugh on it in his place for the length of thirteen days so that they might all listen to the advice he would give.

Thus it was Lugh who freed Ireland of the Formors by killing his grandfather, Balor of the evil eye. From then on, Lugh became King of the De Dananns and High King of Ireland.[5]

Ard Rí of Uisce
Ruled by Fearn

MANANNAN MAC LIR

Meaning

Fire of Water; Spirit dance; the masculine force supported emotionally by the feminine force in life; the full light reflected in the heavens; mature male between age thirty and death; the ebb and flow of life; in touch with the heart center; moving swiftly through life; in the flow; playful; the developed wisdom of Spirit.

The magick of the Faery World will fill you with laughter; the ancient knowledge is given freely to any willing to submerge ego in the abyss to be reborn with second sight.

Card Description

Manannan, the son of the Irish sea god Lir, stands in his boat, Wave-sweeper, which propelled and guided itself wherever its owner wished. The name of his beloved is painted on the prow of the boat in an ancient Irish alphabet. He holds a paddle in his hands, which he uses to beat out a rhythm on the side of the boat, not for stirring. He has pale blue-white hair that catches in the sea breeze and dances about his shoulders. He wears a crown of royalty. His cloak, which is a mantle of invisibility at will, is the color of the ocean, as are his garments.

Dolphins follow him wherever he goes on sea, for he is God of Headlands, and patron to sailors and merchants, who claim him as the first of their guild. A twilight sky, streaked with the colors of the setting sun, foretell the time of day. Before him is a magickal cauldron, containing a luminous mixture. He is also known as a master of skills, wisdom, trickery, illusion, and magick.

The Oghams and Symbols

Fearn is the third letter of the ogham alphabet, and is classified as the second chieftain tree. Fearn is connected to the alder tree. The alder moon month extends from March 18 to April 14, which marks the drying up of the winter floods by the spring sun, symbolic of the fire and its power to reduce water. Fearn is under the astrological rulership of Pisces and Aries.

Principally, the alder is the tree of fire, the power of fire to free the earth from water; and the alder branch in the Cad Goddeu is a token of resurrection—its buds are set in a spiral, representing the continuum of life.

Off the Dingle Peninsula, on the southwestern coast of Ireland, resides a magickal dolphin. He is the only dolphin in the waters. He is a dreamer dolphin and is said to be dreaming the dream of Ireland. The two dolphins represent the dream of Ireland. One dolphin is jumping out of the water, meaning the dream is a conscious dream, whereas the other dolphin is still in the water, symbolizing that all dreams only exist in the subconscious mind.

The red triangle of fire represents Spirit. The blue inverted triangle of water represents the dream: The Spirit of the Dream.

Other Correspondences

Element: water

Sub-element: fire

Element Card Connection: Seven of Aer, Eight of Uisce, Nine of Uisce

Helper Card Connection: Ridire of Uisce, Ridire of Tine, Ainnir of Uisce, Ard Rí of Aer, Ard Rí of Tine, and Banríon of Uisce

Ancient Ones Card Connection: Treoraí, and Seanchailleach Gealach Cnoc

Numerology: 8

Planets: Moon, Saturn, and Jupiter

Energy: willpower/ego/spirit, in flow

Gender: masculine, supported by feminine

his Call to Bran

And there were some that went to Manannan's country beyond the sea, and that gave an account of it afterwards.

One time Bran, son of Febal, was out by himself near his dun, and he heard music behind him. And it kept always after him, and at last he fell asleep with the sweetness of the sound. And when he awoke from his sleep he saw beside him a branch of silver, and it having white blossoms, and the whiteness of the silver was the same as the whiteness of the blossoms.

He brought the branch in his hand into the royal house, and when all his people were with him they saw a woman with strange clothing standing in the house. And she began to make a song for Bran, and all the people were looking at her and listening to her, and this is what she said:

"I bring a branch of the apple-tree from Emhain, from the far island around which are the shining horses of the Son of Lir. A delight of the eyes is the plain where the hosts hold their games, curragh racing against chariot in the White Silver Plains to the south.

"There are feet of white bronze under it, shining through life and time; a comely level land through the length of the world's age, and many blossoms falling on it.

"There is an old tree there with blossoms, and birds calling from among them; every color is shining there, delight is common and music, in the Gentle-Voiced Plain, in the Silver Cloud Plain to the south.

"Keening is not used, or treachery, in the tilled familiar land; there is nothing hard or rough, but sweet music striking on the ear....It is not to all of you I am speaking, though I have made all these wonders known. Let Bran listen from the crowd of the world to all the wisdom that has been told him.

"Do not fall upon a bed of sloth; do not be overcome by drunkenness; set out on your voyage over the clear sea, and you may chance come to the Land of Women."

With that the woman went from them, and they did not know where she went. And she brought away her branch with her, for it leaped into her hand from Bran's hand, and he had not the strength to hold it.

Then on the morrow Bran set out upon the sea, and three companies of nine along with him; and one of his foster-brothers and comrades was set over each company of nine.

And when they had been rowing for two days and two nights, they saw a man coming towards them in a chariot, over the sea. And the man made himself known to them, and he said that he was Manannan Mac Lir. And then Manannan spoke to him in a song, and it is what he said:

"It is what Bran thinks, he is going in his curragh over the wonderful, beautiful clear sea; but to me, from far off in my chariot, it is a flowery plain he is riding on.

"What is a clear sea to the good boat Bran is in, is a happy plain with many flowers toe in my two-wheeled chariot.

"It is what Bran sees, many waves beating across the clear sea; it is what I myself see, red flowers without any fault.

"The sea-horses are bright in summer-time, as far as Bran's eyes can reach; there is a wood of beautiful acorns under the head of your little boat.

"A wood with blossom and with fruit, that has the smell of wine; a wood without fault, without withering, with leaves of the color of gold.

"Let Bran row on steadily, it is not far to the Land of Women; before the setting of the sun you will reach Emhain, of many-colored hospitality."[6]

Ard Rí of Domhan
Ruled by Coll

CONCHOBAR

Meaning

Fire of Earth; Ego and Spirit in union; the masculine force in life married to the feminine force in life; polarity; the quieting light; mature male between age thirty and death; Spirit made manifest; truthful authority in balance; provider; defender of Mother Earth—no compromise.

The magick of the Faery World dances in the bonfire of the commander's camp, giving life to the doorway into alternate realms of existence; join forces with Spirit.

Card Description

King Conchobar sits on an oak throne, outdoors, in a woodland camp. He is dressed in kingly attire; his red kilt and overshirt trimmed with gold, and forest green mantle. The ancient royal battle helmet is upon his head. The torc of royalty is around his neck. Two broaches, both of the elemental world, are pinned on him. He has red hair, and wears a full beard as a symbol of his maturity. From his waist hangs a sheathed dagger.

To his right is a feast table, and to the front of it, resting on the ground, perched against the table's leg, is Conchobar's magickal shield that would cry out when enemies threatened attack.

Oghams and Symbols

Coll is the ninth tree letter and is connected to hazel, the fourth chieftain tree. Hazel's moon month extends from August 5 to September 1, the nutting season, and is under the astrological rulership of Leo and Virgo.

The nut in Celtic legend is always an emblem of concentrated wisdom. The hazel is the tree of wisdom that contains something sweet, compact, and sustaining enclosed in a small hard shell. The saying "this is the matter in a nutshell" is derived from the hazel tree.

The battle helmet bears the sign of the phallus, a symbol of the king's marriage to the land. The chalice on the table is also a symbol of this king's connection to the feminine energy of the land.

On the shield face appears the Uinllean ogham. The magickal characteristics of this ogham are hardness and resistance, the solidity of knowledge, and tried-and-tested actions. It refers to the solidity of ancient wisdom, the cultural or physical foundation that must be in place before any constructions can be made, either physically or figuratively.

The two mushrooms represent a balance between linear thinking and intuitive psychism.

The red triangle or fire represents the masculine energy of creation, while the inverted green triangle, with its red tip, represents the joining of the male with the female.

Other Correspondences

Element: earth

Sub-element: fire

Element Card Connection: Seven of Tine, Eight of Domhan, Nine of Domhan

Helper Card Connection: Ridire of Domhan, Ainnir of Domhan, and Ard Rí of Uisce

Ancient Ones Card Connection: Máthair Bandia Ēiré, Athair
Dia Dagda, Muirneach Deirdre and Naosie, and Brethiúnas

Numerology: 9

Planets: Mars, Sun, and Venus

Energy: willpower/ego/spirit, in polarity

Gender: masculine, supported by feminine

The Birth of Conchobar

Conchobar Mac Nessa was the son of Cathbad the druid, or, as some
say, of Fachtna Fathach, king of Ulster. He was a great and admirable
king, and well indeed he might be, for the hour of his birth was the
hour of the birth of Christ in Palestine. For seven years before his birth
had the prophets foretold that on the same night that Christ should be
born, a notable chief should be born in Erin. And this is the prophecy
of his father, of Cathbad, on the night on which he was born, to Nessa
his wife:

> O Nessa, to art in peril;
> Let every one rise at thy birth-giving,
> Beautiful is the color of thy hands,
> O daughter of Eochaid Yellow-heel.
> Be not sorrowful, O wife,
> A head of hundreds and of hosts
> Of the world will he be, thy son.
>
> The same propitious hour
> To him and to the King of the World.
> Every one will praise him
> For ever to the day of Doom;
> The same night he will be born.
> Heroes will not defy him,
> As hostage he will not be taken,
> He and Christ.
>
> In the plain of Inis thou wilt bear him
> Upon the flagstone in the meadow.
> Glorious will be his story;

He will be the king of grace,
He will be the hound of Ulster,
Who will take pledges of Kings:
Awful will be the disgrace
when he falls.

Conchobar his name,
Whoso will call him.
His weapons will be red;
He will excel in many routs.
There he will find his death,
In avenging the suffering God.
Clear will be the track of his sword
Over the slanting plain of Laim.

Conchobar was called from the name of his mother, Mac Nessa. But her name in the beginning had been Assa, "docile" or "gentle," and it was in this manner that it was changed to Niassa, "ungentle." She was daughter of Eochaid Yellow-heel, king of Ulster, and by his desire she had been trained up by twelve tutors, to whom she was ever docile and full of teachableness. But in one night the entire number of her tutors fell by the hand of Cathbad the druid, who from the southern part of Ulster went on a raid through Erin with three times nine men. He was a man of Knowledge and of druidical skill; moreover, he was endowed with great bodily strength. Now the girl had no knowledge who they were who had slain her guardians, but from that moment she turned woman-warrior, and with her company set out to seek the author of the deed. In the very district of Erin she destroyed and plundered, so that her name was changed to Niassa (Nessa) after that, because of the greatness of her prowess and of her valor.

Once upon a time, she had gone upon a quest into a wilderness, and her people were preparing food. And seeing a clear beautiful spring of water, the maiden went off alone to bathe. Now while she was bathing Cathbad passed by and saw her. And he bared his sword above her head, and stood between the maiden and her dress and weapons.

"Spare me!" she cried.

"Grant then my three requests," replied the druid.

"They are granted," she said.

"I stipulate that thou be loyal to me, and that I have thy friendship, and that for so long as I live thou wilt be my one and only wife," said he.

"It is better for me to consent than to be killed by thee, and my weapon is gone," said the maiden. Then they and their people united in one place. In a favorable hour Cathbad proceeded into Ulster, and the father of the maiden made them welcome and gave them land, namely, Rath Cathbad in the country of the Picts near the river Conchobar in Crith Rois. By-and-by she bore him a son, namely Conchobar son of Cathbad. Cathbad took the boy to his bosom, and gave thanks for him and prophesied to him; and it was then that he uttered this lay:

Welcome the stranger that has come here!
They have told it to you,
He will be the gracious lord,
The son of gentle Cathbad.

The son of gentle Cathbad,
and of Nessa, the young,
Above the fortress of Brig na mBrat,
My son and my grandson.

My son and my grandson,
Grand ornament of the world,
He will be King of Rath Line,
he will be a poet, he will be generous.

He will be a poet, he will be generous,
he will be the head of warriors beyond the sea,
My little bird from the Brug,
My lamb,—welcome![7]

In the West

Ainnir
of Aer
Ruled by Luis

GRAINNE

Meaning

Water of Air; thinking with the heart; emotional energy in balance; inspiration and clarity of feeling; in the dawning of autumn; young female between birth and age thirty; the ability to know what one desires; cunning intellect; clear communication; ready to take action, but willing to remain still if need be; of a royal nature.

The magick of the Faery World exacts the payment of bonds—be careful what you vow yourself to, when such vows are collected by the OtherWorld, they must be upheld.

Card Description

Grainne was the daughter of Cormac, son of Art, High King of Ireland, and no woman in the length and breadth of the country could compare with her in beauty and grace. Many princes and chieftains sought her hand in marriage, but Grainne was proud and she spurned one after the other.

Dressed in royal blue, to show her rank, Grainne stands in the Great Feast Hall of Tara. Her hand rests on the Sword of Truth. A gold chalice also rests on the table, this is the chalice of sleep, in which she placed a potion to enable her the opportunity to speak with Diarmaid.

Oghams and Symbols

Luis in Grainne is a warning that one is subject to interference on the psychic level, but it can also indicate that, if one takes the appropriate precautions, one will not be harmed by the experience. This ogham is very powerful, for it can be used for the development of the power of second sight and protection against enchantment. As the second ogham character, Luis time extends from January 21 to February 17, is the second moon month, and is astrologically ruled by Aquarius and Pisces.

The flame over Grainne's head connects her to her origin, which is that of a sun goddess (*Grain*, a feminine noun, means "sun" in Irish).

Her royal blue dress is not only a sign of her rank, but also represents the feminine gender of the Ainnir cards. Here we have the balanced duality: the Ainnir (water/female) with Aer (air/masculine). The message is to "think with the heart."

Other Correspondences

> **Element:** water
>
> **Sub-element:** air
>
> **Element Card Connection:** Seven of Aer, Eight of Uisce, Nine of Uisce
>
> **Helper Card Connection:** Ridire of Aer, and Ridire of Uisce.
>
> **Ancient Ones Card Connection:** Roth Grian, and Grain Páiste
>
> **Numerology:** 14 or 5

Planets: Moon, Saturn, and Jupiter

Energy: emotional, in thought

Gender: feminine, balanced

Grainne's Lullaby

Manissa, wife to Finn Mac Cumhal, died, and Finn, complaining to some of the fianna of his loneliness, "with no wife to cheer or comfort me," was advised by them to ask Cormac for his daughter, Grannia, in marriage. Finn agreed, and Oisin his son, and Dering O'Bascna, a warrior of the fianna, set out for Tara to take Finn's request to the High King.

When they reached Tara, the King was holding an assembly of his chiefs and nobles, but hearing of the coming of Finn's messengers he put off the assembly until next day, in order to welcome them and to hear their business. But when Oisin told the King that they had come to ask for Grannia as a wife for Finn, he told them that they should go and tell Grannia of Finn's request and get her answer for themselves. "For," he said, "there is hardly in all Ireland a king or son of a king that has not asked for Grannia in marriage, and she has refused them all, and this has made many an enemy for me throughout the land."

So Oisin and Dering went to the apartments of the women, which were at the sunny side of the palace, and Cormac, going with them, said to his daughter: "Here, Grannia, are two warriors of the Fianna whom Finn Mac Cumhal has sent to ask you to be his wife."

And Grannia answered, with as much thought as if it was a lap dog or a pet bird she was being offered: "If you think he is a worthy son-in-law for you, why shouldn't he be a suitable husband for me?"

Oisin and Dering were satisfied with Grannia's answer, and they set out for Allen bearing a message from the King to Finn that he should come and claim his bride at the end of two weeks . . . .All gathered in the King's great banqueting hall. Finn sat at the high table with the Queen and Grannia and other royal persons, while Oisin and Finn's bodyguard sat at a special table set aside for the warriors of the Fianna.

In time, Grannia grew bored with the merry making and spoke with Dara of the Poems, who sat near her. Her eye wandered over the famous warriors of Finn's bodyguard and she asked Dara: "Tell me, O Dara, who this noble company is, for I know none among them but Oisin and his son, Oscar. Tell me, who is the warrior on the right of Oisin?"

"That noble-looking warrior is Goll Mac Morna, the Fierce in battle," he replied. "And who is the graceful, slim warrior next to him?" she questioned. "That is the swiftest runner of all the fianna, Keelta Mac Ronan, and the handsome warrior next to Keelta, with the gray shining eyes, is Diarmaid of the shining Face, the most beloved of women, the most chivalrous and generous of all the warriors of Finn."

In time, Grannia had her serving-maid bring her a large jewel-studded drinking cup that held wine for nine times nine men. And when it was brought to her, Grannia filled it with enchanted wine, gave it to the maid and bade her take the cup to Finn: "And bid him drink it and say it is Grannia who sends it to him."

Warmly, Finn received the cup, toasted, drank and passed the cup. Soon all who drank from the cup fell into a deep slumber. Grannia now rose up and, going to Diarmaid, said to him: "Will you take my love, Diarmaid, and take me away from this house tonight?"

"I will not take you from this house," said Diarmaid, "for you are promised to Finn, and I will not meddle with any woman that is betrothed to him."

"I put you under geis, O Diarmaid, and bonds that no true heroes ever break, to take me out of Tara tonight, and to save me from this marriage with an old man."

"Those are evil bonds, O Grannia, and nothing but evil and strife can come of them." He pleaded with her to withdraw her bonds and to give her love to Finn, but Grannia would not listen, and then Diarmaid said, "Dost thou not know that when Finn sleeps at Tara he keeps by his right and due the keys of the great gates, so that even if we wished it we could not leave Tara?"

"There is a secret wicket-gate in my bower," said Grannia . . . By and by, Diarmaid left with her and over time fell in love with Grannia, who was after all a beautiful maiden. Of course, Finn went crazy and sent trackers to run down Diarmaid and Grannia. They kept on the run for seven years, when they finally settled in Duvros Wood, by a magick rowan tree guarded over by a giant named Sharvan the Surly.

So great was Grannia's love for Diarmaid, that each night when he slept, she slept not, but cradled him in her arms, singing a lullaby that contained all the love in the world, its joys and sorrows, and the triumphant strength that makes it inviolable by society:

Sleep for a little, a very small while,
And fear nothing.
Man to whom I have given my love,
Diarmaid, son of O'Duibhne.
Sleep here, deeply, deeply,
Son of O'Duibhne, noble Diarmaid,
I will watch over your rest,
Charming son of O'Duibhne...
My heart would break with grief
If you should ever lose sight of thee.
To part us would be to wrench
The child from his mother,
Exile the body from the soul,
Warrior of beautiful lake Garman...
The stag in the east does not sleep.
He does not cease to bellow
In the bushes of the black birds.
He does not want to sleep.
The hind without horns does not sleep.
She moans for her dappled child
And runs through the undergrowth.
Sleep for a little, a very small while,
And fear nothing,
Man to whom I have given my love....

But Finn pursued them all over Ireland and finally caught them. He pretended to make peace with Diarmaid, but managed to bring about his death. Grannia died shortly after. However, it is said that Oengus of the Birds took Grannia and Diarmaid to live with him on the Boyne until in the end he went to Finn and asked him to make peace with Diarmaid. And Finn said he was willing, and the High King of Ireland also pardoned Diarmaid and gave Grannia her dowry of land, the cantred of Kesh-Corran in Sligo. And Diarmaid got back his lands and held them without rent or tribute to the King of Erin, and he got a guarantee from Finn that the fianna would not enter them or hunt over them without Diarmaid leave. Then Diarmaid and Grannia went to live in that portion of their lands in the county of Kerry, farthest from Finn and Cormac Mac Airt, and there they built themselves a house called Rath Grannia, where they lived in great peace for many years. And Grannia bore Diarmaid four sons and one daughter, and it was said that there was not a man in Ireland at that time who was richer in silver and in gold, in cattle or in sheep, than was Diarmaid son of Duivne.[8]

Ainnír of Tine

Ruled by Tinne

EMER

Meaning

Water of Fire; emotional ripening; female sexuality; the muted light of twilight; young female between birth and age thirty; great success; pursue all desires; steadfast; wit and charm; player of games.

The magick of the Faery World wafts through the late afternoon, calling to the heart to come alive and prepare to follow the last ray of light into the inner radiant light of the OtherWorld.

Card Description

Emer, daughter of Forgall, the lord of Lusca,[9] stands outside her father's Dun. She is a lovely maiden, who has the six gifts of womanhood: the gift of beauty, the gift of voice, the gift of sweet speech, the gift of needlework, the gift of wisdom, and the gift of chastity. Dressed in red, with a green cloak about her shoulders, she signifies her budding sexuality and connectedness to the land. She appeals to the male libido.

Oghams and Symbols

Tinne as connected to Emer brings strength and power, but in a balanced manner. It has a strong male element, more specifically connected with fatherhood and the consequent ability for souls to be reborn. The Holly indicates that unification must be enacted in the situation in order to receive the balance. Here, we have a fair judge. Holly is placed as the eight ogham letter. Tinne time, the eighth moon month, extends from July 8 to August 4, and is governed by Cancer and Leo.

Emer, hugging the wand—or spear shaft—is very significant, for it shows her willingness to enter into union with a man; note how the shaft of the wand is implanted in the soil. Her willingness to share her sexual expression is also indicated by the red gown and the green cloak symbolizing that in one essence she might even be a goddess of the land.

The chess board symbolizes woman's intelligence and her natural cunning abilities. The raven in the lower left corner is a symbol that appears in all the Tine Helper cards; here it symbolizes the destiny of Emer's mate, which is his mortality. In this meaning, the female is reminded that she must find the male within herself and become married to him as well.

The castle symbolizes the ability to attain great success. The lushness of the land (i.e., vegetation, flowing water, and rich brown soil) represents growth and creativity.

Other Correspondences

> **Element:** water
>
> **Sub-element:** fire
>
> **Element Card Connection:** Seven of Tine, Eight of Domhan, Nine of Domhan
>
> **Helper Card Connection:** Ridire of Tine, Banríon of Uisce, and Ard Rí of Uisce
>
> **Ancient Ones Card Connection:** Carbad na an Morrigu Anand, Réalta Dana, and Breithiúnas
>
> **Numerology:** 8 and 11 or 2
>
> **Planets:** Mars, Sun, and Venus
>
> **Energy:** emotional, in action
>
> **Gender:** feminine

The Wooing of Emer

It was in his festal array that Cu Chulainn went forth one day to address Emer, and to show his beauty to her. As the maidens were sitting on the bench of gathering at the stronghold, they heard coming towards them the clatter of horses' hoofs, with the creaking of the chariot, the cracking of straps, the grating of wheels, the rush of the hero, and the clanking of weapons.

"Let one of you see," said Emer, "what it is that is coming toward us."

"Truly, I see," said Fial, daughter of Forgall, "two steeds alike in size, beauty, fierceness, and speed, bounding side by side. Spirited they are and powerful, pricking their ears: their manes long and curling, and with curling tails. I see a chariot of fine wood with wicker work, moving on wheels of white bronze. A pole of white silver, with a mounting of white bronze. Its frame very high of creaking copper, rounded and firm. A strong curved yoke of gold; two firm-plaited yellow reins; the shaft hard and straight as sword blades.

"Within the chariot a dark sad man, comeliest of the men of Erin. Around him a beautiful crimson five-folded tunic, fastened at its opening on his white breast with a brooch of inlaid gold, against which it heaves, beating in full strokes. A shirt with a white hood, interwoven red with flaming gold. Seven red dragon-gems on the ground of either of his eyes. Two blue-white, blood-red cheeks that breathe forth sparks and flashes of fire. A ray of love burns in his look. Methinks, a shower of pearls has fallen into his mouth. As black as the side of a charred beam each of his eye-brows. On his two thighs rests a golden-hilted sword, and fastened to the copper frame of the chariot is a blood-red spear with a sharp mettlesome blade, on a shaft of wood well-fitted to the hand. Over his shoulders a crimson shield with a rim of silver, chased with figures of golden animals. He leaps the hero's salmon-leap into the air, and does many like swift feats. This is the description of the chariot-chief of the single chariot."

Meanwhile, Cu Chulainn had come to the place where the maidens were. He wished a blessing to them. Emer lifted up her lovely face and recognized Cu Chulainn, and she said, "May God make smooth the path before you!"

"And you," he said, "may you be safe from every harm!"

"Whence comest thou?" she asked.

"From Intide Emna," he replied.

"Where did you sleep?" she asked.

"We slept," he said, "in the house of the man who tends the cattle of the plain of Tethra."

"What was your food there?" she asked.

"The ruin of a chariot was cooked for us there," he replied.

"Which way didst thou come?"

"Between the two Mountains of the Wood," said he.

"Which way didst thou take after that?"

"That is not hard to tell," he said. "From the Cover of the Sea, over the Great Secret of the Tuatha De Danann, and the Foam of the two steeds of Emain Macha; over the Morrigu's Garden, and the Great Sow's Back; over the Glen of the Gream Dam, between the god and his prophet; over the Marrow of the Woman Fedelm, between the boar and his dam; over the Washing-place of the horses of Dea; between the King of Ana and his servant, to Monnchuile of the Four Corners of the World; over Great Crime and the Remnants of the Great Feast; between the Vat and the Little Vat, to the Gardens of Lugh, to the daughters of Tethra's nephew, Forgall, the king of the Fomorians. And what, O maiden, is the account of thee?" said Cu Chulainn.

"Truly, that is not hard to tell," said the maiden. "Tara of the women, whitest of maidens, the paragon of chastity, a prohibition that is not taken, a watcher that yet sees no one. A modest woman is a dragon, which none comes near. The daughter of a king is a flame of hospitality, a road that cannot be entered. I have champions that follow me to guard me from whoever would carry me off against their will, without their and Forgall's knowledge of my act."

"How hast thou been reared in the Gardens of Lugh, O maiden?" asked Cu Chulainn.

"It is not hard to relate that to thee, truly," answered she. "I was brought up in ancient virtues, in lawful behavior, in the keeping of chastity, in rank equal to a queen, in stateliness of form, so that to me is attributed every noble grace of demeanor among the hosts of Erin's women."

"Good indeed are those virtues," said Cu Chulainn. "Why, then should it not be fitting for us both to become one? For I have not hitherto found a maiden capable of holding converse with me at a meeting in this wise."

"One more question," said the maiden. "Hast thou a wife already?"

"Not so," said Cu Chulainn.

Said the maiden, "No one comes to this plain who does not slay as many as a hundred on every ford from the Ford of Scenn Menn at Ollbine to Banchuing Arcait, where swift Brea breaks the brow of Fedelm."

"Fair is this plain, the plain of the noble yoke," said Cu Chulainn.

"No one comes to this plain," said Emer, "who has not achieved the feat of leaping over three walls and slaying three times nine men at one blow, one of each of my brothers being in each group of nine, and yet preserve the brother in the midst of each nine of them alive; and then, accompanied by them and my foster-sister, bring out of Forgall's stronghold my weight in hold."

"Fair is this plain, the plain of the noble yoke," said Cu Chulainn.

"None comes to this plain," said she, "who does not go without sleep from summer's end to the beginning of spring, from the beginning of spring to May-day, and again from May-day to the beginning of winter."

"Even as thou hast commanded, so shall all by me be done," said Cu Chulainn.

"And by me thy offer is accepted, it is taken, it is granted," said Emer.... one year later they were married after Cu Chulainn had performed all her command.[10]

Ainnír of Uisce
Ruled by Gort

NIAMH

Meaning

Water of Water; pure female energy; the emotions in extreme; in the autumn of life; young female between birth and age 30; artistic talents; the juice of eternal youth; fairy tales and fantasy; illusive beauty.

The magick of the Faery World comes alive within the heart and by following the knights and dames of Faery, the world of creative imagination becomes reality.

Card Description

Naimh, of the golden curls, daughter of the Sea God, Manannan Mac Lir, sits atop the white faery horse. She has great beauty. On her head she wears the royal crown. Her brown mantle is of silk, spangled with red-gold stars, covering her feet. Golden rings hang from each curl of her hair. She has clear blue and colorless eyes, with cheeks redder than roses. She is of Sidhe born.

The white steed is covered in a wide, long, smooth garment of red-gold. Golden shoes are mounted to each hoof. A golden bridle fits securely in his mouth. A silver wreath crests his head.

The Faery maiden sits beneath the magickal apple tree, preparing to ride across and under the sea to Tir na nOg, the Land of Immortality, to her father's Faery palace in the west. The Dagda's cauldron rests in the forefront, by the root of the tree.

Oghams and Symbols

Gort, the ivy, is the twelfth ogham character. The ivy month extends from September 30 to October 27, and is under the astrological ruler-ship of Scorpio and Sagittarius. Ivy indicates the second harvest, that of fruits, representing the changes that are necessary for growth, and the requirement that all things be related to the Plains, or earthly realm. Just as it is necessary to till the fields in order to reap a harvest later, so it is necessary to do the groundwork in anything, and to remember that in all things we must think of Mother Earth.

In Irish mythology, an apple branch is given to those mortals to whom the Queen of Faery takes a fancy. This branch, traditionally known as the Silver Branch, is a magickal tool used to shapeshift one's reality.[11]

The white stallion is a totem animal that has the ability to know the ways into the OtherWorld, and to be a good and faithful guide therein.

The double blue water signs (inverted triangles) signify that this card is pure water (water of water), and of an extreme feminine or emotional nature.

The cauldron represents the abundance of the Gifts of Faery, like the apple branch, which is a symbol of being favored by the Queen of Faery, and a key into Tir na nOg.

Other Correspondences

Element: water

Sub-element: water

Element Card Connection: Seven of Uisce, Eight of Tine, Nine of Tine

Helper Card Connection: Ard Rí of Uisce

Ancient Ones Card Connection: Draoi Gebann, and
Seanchailleach Gealach Gnoc

Numerology: 10 or 1

Planets: Venus, Mercury, and Moon

Energy: emotional, in flow

Gender: feminine

Niamh and the Land of Youth

One day the generous Finn my sire, with olden fire led forth the
chase—but our band was small when gathered all, for past recall were
the hosts of our race. 'Twas a summer's morn and a mist hung o'er the
winding shore of sweet Loch Lein, Where fragrant trees perfume the
breeze and birds e'er please with a joyous strain.

We soon awoke the woodland deer that forced by fear fled far away—
keenly our hounds with strenuous bounds o'er moors and mounds pursued their prey. When lo! into sight came a figure bright, in a blaze of
light from the west it rushed—a lady fair of radiance rare whom a white
steed bore to our band, now hush'd! Amazed we halt, though hot the
chase, to gaze on the face of the fair young queen—a marvel to Finn and
his fianna band, who ne'er in the land such beauty had seen!

A golden crown on her brow she bore, a mantle she wore of silken
sheen all studded with stars of bright red gold—ample each fold fell
on herbage green. Her golden hair all fair to view in golden curls on
her shoulders fell—bright and pure were her eyes of blue as drops of
the dew in a blue harebell. Ruddier far her cheek than the rose, her
bosom more white than the swan's so free, sweeter the breath of her
balmy mouth than spice of the south from over the sea.

Her milk-white steed was of worth unto nor bridle of gold did the
charger lack—a saddle all covered with purple and gold lay bright to
behold on the steed's proud back. Four shoes of gold his hoofs did
guard, of gold unmarred by mixture base, a silver wreath on his crest
was shown— such steed was unknown on the earth's fair face.

To Finn's great presence drew the maid thus bright array'd and
softly spake—"O King of the fian host," she cried "far have I hied for
sweet love's sake!"

"Who art thou, pray, O princess rare, of form most fair, of face divine? Gently thy errand to us make known—what land's thine own, what name is thine?"

"Niamh the Golden-haired I'm named, O Finn far-famed for wisdom and truth!—My praise harps ring, and bards e'er sing, and my sire's the King of the Land of Youth!"

"Then tell us, most lovely lady now, why comest thou o'er seas so far? Has heartless husband left thee to weep with grief most deep, thy mind to mar!"

"No husband has left me, O lordly Finn, My heart within ne'er man did gain, till hero of Erin, thy famous son, its young love won, for aye to reign!"

"On which of my gallant sons, O maid, is thy heart's love laid, so frankly free? Now hide not from us, O princess dear, the causes clear of thy visit to me!"

"His name, O Finn, then I'll declare—'tis thy famed son, so fair, so brave, Oisin the warrior, Erin's bard, my fair reward for crossing the wave!"

"Then why hast thou hastened to give thy love, O maiden above all maids most fair—to Oisin my own beyond all known of princes high both rich and rare?"

"Good cause I ween for my course shall be seen, O king of the Fian, when I tell thee truth: Oisin's high deeds and noble name have won him fame in the Land of Youth. Full many a prince of high degree hath offered me both heart and hand; but whoso appealed, I ne'er did yield but my heart kept sealed for my hero grand!"

O how my soul did yearn and with ardor burn for the peerless maid—no shame to tell each word was a spell, that bound me well past mortal aid. I took her gentle hand in mine and with every sign of love I said, "Welcome a hundred thousand times, from fairy climes, O royal maid! O women the rarest, fairest seen, thou art O queen, without compeer! My soul, my life, my chosen wife, Star of my way of ray most clear!"

"Request refused by no true knight who knoweth aright the knightly vogue, I make of thee now—'tis hence to speed with me on my steed to Tir na nOg!

Delightful land beyond all dreams!
Beyond what seems to thee most fair—
Rich fruits abound the bright year round
And flowers are found of hues most rare.

Unfailing there the honey and wine
And draughts divine of mead there be,
No ache nor ailing night or day—
Death or decay thou ne'er shalt see!

The mirthful feast and joyous play
And music's sway all blest, benign—
Silver untold and store of gold
Undreamt by the old shall all be thine!

A hundred swords of steel refined,
A hundred cloaks of kind full rare,
A hundred steeds of proudest breed,
A hundred hounds— thy meed when there!

A hundred coats of mail shall be thine,
A hundred kine of sleekest skin,
A hundred sheep with fleece of gold,
And gems none hold these shores within.

A hundred maidens young and fair
Of blithesome air shall tend on thee,
Of form most meet, as fairies fleet
And of song more sweet than the wild thrush free!

A hundred knights in fights most bold
Of skill untold in all chivalry,
Full-armed, bedight in mail of gold
Shall in Tir na nOg thy comrades be.

A corslet charmed for thee shall be made
And a matchless blade of magic power,
Worth a hundred blades in a hero's hands,
Most blest of brands in battle's hour!

The royal crown of the King of Youth
Shall shine in sooth on thy brow most fair,

All brilliant with gems of luster bright
Whose worth aright none might declare.

All things I've named thou shalt enjoy
And none shall cloy—to endless life—
Beauty and strength and power thou'lt see
And I'll e'er be thy own true wife!"

Refusal of mine thou ne'er shalt hear,
O maid without peer, of the locks of gold!
My chosen wife for life I know
And gladly I'll go to Tir na nOg![12]

Ainnir of Domhan

Ruled by Saille

DEIRDRE

Meaning

Water of Earth; fertility of the land; the heart made manifest in life; the midnight of youth; young female between birth and age thirty; the virgin earth goddess; a synthesis of the elemental world into manifested form.

The magick of the Faery World is often deep and dark and mysterious, but any who hold fear in their hearts will not be allowed entrance; when alignment with the earth's heart center is achieved the Other-World is revealed.

Card Description

Deirdre, the daughter of Malcolm, stands in a wooded area near a cloghan, her home of exile. She is dressed in beautiful woolen garments. She wears a shawl loosely draped over her wavy, dark brown hair that falls loosely about her shoulders.

A shield is hung on the trunk of a tree. She touches it with her left hand, as if touching an oracle. She intently peers at the face of the shield.

Oghams and Symbols

Saille, the willow, is the third peasant tree. Willow month begins on April 15 and ends on May 12, the sacred moon month of the goddess. Saille is under the astrological rulership of Aries and Taurus. Saille is a vibration that shows that, through flexibility, harmonious amenability with the conditions to which it is subjected can be achieved. Its power of divination is greater at night than in daytime, except when the moon is visible during the day. Willow's power fluctuates with the cycle of the moon's phases, and the time of day and moon phase will indicate whether the energy is flowing or ebbing.

The five-pointed star on the shield, which Deirdre is touching, represents the synthesis of the four elements into the fifth—that of ether or Spirit. This symbol is of manifestation, abundance, and pure fertility. On the shield we also see the Uinllean ogham, which has the magickal characteristics of hardness and resistance, the solidity of knowledge, and tried and tested actions. It refers to the solidity of ancient wisdom, the cultural or physical foundation that must be in place before any constructions can be made, either physically or figuratively.

The three mushrooms are symbolic of magickal vision or second-sight, which certain types of mushrooms are known to produce when eaten. Here they symbolize the ability of prophecy.

The two inverted triangles—the top one blue and the bottom one half-green, half-red—represent the qualities of water and earth, symbolizing the creative or fertile qualities of life.

Other Correspondences

Element: earth

Sub-element: water

Element Card Connection: Seven of Domhan, Eight of Aer, Nine of Aer

Helper Card Connection: Ridire of Domhan and Ard Rí of Domhan

Ancient Ones Card Connection: Máthair Bandia Ēiré,
Muirneach Deirdre and Naosie, and Uisce Coisrīchthe

Numerology: 16 or 7

Planets: Saturn, Jupiter and Mars

Energy: emotional, in creation

Gender: feminine

The Story of Deirdre

Because of the Druidic prophecy spoken at her birth, Deirdre and her foster mother dwelt in the dun mid the hills without the knowledge or the suspicion of any living person about them and without anything occurring, until Deirdre was sixteen years of age. Deirdre grew like the white sapling, straight and trim as the rash on the moss. She was the creature of fairest form, of loveliest aspect, and of gentlest nature that existed between earth and heaven in all Ireland; and whatever color of hue she had before, there was nobody that looked into her face but she would blush fiery red over it.

The woman who had charge of her gave Deirdre all information and skill of which she herself had knowledge and skill. There was not a blade of grass growing from root, or a bird singing in the wood, or a star shining from heaven but Deirdre had a name for it. Yet one thing the woman did not wish her to have either part or parley with—any single living man of the rest of the world.

But by and by, as the story goes, Deirdre met Naosie, son of Uisnech, whom she immediately fell in love with, and asked, "Naosie, son of Uisnech, will you leave me?"

Upon their meeting, Deirdre kissed Naosie three times, and a kiss each to his brothers. With the confusion that she was in, Deirdre went into a crimson blaze of fire, and her color came and went as rapidly as the movement of the aspen by the stream side. Naosie thought he never saw a fairer creature, and Naosie gave Deirdre the love that he never gave to thing, to vision, or to creature but to herself. Then Naosie placed Deirdre on the topmost height of his shoulder, and told his brothers to keep up their pace, and they kept up their pace, and left Erin for Alba. There they lived in exile, until one day they received news that Conchobar, King of Ulster, was willing to forgive Naosie for stealing Deirdre away from him.

Upon hearing the news, Naosie exclaimed, "We will go with you!" But Deirdre did not wish to go with Fergus Mac Roy, and she tried every prayer to turn Naosie from going with him. She said: "I saw a vision, Naosie, and do you interpret it to me." Then she sang:

O Naosie, son of Usinech, hear
What was shown in a dream to me.
There came three white doves out of the South,
Flying over the sea,
And drops of honey were in their mouth
From the hive of the honey-bee.
O Naosie, son of Uisnech, hear
What was shown in a dream to me.
I saw three gray hawks out of the South
Come flying over the sea,
And the red drops they bare in their mouth
They were dearer than life to me.

Said Naosie: "It is naught but the fear of woman's heart, and a dream of the night Deirdre."

And so, unable to persuade Naosie from his return to Erin, Deirdre also prepared to go, but as they prepared to depart, she tried once more to persuade her beloved, and went to Naosie. Deirdre wept tears in showers and she sang:

Dear is the land, the land over there,
Alba full of woods and lakes;
Bitter to my heart is leaving thee,
But I go away with Naosie.

Fergus did not stop till he got the sons of Uisnech away with him, despite the suspicion of Deirdre.

The coracle was put to sea,
The sail was hoisted to it;
And the second morrow they arrived
On the white shores of Erin.

They found themselves in ambush, and the three heroes stripped and tied their clothes behind their heads, and Naosie placed Deirdre on the top of his shoulder.

They stretched their sides to the stream,
And sea and land were to them the same;
The rough gray ocean was the same
As the meadow-land green and plain.

Conchobar elicited the magick of the druid, who froze the gray-ridged sea into hardy rocky knobs, the sharpness of sword being on the one edge and the poison power of adders on the other.

The first of Naosie's brothers, Arden, died, and then not long after, the weakness of death came upon his second brother, Allen. Naosie looked around, and when he saw his two well-beloved brothers dead, he cared not whether he lived or died, and he gave forth the bitter sigh of death, and his heart burst.

"They are gone," said Duanan Gacha Druid to the King, "and I have done what you desired me. The sons of Uisnech are dead and they will trouble you no more; and you have your wife hale and whole to yourself."

"Blessings for that upon you and may the good results accrue to me, Duanan. I count it no loss what I spent in the schooling and teaching of you. Now dry up the flood, and let me see if I can behold Deirdre," said Conchobar.

And Duanan Gacha Druid dried up the flood from the plain and the three sons of Uisnech were lying together dead, without breath of life, side by side on the green meadow plain and Deirdre bending above showering down her tears.

Then Deirdre said this lament: "Fair one, loved one, flower of beauty, beloved upright and strong, beloved noble and modest warrior. Fair one, blue-eyed, beloved of thy wife, lovely to me at the trysting place came thy clear voice through the woods of Ireland. I cannot eat or smile henceforth. Break not today, my heart. Soon enough shall I lie within my grave. Strong are the waves of sorrow, but stronger is sorrow's self, Conchobar."

The people then gathered around the heroes' bodies and asked Conchobar what was to be done with the bodies. The order that he gave was that they should dig a pit and put the three brothers in it side by side.

Deirdre kept sitting on the brink of the grave, constantly asking the gravediggers to dig the pit wide and free. When the bodies of the brothers were put in the grave, Deirdre said:

Come over hither, Naosie, my love,
Let Arden close to Allen lie;
If the dead had any sense to fee,
Ye would have made a place for Deirdre.

The men did as she told them. She jumped into the grave and lay down by Naosie, and she was dead by his side.

The King ordered the body to be raised from out of the grave and to be buried on the other side of the loch. It was done as the King bade, and the pit closed. Thereupon a fir shoot grew out of the grave of Deirdre and a fir shoot from the grave of Naosie, and the two shoots united in a knot above the loch. The King ordered the shoots to be cut down, and this was done twice, until, at the third time, the wife whom the King had married caused him to stop this work of evil and his vengeance on the remains of the dead.[13]

In the North

Banrion of Aer
Ruled by Gort

MAEVE

Meaning

Earth of Air; feminine intelligence; assertion of ideas; quick to communicate one's mind; will stop at nothing to achieve one's goals; the first light of winter; mature female between age thirty and death; communication skills perfected; tamer of wild beasts; ruler of domain; strong enemy; need for total freedom; not afraid to show true colors.

The magick of the Faery World can often tempt one into pursuing matters of insignificance when done so through the mind only; seek to find spiritual enlightenment; walk your talk.

Card Description

Queen Maeve, with her long chiseled face, beautiful flaming red hair, and sky blue eyes, sits upon the black bull of Cuilgne in the plain of Muirthnerme. Dressed in royal blue, with a yellow undershirt and orange cloak about her shoulders, she is the epitome of female rulership.

Her crown is that of a diamond-encrusted sword hilt. Her broach is the spiral. The sword held in her right hand symbolizes her willingness to fight for that which she desires and thinks is hers by right. She is a sharp-witted woman, quick-thinking and cunning.

Two golden hoops circle the bull's horns, showing that he is her prized possession. Directly behind the bull stands the pillar stone of Cu Chulainn, the same stone to which the champion tied himself at the time of his death.

Oghams and Symbols

Gort, the ivy, is the twelfth ogham character. Its moon months extend from September 30 to October 27, under the astrological rulership of Libra and Scorpio. Gort represents the changes that are necessary for growth, and the requirement that all things be related to the Plains, or earthly realm.

The diamond sword-hilt crown represents the attitude of the warrior, ruthless at times and one that is focused on success. The single spiral, among the most sacred signs of Neolithic Europe, appears in a yellow triangle. The spiral is the cosmic symbol for the natural form of growth, a symbol of eternal life, reminding us of the flow and movement of the cosmos. The whorls are continuous creation and dissolution of the world; the passages between the spirals symbolized the divisions between life, death, and rebirth. The yellow triangle represents the masculine energy of fire utilized totally in a mental way.

The half-green, half-red inverted triangle signifies the earthly realm and earth element, while the half-yellow, half-white triangle signifies the air element and the mental body.

Other Correspondences

Element: air

Sub-element: earth

Element Card Connection: Ten of Domhan, Two of Aer, Three of Aer

Helper Card Connection: Ridire of Tine and Ard Rí of Uisce

Ancient Ones Card Connection: Cuardaitheoir and Carbad na an Morrigu Anand

Numerology: 10 or 1

Planets: Mercury, Moon, and Saturn

Energy: physical/cycles/spirituality, in thought

Gender: feminine, supported by masculine

The Battle of the Bulls

Though Ailell was king, Maeve was the ruler in truth, and ordered all things as she wished, and took what husbands she wished, and dismissed them at pleasure; for she was as fierce and strong as a goddess of war, and knew no law but her own wild will. She was tall, it is said, with a long, pale face and masses of red hair. When Fergus came to her in her palace at Rathcroghan in Roscommon she gave him her love, as she had given it to many before, and they plotted together how to attack and devastate the Province of Ulster.

Now it happened that Maeve possessed a famous red bull with white front and horns named Finnbenach, and one day when she and Ailell were counting up their respective possessions and matching them against each other he taunted her because the Finnbenach would not stay in the hands of a woman, but had attached himself to Ailell's herd. So Maeve in vexation went to her steward, Mac Roth, and asked of him if there were anywhere in Erin a bull as fine as the Finnbenach. "Truly," said the steward, "there is—for the Brown Bull of Coolny, that belongs to Dara son of Fachtna, is the mightiest beast that is in Ireland." And after that Maeve felt as if she had no flocks and herds that were worth anything at all unless she possessed the Brown Bull of Coolny. But this was in Ulster, and the Ulster men knew the treasure they possessed, and Maeve knew that they would not give up the bull without fighting for it. So she and Fergus and Ailell agreed to make a foray against Ulster for the bull, and thus to enter into war with the province, for Fergus longed for vengeance, and Maeve for fighting, for glory, and for the bull, and Ailell to satisfy Maeve.

The bull is defended by the solar halo Cu Chulainn, who, however, is ultimately overthrown and the bull is captured for a season. The Brown Bull is described as having a black hide the darkness of night, a back broad enough for fifty children to play on, and when he is angry with his keeper he stamps the man thirty feet into the ground. He is likened to a sea wave, to a bear, to a dragon, a lion.

The first attempt of Maeve to get possession of the bull was to send an embassy to Dara to ask for the loan of him for a year, the recompense offered being fifty heifers, besides the bull himself back, and if Dara chose to settle in Connacht he should have as much land there as he now possessed in Ulster, and a chariot worth thrice seven cumals,[14] with the patronage and friendship of Maeve.

Dara was at first delighted with the prospect, but tales were borne to him of the chatter of Maeve's messengers, and how they said that if the bull was not yielded willingly it would be taken by force; and he sent back a message of refusal and defiance. "'Twas known," said Maeve, "the bull will not be yielded by fair means; he shall now be won by foul." And so she sent messengers around on every side to summon her hosts for the Raid.

And there came all the mighty men of Connacht—first the seven Mainés, sons of Ailell and Maeve, each with his retinue; and Ket and Anluan, sons of Maga, with thirty hundreds of armed men; and yellow-haired Ferdia, with his company of Firbolgs, boisterous giants who delighted in war and in strong ale. And there came also the allies of Maeve—a host of the men of Leinster, who so excelled the rest in warlike skill that they were broken up and distributed among the companies of Connacht, lest they should prove a danger to the host; and Cormac son of Conor, with Fergus Mac Roy and other exiles from Ulster, who had revolted against Conor for his treachery to the sons of Usna.

By and by, the battle was engaged, during one of Cu Chulainn's duels with a famous champion, Natchrantal, Maeve, with a third of her army, makes a sudden foray into Ulster and penetrates as far as

Dunseverick, on the northern coast, plundering and ravaging as they go. The Brown Bull, who was originally at Quelgny (Co. Down), has been warned at an earlier stage by the Morrigu, to withdraw himself, and he has taken refuge, with his herd of cows, in a glen of Slievegallion, Co. Armagh. The raiders of Maeve find him there, and drive him off with the herd in triumph, passing Cu Chulainn as they return. Cu Chulainn slays the leader of the escort—Buic son of Banblai—but cannot rescue the bull, and "this," it is said, "was the greatest affront put on Cu Chulainn during the course of the raid."[15]

Banríon of Tine

Ruled by Fearn

THE BADB

Meaning

Earth of Fire; feminine force of nature aligned with masculine force; polarity; Spirit made manifest; spiritual pursuits are top priority; defender of the natural world; caretaker of life; female minister; assertive feminine energy; the full moon at midnight; mature female between age thirty and death; successful woman; commander of forces; in touch with the OtherWorld; will fight when necessary to uphold the truth; creative energy; aligned with heart-center of earth.

The magick of the Faery World touches your heart; the call of the Morrigu reaches the ears of those individuals who are attuned to the south winds; become the warrior of the Ancient Ones; one who is walking their talk without hesitation.

Card Description

Badb, the "Fury," is a war goddess who symbolizes the moon, deemed by early races to have preceded the sun, and worshiped with magickal and cruel rites. She is represented as going fully armed, and carrying a spear in her hand. Wherever there was war, either among gods or men, she, the great queen, was present, either in her own shape or in her favorite disguise, that of a "hoodie" or carrion crow.

Outfitted for war, Badb sits upon a throne made from bones. Like all warriors, she bears the blue tattoo, under both eyes and around both arms. Three crows sit aback the throne. In the background rises a rath, upon which stands a stone fort.

Oghams and Symbols

Fearn, the alder, is classified as the second chieftain tree, and is the third ogham of the alphabet. Alder moon month extends from March 18 to April 14, under the astrological rulership of Pisces and Aries. Green alder branches make good whistles and were used by the cunning women to conjure up destructive winds, especially from the north, in opposition to invaders.

Alder, the tree of strength, represents protection that is needed in a personal conflict, and that one must be willing to free oneself from the binding. Fearn brings the solution by highlighting what is being held on to and clarifying whether it is truly needed.

The war tattoos under both eyes and the wave-like tattoos around both arms signify that the Badb has passed a spiral barrier into an inner sanctuary on her journey of the sacred dance through the labyrinth. She has entered the sacred realms beyond the center. She has touched the still center of the labyrinth, and received the knowledge only in the correct way—initiation. At the center there is a complete balance: the point where heaven and earth are joined. Badb is this point.

The three crows not only represent the Triple Morrigu, which Badb is an aspect of, but can also be seen as totem animals. Crow is known as the protector of the sacred records and is connected to the attribute of respect. Crow teaches skill, cunning, and single-mindedness. Crow is a companion to the OtherWorld. Through the lesson of crow, one can receive wise and knowledgeable information, but do so with great caution. Crow is the sacred law.

The triple spiral necklace signifies her triune nature.

The half-green-half-red inverted triangle signifies the earthly realm and earth element, as well as the feminine nature of the card. The red triangle represents the fire element and Spirit; thus we see the energy—feminine supported by masculine, Spirit made manifest, as well as spirituality in action.

Other Correspondences

Element: fire

Sub-element: earth

Element Card Connection: Ten of Uisce, Two of Tine, and Three of Tine

Helper Card Connection: Ridire of Tine, Ard Rí of Aer, and Banríon of Uisce

Ancient Ones Card Connection: Bansagart Ard Brigid and Carbad na an Morrigu

Numerology: 8

Planets: Mars, and Sun

Energy: physical/cycles/spirituality, in action

Gender: feminine, supported by masculine, in polarity

The hoodie-Crow

Nemon, Badb, and Macha are the triple aspects of the Morrigu. Together they incite the warrior, as this old poem shows:

Over his head is shrieking
A lean hag, quickly hopping
Over the points of the weapons and shields;
She is the gray-haired Morrigu!

An account of the Battle of Clontarf, fought by Brian Boru, in 1014 against the Norsemen, gives a gruesome picture of what the Gaels believed to happen in the spiritual world when battle lowered and men's blood was aflame. "There arose a wild, impetuous, precipitate, mad, inexorable, furious, dark, lacerating, merciless, combative, contentious badb, which was shrieking and fluttering over their heads. And there arose also the satyrs, and sprites, and the maniacs of the valleys, and the witches and goblins and owls, and destroying demons of the air and firmament, and the demonic phantom host; and they were inciting and sustaining valour and battle with them." When the fight was over, they reveled among the bodies of the slain; the heads cut off as trophies were called "Macha's acorn crop." These grim creations of the savage mind had immense vitality. While Nuada, the supreme war god, vanished early out of the Irish Pantheon—killed by the Fomors in the great battle fought between them and the gods—Badb and the Morrigu lived on as late as any of the deities. Indeed, they may be said to still survive in the superstitious dislike and suspicion shown in all Celtic-speaking countries for their avatar, the hoodie-crow.

Whether the Tuatha De Danann came from earth or heaven, they landed in a dense cloud upon the coast of Ireland on the mystic first of May without having been opposed, or even noticed by the people whom it will be convenient to follow the manuscript authorities in calling the Fir Bolgs. That those might still be ignorant of their coming, the Morrigu, helped by Badb and Macha, made use of the magic they had learned in Findias, Gorias, Muirias, and Falias. They spread "druidically formed showers and fog-sustaining shower-clouds" over the country, and caused the air to pour down fire and blood upon the Fir Bolgs, so that they were obliged to shelter themselves for three days and three nights.[16]

Banríon of Uisce
Ruled by Duir

FAND THE FAERY QUEEN

Meaning

Earth of Water; fertility of woman; spirituality actively supported by the emotional nature of the masculine force in life; the female body; in the autumn of life; twilight of beauty; a mature woman between age thirty and death; woman's intuition flowing; the psychic's card; natural beauty; romance; being in the Beauty way.

The magick of the Faery World is all around you; the Queen of Faery and her minions will gladly become co-walkers in your world if you open to their presence; trust intuition; develop your psychic ability; open totally to the natural world; attune to the time of twilight when the entrance between the worlds opens every day.

Card Description

Beautiful Fay Fand sits upon her swan thrown. She has long, flowing blue-white hair held back with a pearl and scallop shell crown. She wears the inverted triangle. Her gown is of the finest seafoam, an iridescent tendril-like garment, trimmed with seaweed and adorned with pearls and scallop shell.

Behind her is the sea, and her husband, Manannan Mac Lir's Wavesweeper. On the sands before her is the magickal cauldron of flowing light, containing the elixir of eternal youth.

Oghams and Symbols

Duir, oak, is the seventh sacred tree of the oghams. The oak is the most powerful of the trees, and classified as the third noble, or chieftain tree. The seventh moon month begins on June 10 and ends on July 7, containing the high point of the year, summer solstice or midsummer, esoterically known as the door of the year. Duir is under the astrological rulership of Gemini and Cancer.

The western sea is known as the entrance into the Land of Faery, and here, as with Niamh, Manannan Mac Lir, and Oengus Og, Fand sits in the West.

The double swan throne shows that the entrance betwixt and between our world and the OtherWorld can be easily achieved through the guidance of Fand, who can give you the elixir of immortality, as symbolized by the cauldron filled with white light.

The half-green, half-red inverted triangle symbolizes the earth element, while the blue inverted triangle is the water element: total fertility. The inverted triangle necklace, which is gold containing green, represents the yoni as well as earth, thus communicating that Fand is the feminine principle of life (i.e., the vagina of Mother Earth).

Other Correspondences

Element: Water

Sub-element: Earth

Element Card Connection: Ten of Aer, Two of Uisce, Three of Uisce

Helper Card Connection: Ridire of Tine, Ainnir of Tine, Ard Rí of Uisce, and Banríon of Domhan

Ancient Ones Card Connection: Máthair Bandia Éiré, and Réalta Dana

Numerology: 12 or 3

Planets: Sun, Venus, and Mercury

Energy: Physical/Cycles/Spirituality, in wisdom

Gender: Feminine, supported by Masculine

Fand and Cu Chulainn

Cu Chulainn went forth to the pillar, and then saw he the woman in the green mantle come to him. "This is good, O Cu Chulainn!" said she.

"It is no good thing in my thought," said Cu Chulainn. "Wherefore camest thou to me last year?"

"It was indeed to do no injury to thee that we came," said the woman, "but to seek for thy friendship. I have come to greet thee," she said, "from Fand, the daughter of Aed Abrat; her husband, Manannan Mac Lir, has abandoned her, and she has thereon set her love on thee. My own name is Liban."

Cu Chulainn sent his charioteer, Loeg, with Liban to Mag Mell, the place where Fand was to see who this Fand was and report back to himself.

Fand was the daughter of Aed Abrat; Aed means fire, and he is the fire of the eye: that is, of the eye's pupil: Fand moreover is the name of the tear that runs from the eye; it was on account of the clearness of her beauty that she was so named, for there is nothing else in the world except a tear to which her beauty could be likened.

By and by, when Fand bade welcome to Loeg, she asked "How is it that Cu Chulainn has not come with thee?"

"It pleased him not," said Loeg, "to come at a woman's call; moreover he desired to know whether it was indeed from thee that had come the message, and to have full knowledge of everything."

Upon his return to Cu Chulainn, Loeg describes the Faery world and Fand thus:

There is a well in that noble palace of the fairy-mound.
There you will find thrice fifty splendid cloaks,
With a brooch of shining gold
To fasten each of the cloaks.

There is a cauldron of invigorating mead,
For the use of the inmates of the house.
It never grows less; it is a custom
That it should be full forever.

There is a woman in the noble palace.
There is no woman like her in Erin.
When she goes forth you see her fair hair.
She is beautiful and endowed with many gifts.

Her words, when she speaks to anyone,
Have a marvelous charm.
She wounds every man to the heart
With the love she inspires.

The noble lady said,
"Who is the youth whom we do not know?
Come hither if it be thou
That art the servant of the warrior of Muirthemne."

I yield to her request with reluctance;
I feared for my honor.
She said to me, "Will he come,
The only son of the excellent Dechtire?"

It is a pity that thou hast not gone, O Cu Chulainn!
Everyone asks for you.
You yourself should see how it is built,
The grand palace that I have seen.

If I owned the whole of Erin,
With supreme sovereignty over its fair inhabitants,
I would give it up—the temptation would be irresistible—
I would go and live in the country where I have just been.

And Cu Chulainn, when he had heard the report, went on with Liban to that land, and he took his chariot with him; and Fand gave an especial welcome to Cu Chulainn. Cu Chulainn slept with Fand, and he abode for a month in her company, and at the end of the month he came to bid her farewell. "Tell me," she said, "to what place I may go for our tryst, and I will be there"; and they made tryst at the yew tree by the strand that is known as Iubar Cinn Trachta (Newry).

Now word was brought to Emer of that tryst, and knives were whetted by Emer to slay the fairy woman. When she arrived she spoke thus to Cu Chulainn. "Truly, the woman to whom thou dost cling is in no way better than am I myself! Yet fair seems all that's red; what's new seems glittering; and bright what's set o'erhead; and sour are things well known! Men worship what they lack; and what they have seems weak; in truth thou hast all the wisdom of the time! O Youth! Once we dwelled in honor together, and we would so dwell again, if only I could find favor in thy sight!" Her grief weighed heavily upon her.

"By my word," said Cu Chulainn, "thou dost find favor, and thou shalt find it as long as I am in life."

"Desert me, then!" cried Fand.

"No," said Emer, "it is more fitting that I should be the deserted one."

"Not so, indeed," said Fand. "It is I who must go, and danger rushed upon me from afar." And an eagerness for lamentation seized upon Fand, and her soul was great within her, for it was shame to her to be deserted and straightway to return to her home; moreover, the mighty love that she bore to Cu Chulainn was tumultuous in her, and in this fashion she lamented, and lamenting sang this song:

I it is that will go on the journey;
I give assent with great affliction;
Though there is a man of equal fame,
I would prefer to remain.

I would rather be here,
To be subject to thee, without grief,
Than to go, though you may wonder at it,
To the sunny palace of Aed Abrat.

O Emer! the man is thine,
And well mayst thou wear him, thou good woman,
What my arm cannot reach,
That I am forced to wish well.

Many were the men that were asking for me,
Both in the court and in the wilderness;
Never with those did I hold a meeting,
Because I it was that was righteous.

Woe! to give love to a person,
If he does not take notice of it;
It is better for a person to turn away
Unless he is loved as he loves.

With fifty women hast thou come hither,
O Emer of the yellow hair,
To capture Fand—it was not well—
And to kill her in her misery.

There are thrice fifty, during my days,
Of women, beautiful and unwedded,
With me in my court together;
They would not abandon me.

Now upon this it was discerned by Manannan that Fand was engaged in unequal warfare with the women of Ulster, and that she was like to be left by Cu Chulainn. And thereon Manannan came from the east to seek for Fand, and he was perceived by her, nor was there any other conscious of his presence saving Fand alone. And when she saw Manannan, Fand was seized by great bitterness of mind and by grief, and made this song:

. . . I bid thee farewell, O beautiful Cu;
We depart from thee with a good heart;
Though we return not, be thy good will with us;
Everything is good, compared with going away.

It is now time for me to take my departure;
There is a person to whom it is not a grief;
It is, however, a great disgrace,
O Loeg, son of Riangabar.

I shall go with my own husband,
Because he will not show me disobedience.
Now that you may not say it is a secret departure,
If you desire it, now behold me.

Then Fand rose behind Manannan as he passed, and Manannan greeted her: "O woman! Which wilt thou do? Wilt thou depart with me, or abide here until Cu Chulainn comes to thee?"

"In truth," answered Fand, "either of the two of you would be a fitting husband to adhere to; and neither of you is better than the other; yet, Manannan, it is with thee that I go, nor will I wait for Cu Chulainn, for he has betrayed me; and there is another matter, moreover, that weigheth with me, O noble prince! And that is that thou hast no consort who is of worth equal to thine, but such a one hath Cu Chulainn already."

And Cu Chulainn saw Fand as she went from him to Manannan, and he cried out to Loeg: "What does this mean that I see?"

"Tis no hard matter to answer," said Loeg. "Fand is going away with Manannan Mac Lir, since she hath not pleased thee!"

Then Cu Chulainn bounded three times high into the air, and he made three great leaps toward the south, and thus he came to Tara Luachra, and there he abode for a long time, having no meat and no drink, dwelling upon the mountains, and sleeping upon the high-road that runs through the midst of Luachra.

Then Emer went on to Emain, and there she sought out king Conchobar, and she told him of Cu Chulainn's state, and Conchobar sent out his learned men and his people of skill, and the druids of Ulster, to find Cu Chulainn, and to bind him fast, and bring him with them to Emain. And Cu Chulainn tried to kill the people of skill, but they chanted wizard and fairy spells against him, and they bound fast his feet and his hands until he came a little to his senses. Then he begged for a drink at their hands, and the druids gave him a drink of forgetfulness, so that afterwards he had no more remembrance of Fand nor of anything else that he had then done; and they also gave a drink of forgetfulness to Emer that she might forget her jealousy, for her state was in no way better than the state of Cu Chulainn. And Manannan shook his cloak between Cu Chulainn and Fand, so that they might never meet together again throughout eternity.[17]

Banríon
of Domhan
Ruled by Beth

Ēiré

Meaning

Earth of Earth; exalted feminine force in the natural world; nature; in the winter of life; mature female between age thirty and death; happiness; abundance; Mother Earth; a time of celebration; the matriarch; the wife and mother; manifestation.

The magick of the Faery World is here; you are a co-walker; wake up to this reality; working within the natural cycles of life; controller of the natural world; earth wisdom; green witch.

Card Description

Ēiré, the Earth Mother of Ireland, sits upon her birch throne in a magickal forest of Erin. Dressed in the faery green, she wears the horned crown of the Goddess. She is abundance, as represented by her full bosom.

As the Elf Queen, wearing a double-spiral brooch, her throne is inscribed with double spirals and the Wheel of the Year. The cushion of the throne is red. Four gold poles stand around the throne, each representing a cardinal direction, though all flags are green. On one of the front poles rests a shield.

Oghams and Symbols

Beth, the birch, is the first tree letter of the Irish ogham alphabet. The birch month extends from December 24 to January 20, fixing its beginning just after the winter solstice, the midwinter day of purification and renewal. Beth is under the astrological rulership of Sagittarius and Capricorn. Birch protects against all harms, physical and spiritual.

The double spirals, or spiral oculi, represent eyes. These eyes are those of the Otherworld. The duality of the spiral also represents the concept "As above, so below," mirroring the macrocosmic order of the heavens.

The Wheel of the Year carvings represent the four sacred holidays of the natural world. The mushrooms represent an altered state of consciousness or the paradigm shift one encounters consciously when communing with the natural world.

The lozenge symbol worn as a necklace further demonstrates Eiré's connection to the fertility of the earth, as her crown, the symbol of the Triple Goddess or Moon Goddess, represents the fertility of woman.

The two inverted triangles, both which are half-green, half-red, is the earth-earth energy: Earth Mother, Mother Earth, Ireland, and so on.

Other Correspondences

> **Element:** earth
>
> **Sub-element:** earth
>
> **Element Card Connection:** Ten of Tine, Two of Domhan, Three of Domhan
>
> **Helper Card Connection:** Ridire of Domhan, Ainnir of Domhan, Ard Rí of Aer, and Banríon of Uisce
>
> **Ancient Ones Card Connection:** Máthair Bandia Eiré, Roth Grian, Rúndaigne Banba, Crochadóir Amorgen, and Seanchailleach Gealach Cnoc

Numerology: 5
Planets: Saturn, Jupiter, and Mars
Energy: physical/cycles/spirituality, in matter
Gender: feminine, supported by masculine, in extreme

The Naming of Ireland

When the Milesians began their march on Tara, which was the capital of the Tuatha De Danann, as it had been in earlier days the chief fortress of the Fir Bolgs, and would in later days be the dwelling of the high kings of Ireland. On their way they met with a goddess called Banba, the wife of Mac Cuill. She greets Amorgen. "If you have come to conquer Ireland," she said, "your cause is no just one." "Certainly it is to conquer it we have come," replied Amorgen, without condescending to argue upon the abstruse morality of the matter. "Then at least grant me one thing," she asked. "What is that?" replied Amorgen. "That this island shall be called by my name." "It shall be," replied Amorgen.

A little farther on, they met a second goddess, Fotla, the wife of Mac Cecht, who made the same request, and received the same answer from Amorgen.

Last of all, at Uisnech, the center of Ireland, they came upon the third of the queens, Éiré, the wife of Mac Greine. "Welcome, warriors," she cried. "To you who have come from afar this island shall henceforth belong, and from the setting to this rising sun there is no better land. And your race will be the most perfect the world has ever seen." "These are fair words and a good prophecy," said Amorgen. "It will be no thanks to you," broke in Donn, Mil's eldest son. "Whatever success we have we shall owe to our own strength." "That which I prophesy has no concern with you," retorted the goddess, "and neither you nor your descendants will live to enjoy this island." Then turning to Amorgen, she, too, asked that Ireland might be called after her. "It shall be its principal name," Amorgen promised.

And so it has happened. Of the three ancient names of Ireland—Banba, Fotla, and Erie—the last, in its genitive form of "Erinn," is the one that has survived.

The Milesians arrived at Tara and agreed to undergo a test of worthiness and when the signal was given, they retreated to their ships.

The signal was given, and the sons of Mil bent to their oars. But they had hardly started before they discovered that a strong wind was blowing straight towards them from the shore, so that they could make no progress in retaking Ireland. At first they thought it might be a natural breeze, but Donn smelt magic in it. He sent a man to climb the mast of his ship, and see if the wind blew as strong at that height as id did at the level of the sea. The man returned, reporting that the air was quite still "up aloft." Evidently it was a druidical wind. But Amorgen soon coped with it. Lifting up his voice, he invoked the goddess of Ireland herself, a power higher than any other.

I invoke the land of Erie!
The shining, shining sea!
The fertile, fertile hill!
The wooded vale!
The river abundant, abundant in water!
The fishful, fishful lake!

The incantation proved effectual. The Land of Ireland was pleased to be propitious, and the druidical wind dropped down. By-and-by the Milesians were successful at taking Ireland, although several ships were lost in the cause. Donn was among the lost, thus fulfilling Erie's prophecy, and three other sons of Mil also perished.[18]

Spreads for Personal Development Using the Element and helper Cards

The tarot spreads outlined in this section were designed with the intent of using just the Element and Helper Cards when performing a reading. Helper Cards now bring one of three things into your readings:

- Other people.
- An added insight into the energy surrounding a situation.
- A divine archetype to contemplate for added clarity in spiritual endeavors.

Fifty percent of the time, Helper Cards will represent other people. Thirty percent of the time they will represent the energy surrounding a situation, and twenty percent of the time they will represent a divine archetype. You must use your intuition in defining which one of the three roles a Helper Card plays. Here is a key to follow.

If you tend to focus on the face of the Helper Card when first looking at it, it most likely represents another person. If you tend to focus on the ogham or other symbols in the picture, it most likely represents the energy of the situation. If you tend to focus on the name of the card, it most likely will represent the divine archetype of the card, in which case, serious contemplation would be given to the Faery Lore of the card found in the card's myth.

The Five-Fifths Spread

The Five-Fifths Spread is unique in that when performing it, you begin with the Element and Helper Cards separated (figure 12, page 229) Using the Helper Cards first, focus on pulling the Divine Archetype that you need to work with at this time in your life. When you are ready, draw one Helper Card and place it in the first position. Interpret the card, then read the card's myth in this book.

Next, combine the Element and Helper Cards thoroughly before pulling a card for the four remaining positions. When pulling the cards, ask the Divine Archetype to provide the answers.

The second position will provide insight and clarity into the question asked or situation being examined.

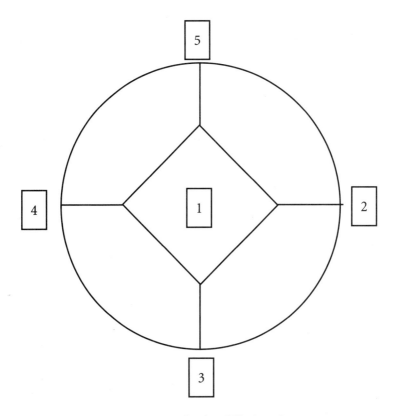

FIGURE 12. *The Five-Fifths Spread.*

Position 3 will indicate how you are using your personal power in the situation.

Position 4 will provide the area of focus required, which is not being taken into consideration, that will help the situation.

Position five will indicate the actions you need to take in the situation.

The Key Pattern Spread

Begin this spread with the Element and Helper Cards combined (figure 13, page 230). Focus on your area of inquiry and when ready pull a card for each position. Interpret the cards accordingly.

Positions 1 and 2 represent something from the past that is affecting the current situation, and needs to be taken into consideration.

Positions 3, 4, and 5 represent the area needing attention in the present, which you may not be considering.

Positions 6 and 7 represent the probable event preparing to take place.

This reading can act as a preparatory reading to determine what question needs to be worked with next. If this is the case, the appropriate spread could then be chosen.

FIGURE 13. *The Key Pattern Spread.*

The Revised Celtic Cross

No book of tarot would be complete without a Celtic Cross spread. However, the *Faery Wicca Tarot* Celtic Cross has been slightly revised (figure 14, page 231). Use both the Element and Helper Cards for this spread and decide whether you will use a significator card. If so, pull it, and place it in the first position. Continue with the reading by pulling a card for all positions. Interpret the cards accordingly.

Position 1: the base of the situation.

Position 2: the energy querent is bringing to the situation.

Position 3: what could come into being, or will eventually happen.

Position 4: the strength of the situation, or foundation.

Position 5: the element of change, what might be leaving, or changing into the third position.

Position 6: the unexpected; what needs to be considered.

Position 7: other people and how they are relating to querent.

Position 8: self; how querent is relating to others involved in the situation.

Position 9: what element needs to shift between querent and others.

Position 10: probable future if all positions are worked with.

Positions 11, 12, and 13: summarize the situation.

Position 14: confirms position 10.

To determine timing in this spread look to see if an Ace Element Card falls in either position 5 or 6. If one does, it will indicate a season. Then, the card in position 10 will indicate the number of weeks into the season indicated by the Ace Element Card. If the card happens to be a Helper Card, this would indicate timing is based on another person's actions.

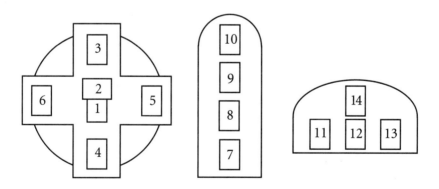

FIGURE 14. *The Revised Celtic Cross Spread.*

The Holy Mountain Spirit Walk

This spread uses all the Element and Helper Cards in the layout. It is a "karma" reading and can be performed annually on your birthday for the upcoming year.

Create the Holy Mountain by laying the cards out according to figure 15, page 233. When you are ready to begin, position yourself at the eastern face of the mountain, where the Aer Element Cards are laid out. Close your eyes. Connect with Sacred Self and Deity. Ask what lesson you will receive from Air this year. When you are ready, open your eyes and look at the Aer Cards. The first card you see becomes your Mental Lesson Card for the entire year. Repeat this process for the other three suits, pulling cards for:

> **Your Fire Lesson (Tine Card):** if it is an Element card, the lesson will be an Ego lesson; if it is an Helper card, the lesson will be a Spirit lesson.

> **Your Water Lesson (Uisce Card):** this shows your Heart lesson based on emotions.

> **Your Earth Lesson (Domhan Card):** indicates a Physical lesson if it is an Element Card; if it is a Helper Card, it will be a Spiritual lesson.

Work with these four cards throughout the year, paying particular attention when they come up in all other readings. You may find it important to meditate on them once a month at either the Dark (new) Moon or Full Moon time to gain added insight and clarity.

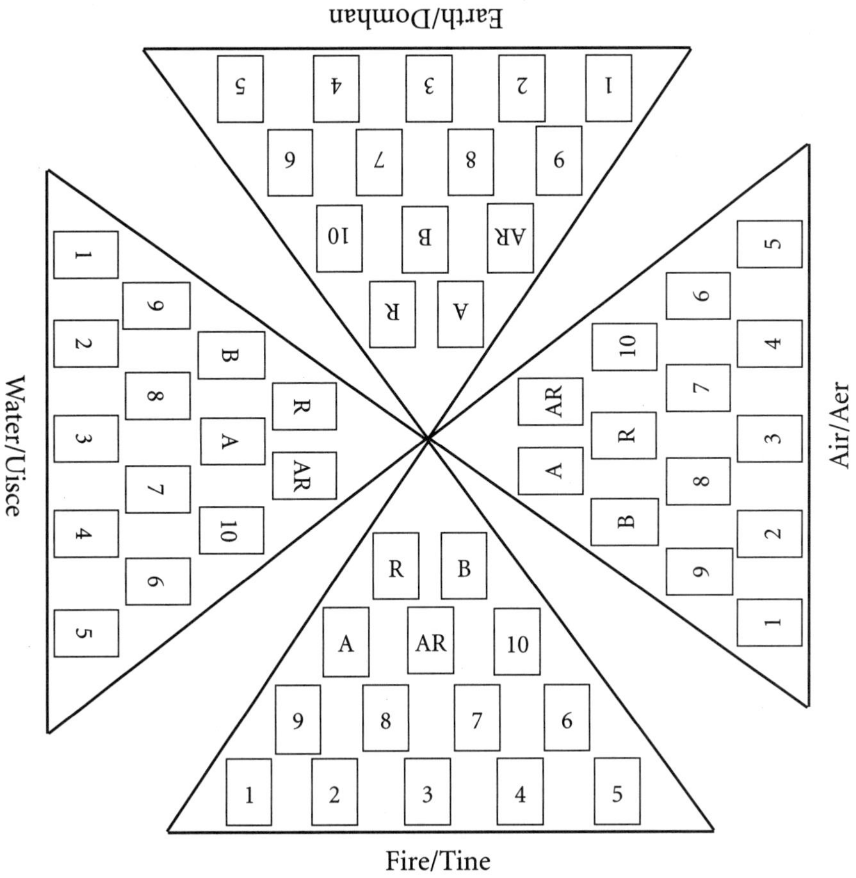

FIGURE 15. *The Holy Mountain Spirit Walk Spread.*
Legend:
R: Ridire card
B: Banríon card
A: Ainnir card
AR: Ard Rí card

Part Three
The Land of Faery:
The Ancient Ones Cards

The Sons of Mil

LXIII.

I seek the land of Ireland,
Coursed be the fruitful sea,
Fruitful the ranked highland,
Ranked the showery wood,
Showery the river of cataracts,
Of cataracts the lake of pools,
Of pools the hill of a well,
Of a well of a people of assemblies,
Of assemblies of the king of Temair;
Temair, hill of peoples,
Peoples of the Sons of Mil,
Of Mil of ships, of barks;
The high ship Eriu,
Eriu lofty, very green,
An incantation very cunning,
The great cunning of the wives of Bres,
Of Bres, of the wives of Buaigne,
The mighty lady Eriu,
Erimón harried her,
Ir, Eber sought for her—
I seek the land of Ireland.

—*Lebor Gabala Erenn*
Vol. XLIV, Part V., Sec. VIII

The Ancient Ones

The Ancient Ones Cards—traditionally known as the major arcana, greater secrets, or trump cards—crest the Crown of the Holy Mountain like the stars enmeshed in the Milky Way. They are located on the OtherWorld Tree of Life (figure 1, page 4) and are divided into three groups, each representing one of the Three Realms of the Land of Faery.

We move up the Threshold, the Spindle of Necessity—the trunk of the tree—working first with a power card, one of the additional cards unique to *Faery Wicca Tarot*, known as Crann na beatha, Tree of Life. From this point at the center, we move forward into the Solar Realm, leading to the Heavenly Realm. Here we experience the Spiritual lesson and evolution of the eons.

As the Cuardaitheoir, or the seeker, the neophyte makes their journey through each station of ancestral wisdom, encountering the teachings of the ancient Bardic College of Ireland. The stations or cards encountered in the Solar Realm are:

Draoi Gebann: the Druid Gebann, the magician

Bansagart Ard Brigid: the High Priestess Brigid, the high priestess

Máthair Bandia Éiré: Mother Goddess Éiré, the empress

Athair Dia Dagda: Father God Dagda, the emperor

Treoraí: Guide, the hierophant

Muirneach Deirdre and Naosie: Beloved Deirdre and Naosie, the lovers

Carbad na an Morrigu Anand: Chariot of the Morrigu Anand, the chariot

Fíorcheart Macha: Poetical Justice of Macha, justice

Díthreabhach Arias: the Holy Man Arias, the hermit

The Cuardaitheoir moves through the second threshold card, Roth Grian, the sun wheel or wheel of fortune card, and into the Lunar Realm, moving into the UnderWorld, wherein the Cuardaitheoir undergoes the challenge of Spirit tests. The cards found in the Lunar Realm are:

Rúndaigne Banba: Banba's Strength of Will, strength

Crochadóir Amorgen: Hangman Amorgen, the hanged man

Bean Sidhe Cailleach: The Banshee Cailleach, death

Uisce Coisriĉhthe: Holy Waters, temperance

Áibhirseoir Cernunnos: Cernunnos The Old One, the devil

An Clogás: The Round Tower, the tower

Réalta Dana: Dana's Star, the star

Seanchailleach Gealach Cnoc: Old Witch Moon Hill, the moon

Grain Páiste: Sun Child, the sun

Breithiúnas: Judgment, judgment

Ending the Lunar Realm, the Cuardaitheoir thus ends the apprenticeship and is initiated by the third threshold card: Fíodóir Bandia, the Weaver Goddess or the world card, and is ready to begin the journey again, now as an Initiate or the Draoi Gebann.

The emphasis of the *Faery Wicca Tarot* is placed on magickal archetypes; mystical symbols; ancestral wisdom; and the wisdom of the Ancient Ones, the gods and goddesses of ancient Ireland. The meaning of each card takes us deeper into the Spiritual forces and essence of all things visible and invisible, our Spiritual evolution, and a deepening between self, Sacred Self, and the Great Weaver Goddess, She Who Weaves the Web of Life.

The beauty and richness of each card reflects clarity and wisdom. Each image and symbol has a message designed to empower us Spiritually and make everyday and special life decisions easier.

In keeping with the natural order of nature, and balanced polarity, the number 8 card is Fíorcheart Macha, while the number 11 card, leading off the second circle—the Lunar Realm—is connected to the goddess and energy of the feminine principle of life, Rúndaigne Banba.

The *Faery Wicca Tarot* cards will continually guide aspirants into deeper levels of inner knowing and health simply by contemplating the symbology of each card. Most importantly, there is at last a tarot deck containing the ancestral wisdom and earth wisdom of balanced polarity, which affects the psyche consciously and unconsciously through the heart-mind and body-soul connections.

The Circles Of Becoming

The 23 major arcana, or Ancient Ones cards of *Faery Wicca Tarot* contain powerful teachings from the UnderWorld. A study layout that enhances one's deep understanding of the cards is the lemniscate, or infinity sign (figure 16, below), which is called the Circles or Wheels of Becoming.

The lemniscate is a holy symbol usually shown as two serpents, or one, swallowing each other's tails. The direction of the serpents' coiled bodies show that one circle moves clockwise, with the other counter-clockwise.

Each card has a special and important position on the lemniscate, as well as a corresponding card that can be thought of as a mirror reflection. These companion cards help elucidate the deeper meaning of each card.

When working with the Circles of Becoming it is important to divide the Ancient Ones Cards into three distinct classifications:

- Threshold Cards
- Solar Cards
- Lunar Cards

The Threshold Cards of *Faery Wicca Tarot* include the Crann na beatha, the Tree of Life card, unique to this deck, which is given a 00 position, as well as the Roth Grain, or Wheel of Fortune card, which is

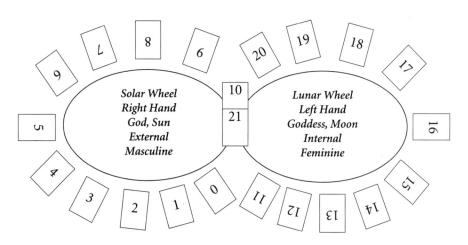

FIGURE 16. *The Circles of Becoming.*

a 10 position, and the Fíodóir Bandia, or Weaver Goddess, card, which is given the 21 position.

Each card is located on the Spindle of Necessity (figures 17 a, b, and c, pages 242–244). Crann na beatha, the first Ancient Ones card, is the Center of the Spindle of Necessity, the threshold into the Sacred Center, the Plains and earth wisdom. This card puts one in touch with the lessons of the Element Cards, which are reflections of the teachings the Tuatha De Danann brought with them from the Four Great Cities of the OtherWorld. Crann na beatha orients one to the primal land and the cardinal directions, raw elemental powers, and the wholism of the land.

Roth Grain, the tenth Ancient Ones card, is located at the Roots of the Spindle of Necessity and is the threshold into the UnderWorld and ancestral wisdom. This card puts one in touch with the lessons of the Helper Cards when they are worked with as archetypes of the Irish Pantheon and as energies resonating with ancestral teachings. Roth Grain is the Lunar Realm energy, the conscious realm of the psyche and subconscious awakening.

Fíodóir Bandia, the twenty-first Ancient Ones card, is located in the Branches of the Spindle of Necessity, and is the threshold into the OtherWorld, or Heavenly Realm and the wisdom of the gods. This card puts one in touch with the lessons of the Ancient Ones Cards when they are worked with in their companionships and as the holy stations an apprentice would encounter when undergoing initiation into the mysteries. Fíodóir Bandia is the Solar Realm energy, the awakened subconscious of the psyche fully operating on a conscious level.

The Solar Cards of the *Faery Wicca Tarot* when laid out in the Circles of Becoming Study Spread face outward, toward the material world. The cards 0 through 9 move in the clockwise direction. This circle follows the sun, representing the right-hand path of the God or masculine force in the world. It is the circle of the daytime world of outward appearances. These are the lessons of subconscious awakening.

The Lunar Cards of the *Faery Wicca Tarot* are placed facing inward, toward the Spiritual realm of inner meanings. The cards 11 through 20 move in the counter-clock wise direction, or moonwise. The lunar circle represents the left-hand path of the Goddess or feminine force in the world. It is the night world of mystery, fate, the soul, and true inner meanings, the way of goddess. These are the lessons of conscious awareness.

The Ancient Ones cards are a call for a return to the feminine principle. The Circles of Becoming governed by the karmic wheels, or the
solar and lunar paths eternally circling and merging one into the other,
refer to a secret doctrine of eternal rebirth, or the Transmigration of
Souls.[1] In Faery Wicca it is recognized that each living creature spends
a period in the daylight world, on what is called the sublunar sphere,
then spends another period in the OtherWorld awaiting new birth. The
corollary belief is that all flesh is alike in essence, and so is all Spirit.
Forms change, but the basic material of life is forever the same.

The stages of initiation, the seven veils of enlightenment, the
descent into the UnderWorld, the internal mysteries of the feminine
intuition—the intelligentsia of the planet—are the secrets of the
Ancient Ones cards. For the evolution of the soul, for consciousness,
and for students of esoterica today who travel the path of Spiritualism,
understanding this system as expressed through the Ancient Ones
cards and the Circles of Becoming is imperative—this is representative
of the actual initiation ceremony apprentices of esoterica undergo.

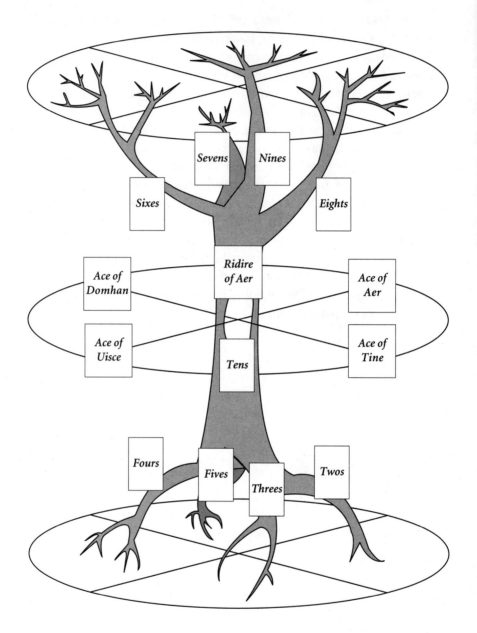

FIGURE 17A. *The Element Card positions on the Tree of Trees.*

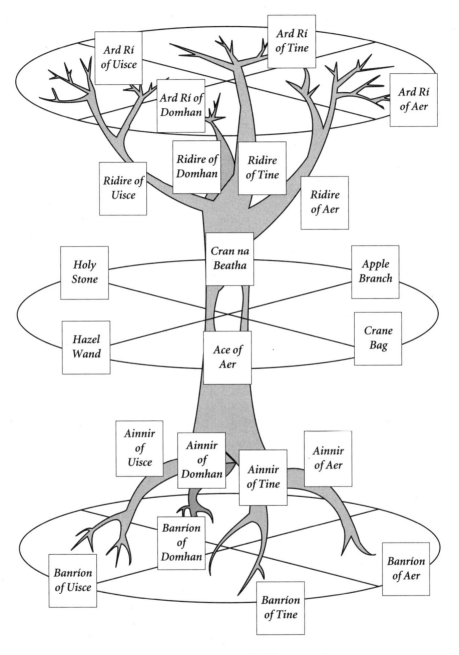

FIGURE 17B. *The Helper Card and Gift of Faery Card positions on the Tree of Trees.*

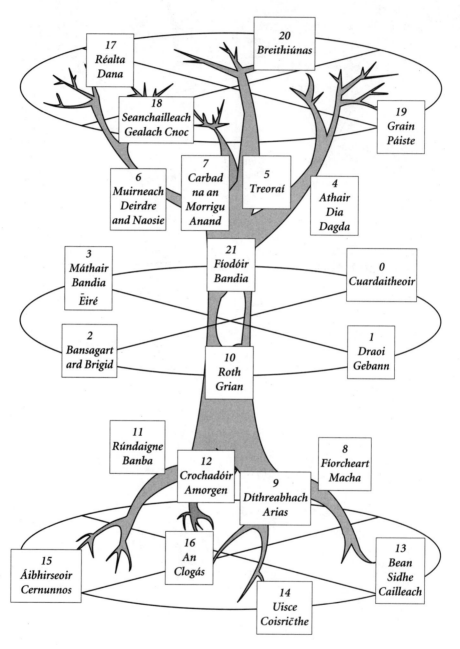

FIGURE 17C. *The Ancient Ones positions on the Tree of Trees.*

The Companion Cards

As noted in the previous chapter, each Ancient Ones Card has a companion card located opposite it in the other Circle of Becoming.[2] These sub-relationships create important insights into the active world of Spiritual evolution—or the wisdom of the gods. The companion groupings are shown in the following table.

Solar Circle	Lunar Circle
0–Cuardaitheoir	20–Breithiúnas
1–Draoi Gebann	19–Grain Páiste
2–Bansagart ard Brigid	18–Seanchailleach Gealach Cnoc
3–Máthair Bandia Éiré	17–Réalta Dana
4–Athair Dia Dagda	16–An Clogás
5–Treoraí	15–Áibhirseoir Cernunnos
6–Muirneach Deirdre and Naosie	14–Uisce Coisrĭcthe
7–Carbad na an Morrigu Anand	13–Bean Sidhe Cailleach
8–Fíorcheart Macha	12–Crochadíor Amorgen
9–Díthreabhach Arias	11–Rúndaigne Banba

The purpose of knowing each card's companion is to bring into each reading the energy of its reflection. The particular card laid out gives insight into whether certain lessons are being "actively," or consciously, worked with. The integration of the lesson would then depend on the companion card. A card located in the Lunar Circle explains how a Spirit lesson is being dealt with through internal processes, as well as highlighting a paradigm shift taking place.

Lunar Cards show us why the lesson is being experienced. In Faery Wicca, we recognize every lesson or experience in life to be a reflection of an awakening taking place in our subconscious, even if we are not always cognizant of it at the time. There are no coincidences in life, therefore every situation is a result of choices made that may have aligned an individual to the opportunity of experience.

Spirit and Evolution

When we undergo challenging times, we can look upon such challenges as Spirit Tests. When viewed from this perspective the challenges can be lessened.

In Faery Wicca, Spirit Tests are accepted as valuable times of Spiritual growth. The gods challenge us, or put us through a Spirit test, when an aspect of our native composition that was of a weak nature is ready to be transformed into a strength. Spirit tests are likened to the saying "Walk your talk"—for it's our "talk" that is challenged.

Numerology and Energy

As with the Element Cards, the Ancient Ones Cards are assigned numbers. In tarot, the numbers assigned a card become representative of an energy aspect applicable to the meaning of that card.

In Part One, a basic interpretation of numbers 1 through 9 was provided, which can also be applied to the Ancient Ones cards. However, in the case of certain Ancient Ones cards, it becomes important to take into consideration Celtic Numerology.[3]

In most instances, when an Ancient Ones Card is a double digit number, the number is broken down into its primary number. For example: the number 15 would be broken down into 6 (1 + 5 = 6). However, the 13 and 17 cards will remain in their whole state as both numbers have special Celtic meaning.

Celtic Numerology places its main emphasis on 4/5, 8/9, 12/13, 16/17, 27, and 32/33. This system is based on multiples of even numbers, plus an odd number, except for 27, which is perfectly divided by 9 three times, enacting the ancient magickal teaching of "by the powers of three times three."

The implications that each of the odd numbers is completed by the addition of 1 is borne out by the fact that the unit (even number) is transformed into an odd number when added to the sacred center or leader, which is considered the unifying principle. Following are brief descriptions of 5, 9, 13, and 17.

5

In Celtic numerology, 5 represents "wholism," the 4 + 1. The 4 represents the four elements and directions, while the fifth, the completing factor, represents the center where the four quarters meet and become whole. Synthesis; a unification of polarities; expansion; awareness; the five senses.

9

This number figures so prominently in Celtic tradition that it can be described as the northern counterpart of the sacred seven of Eastern traditions. Nine, like five, symbolized the whole. In this case, however, it is the group of 8 + 1—the leader. Wisdom; coalition; healing; space; servant to the Universe.

13

The figure of twelve individuals around a king is ancient. In Ireland, the ancient king-idol, Crom Croich, was made of gold and twelve stone idols were placed around him. The twelve subsidiary idols were arranged in four rows of three, forming the familiar pattern of a center and three in each direction, or the Celtic Cross. However, here 13 represents the natural cycles of life on earth. There are four seasons (3+1) that comprise one year, yet, within each year there are 13 lunations, or lunar months. The four seasons are duly honored through the observance of the completion of the 13 lunations of the moon.

In the science of numerology, the vibration of 13, or 4, is that of boundary. Four is the first manifestation in matter, as well as the formation of Spirit, Soul, Mind, and Body. The earth is considered the square of the 4, or the boundary in which the physical manifests. The lesson of the 4 is to learn to cooperate within the physical, and that of 13 is to recognize that the physical will give way and return back to its elemental or natural state.

17

In Celtic numerology, 17 represents kingdoms, as well as a sense of time duration. Seventeen is the result of 16 + 1, symbolizing the sixteen regions of the Heavenly Realm plus the cosmologies, or the sacred center, denoting the seventeenth region. The year was also looked upon as 17: the thirteen lunar months plus the four seasons.

Seventeen is also the number of generations; interestingly enough, 1 + 7 = 8, the number of humankind. In the science of numerology, eight is the vibration of manifestation; the power to create or move the forces of matter and the balanced judgment to use them for the good of humankind—and in the Irish sense, unto seventeen generations.

In the lesson of 17, the key to success is in considering the effects one's decisions and actions will have on the kinship of the seventeenth generation (not unlike the American Indian consideration of seventh generation caretaking).

The Application of Astrology

Because astrological significance in Celtic mythology was more attached to the ogham moon months, then zodiacal signs, the astrological system that one could apply to the Ancient Ones cards, would be the standard astrological affiliations generated through the Golden Dawn system of tarot. Therefore, the signs of the zodiac would be applied as follows:

Athair Dia Dagda: Aries, sight

Treoraí: Taurus, hearing

Muirneach Deirdre and Naosie: Gemini, smell

Carbad na an Morrigu Anand: Cancer, speech

Rúndaigne Banba: Leo, taste

Díthreabhach Arias: Virgo, sexual love

Fíorcheart Macha: Libra, work

Bean Sidhe Cailleach: Scorpio, movement

Uisce Coisricthe: Sagittarius, anger

Áibhirseoir Cernunnos: Capricorn, mirth

Réalta Dana: Aquarius, imagination

Seanchailleach Gealach Cnoc: Pisces, sleep

The seven primary planets used by ancient astrologers would be applied as follows:

Draoi Gebann: Mercury, life-death

Máthair Bandia Éiré: Venus, peace-maker

Bansagart Ard Brigid: the Moon, wisdom-folly

Roth Grian: Jupiter, riches-poverty

An Clogás: Mars, grace-indignation

Grain Páiste: the Sun, fertility-barrenness

Fíodóir Bandia: Saturn, power-servitude

Oghams and Celtic Symbols

In esoteric studies, the most enthralling information for the novice is found in the magickal symbols, runes, and alphabets once used to encode the teachings of the Mysteries. Such items are indeed codes, not only used as a secret language to communicate information between adepts, but also to empower working tools and spellcraft, as well as for divination.

The *Faery Wicca Tarot* is encoded with the secret language of the Bards as represented through the use of the Irish oghams (see Part One, pages 20-21, for information on the ogham alphabet), ancient Gaelic alphabets, and sacred symbols.

The art of understanding magickal and sacred symbolism has always fascinated humankind. Symbols represent an image that links us to higher levels of subjective intuitive experience, as well as to our immediate conscious awareness. Symbols can be thought of as the midway point between what is outside ourselves and what is deeply etched within.

Through symbolism, we can see the soul awakening to the realization of true purpose, leading us to a higher level of Spiritual evolution.

The study of symbols allows one to experience the symbol as the gateway to deeper thinking and living, we become aware that we have transcended the personality and touched deeply on our soul quality. When this happens, we recognize that it is through the self that we make an inner contact with the Ancient Ones on a level beyond reason or intellect. We become part of the whole, and recognize that the whole is also part of us.

Throughout the Ancient Ones Cards, the secret language of the Bards can be seen. Deeper meditation on this language, whether represented through an ogham, Gaelic word, or sacred symbol, will bridge an attunement to the Spiritual vibration of the Faery lesson depicted beneath the surface of the card illustration, and that of the core of each card's Faery Lore.

Continual meditation on an Ancient Ones Card will bring forth the knowledge of the OtherWorld, inviting the Faery to become co-walkers in your world, while assisting you in becoming a co-walker in theirs.

The Border Oghams of the Ancient Ones Cards

On the border of each of the Ancient Ones cards are four oghams. In the upper left-hand corner, in a green circle, is the ogham Ailm, the elm or silver fir, which is the station of the Winter Solstice—Season of Rebirth. Ailm's qualities are boldness, fidelity, and good luck. Elm represents the god-like strength that one needs to rise above adversity, like the elm tree, to create a viewpoint from a higher level—the god-like capabilities of healing and perception of future trends. If Ailm stands out, it means that one must stand up for oneself by voicing their truth.

In the upper right-hand corner, in a yellow circle, is the ogham Ohn, gorse or furze, station of the Spring Equinox, Season of Spring. The religious importance of furze, or gorse, is enhanced by its flowers being frequented by the first bees of the year, as the ivies are by the last. Ohn takes on the symbolical meaning of continuous fertility. Gorse or furze represents carrying on one's activities despite the surrounding of conditions, in the aspect of "standing out" against the background, as does the gorse bush. Magickally, this ogham represents collecting and retaining of one's strength through adversity. The collection and dispersal of the gorse seeds by ants expresses the necessity for gathering small and separate things together. If Ohn stands out it warns against allowing minor obstacles to stop your progress. Focus with determination on your goal.

In the bottom right-hand corner, in a red circle, is the ogham Ur, heather, Station of the Summer Solstice, Season of Summer. The heather is the midsummer tree, red and passionate, and is associated with mountains and bees. The goddess is, herself, a queen bee about whom male drones swarm in midsummer. Heather often represents a lucky charm. The white heather is a lucky charm of protection against danger, while the purple heather represents beauty in solitude and admiration. In divination, heather brings luck and freshness to any venture it is applied to. In magickal practices, it is the entrance point to the inner worlds. If Ur stands out, it indicates moving forward, remembering to let Spirit guide you.

In the bottom left-hand corner, in a blue circle, is the ogham Eadha—aspen or white poplar, Station of the Autumnal Equinox, Season of Autumn. Aspen is the shield-maker's tree and has the qualities of hardy resistance to a variety of seemingly inhospitable conditions. The poplar or aspen was used widely in divining, along with the silver fir. The fir stood for hope and the poplar for loss of hope. In ancient Ireland, the *fé*, or measuring rod used by coffin makers on corpses, was of aspen, a reminder to the souls of the dead that this was not the end, but rather a transcending into a new Circle of Existence. Magickally, aspen is seen as a preventer of death. At its most powerful, it signifies the power of one's will overriding destiny, the possibility of the power of the mind overriding the inertia of matter (i.e., mind over body, or the body-mind connection).

At the Threshold of the Solar Circle and the Path of the Sun

Ancient Ones Cards 00 through 9

The Path of the Sun

The Ancient Ones Cards form a holy procession that carries certain divine images. These images are attuned to supernatural entities. Each illustration is meant to be a new revelation in the process of initiation.

Standing at the threshold of the Crann na beatha card, the Cuardaitheoir is ready to begin the journey. Here, the Cuardaitheoir represents the magickal neophyte who will be introduced on their journey by the Draoi Gebann to the four Lunar and Solar Goddesses and Gods. The Ordeals of Initiation into Spiritual rebirth through alchemical transmutation is next depicted. The neophyte will be instructed in the Solar Realm by the Draoi Gebann, and helped to unbind herself or himself from societal mind conditioning.

OO

Crann na Beatha
The Tree of Life

Meaning

Come into the center of the sacred; stand tall and firm like a tree, with your roots solidly planted in MaMa Earth's soil, and your branches aspiring to new heights; prepare to align with the primal land by orienting yourself to the cardinal directions; become the power of the provinces; move forward into the Plains. It is time to begin your apprenticeship into Faery Wicca.

Card Description

This is the first card added to the *Faery Wicca Tarot*. An ancient oak tree stands on the western shore of Ireland. A swan waits near shore in the water. The horizon reflects the colors of what could be sunrise or sunset. Votive offerings to Dia Dana (God Dana) are tied in the branches of the oak tree. On the trunk is carved the Tree Cross. The trunk also has a doorway, which is slightly open, emitting an illuminating light from the OtherWorld. At the root of the oak is a leprechaun with a pipe in his mouth, wearing a red cap and a green vest, a bag full of gold and silver coins (see Nine of Domhan, page 125 for more information), and two mushrooms.

Oghams, Alphabets, and Symbols

For border oghams, see The Border Oghams of the Ancient Ones Cards on page 250. For the meaning of the bag of gold see the Nine of Domhan card description and meaning (page 125).

The votive offering is a symbol representing one's prayers to the Ancient Ones. Votive offerings are often tied to the guardian tree around sacred wells in Ireland. Such wells are seen as healing sites or entrances into the UnderWorld (see Rúndaigne Banba, page 307). Here, the votive offerings symbolize one's desire to gain admittance into the Plains, and to become oriented to the primal land, the elemental world, and the five provinces of Ireland.

The Tree Cross combines two of the most ancient symbols, each uniting a pair of opposites. The Tree unites the mundane earth with the Spiritual sky or Heavenly Realm, as well as with the UnderWorld. The Cross unites the masculine trunk with the horizontal feminine branches, which bear protective leaves and nourishing fruit. The Tree is highly significant in the Bible with the Tree of Life (the earthly paradise and its seductive fruits) and the Tree of Knowledge of good and evil (the lure of the other reality where opposites unite, ultimately the lure of Sophia, the feminine, of wisdom). Tree worship, throughout the Bronze Age from Palestine to Ireland, was associated with the worship of the Triple Moon Goddess. As a Tree, the annual renewal of foliage promises rebirth; as a Cross, it signifies resurrection—the victory of life over death.

> We must find some place upon the Tree of Life high enough for the passion that is exaltation and for the wings that are always on fire.[4]

Leprechauns were generally described as fairy shoemakers—a red-capped fellow who stays around pure springs and is known to haunt cellars. He spends his time drinking and smoking. One branch of the Leprechaun is known as the Fir Darrig, who is a practical joker; both are of the Solitary Fairies. Leprechauns have also been associated with the earth elemental, Gnome, and when so done, is described as a merry little fellow dressed in green. Instead of wearing a red cap, he wears a leather apron, drab clothes, and buckled shoes. Leprechauns have been known to harbor the secret treasures of the earth, and when favor is gained from them, often one is rewarded with Faery Gold!

The mushrooms represent the magick mushroom, which often shifts one's awareness. In Faery Lore, magick mushrooms are an important ingredient in the Faery Eye Ointment, which allows one to see the alternate reality of the Land of Faery superimposed on our reality or this world.

The opening in the trunk of the tree emanates the earth light, a source of light connected to the stars inside the earth. Through this door, one gains entrance into the sacred center of the Plains—the Hill of Uisneach in Ireland.

Swans are often believed to be Faeries. Here, the swan represents a totem animal of the Plains. When one is ready to become oriented to the primal land, swan will become their ally. Swan is known in Faery lore as the power of woman and is connected to the attribute of grace. It teaches us to surrender to the grace of the rhythm of the universe and to shapeshift from the physical body into the OtherWorld. Through the lesson of swan, one can learn to move into the spiraling beauty and Spirit of the All. Swan is Spiritual Power.

Faery Lore

There was a very high oak tree in Kildare that Brigid loved much and blessed: of which the trunk still (c. A.D. 980) remains. No one dares to cut it with a weapon but he who can break off any part of it with his hands deems it a great advantage, hoping for the aid of God by means of it, because through the miracles of Brigid, many miracles have been performed by that wood.[5]

There are many stories told to illustrate the immortality of the sacred trees of Ireland. It would be regarded as sacrilege to injure or even to insult the sacred tree, for everyone knows that "Faery Folks are in old oaks." The older the oak tree, the more sacred and renowned its powers.

In Lough Gur, the Irish version of the Tree of Trees, or of Life, was believed to be rooted into the lake bed. The Lough was believed to disappear by magick once every seven years. At these times the supernatural tree was revealed, growing from the bottom of the Lough. This tree at Lough Gur, the magic tree, "is covered with a green cloth," as the following tale proclaims:

A certain bold fellow was at the spot one day at the very instant when the spell broke, and he rode his horse towards the tree and snatched away the Brat Uaine, or Green Cloth, that covered it. As he turned his horse and fled for his life, the Woman who sat on the watch, knitting, under the cloth at the foot of the tree cried out:

> *Chughat, chughat, a bhuaine bhalbh!*
> *Marcach ó Thir na mBan Barbh*
> *F'fuadach an bhruit uaine dhom bhathas.*
>
> *Awake, awake, thou silent tide!*
> *From the Mortal Women's Land a horseman rides,*
> *From my head the green cloth snatching.*

At these words, the waters rose; and so fiercely did they pursue him, that as he gained the edge of the lake one half of his steed was swept away, and with it the Brat Uaine which he was drawing after him. Had that been taken, the enchantment would be ended forever.

Supernatural trees played a central role in the Irish imagination until late medieval times. Mythologically speaking, the country revolved around them. The tree of Eo Rossa was praised as 'a king's wheel, a prince's right, a wave's noise, best of creatures. . .a firm-strong god . . . a measure's house, a mother's good . . . a fruitful sea, Banba's renown, judgment of origin, judicial doom, faggot of sages . . . dearest of bushes, vigor of life, spell of knowledge . . . shout of the world.'

The Lough Gur tree stands for a divinely renewable prosperity. It is envisaged in poetic form because poetry is the language of the gods. Especially when sun, poetry takes us beyond categorization, and allows us back into the primordial forest where the Tree of Life is synonymous with the Tree of Knowledge. [6]

0

CUARDAITHEOIR
The Seeker

Meaning

The Amadan-Dhu has perhaps called to you. Time to visit the wilderness and reconnect with the soul of nature. A new journey is at hand, one that will guide you down the pathways of the gods. A true initiation is at hand, but first you must enter the labyrinth of the mind and find your heart. All that you need in life you already carry with you. Let Spirit guide you.

Card Description

A three-headed figure dressed in blue and carrying a green napsack inscribed with a word has entered the sacred landscape of the Great City of Gorias, located in the east (see Ace of Aer, page 33). The seeker of knowledge has come to a crossroads. A host of trooping faery, dressed in green, point the seeker into every direction, knowing that no matter what direction the seeker chooses, a significant lesson in life will be learned.

However, not too far up the eastern road, a stone circle can be seen, indicating that this way would be the most obvious to choose. Also, in the middle of the pathway is a black crow feather, a second indicator for right choice. At the foot of the eastern path, where it meets the others, is a stone, marked with an inverted triangle, the third indicator—messages, warnings, incantations, and the like, are always given or said in threes.

Oghams, Alphabets, and Symbols

For border oghams, see The Border Oghams of the Ancient Ones Cards on page 250.

The napsack is green to symbolize that it contains "magickal" items that are oriented to the primal land. The word that is inscribed on the bag is written in an ancient Gaelic alphabet, each letter representing a tree, number, color, animal totem, and time of year (figure 5, page 23).

A particular aspect of triplism was the practice of producing images of gods with three heads or three faces on a single head. It is known that the head was a potent symbol for the Celts, and thus it is logical for the head sometimes to have been represented with its power multiplied to the power of three.

Three-headed images had particular power. Such heads could look in three directions and possessed the normal potency of the human head, but tripled.

The significance of the triple head indicates that the path of knowledge is magickal. Each face represents an aspect of life. The face to the left is a female face, while the face to the right is that of a man. The center face, however, is the face of Spirit, a union of the feminine and masculine principles in life, which renders it angelic or youthful in appearance. This symbol of trinity also symbolizes that the path of the seeker of knowledge is one blessed and guarded by all Goddesses and Gods of a triune nature.

This triad of the head indicates that the seeker must also find a true union or merging between the mind and the heart to manifest Spirit. Here the emphasis is placed on the head, showing that such a concept is first experienced in the mind, which is also indicated by being in the landscape connected to the mind. The blue clothing represents the need to connect the mind to the heart, as blue is the color connected to the west, the province of the heart. The stone at the foot of the eastern path, with the inverted triangle, also symbolizes the need for balance between the mind and heart—the inverted triangle is traditionally known as the symbol for the element of water.

In this card, the seeker is surrounded by the primal elements of the land:

Air is symbolized by the landscape of Gorias, dawn, the crow feather, and the triane head.

Fire is symbolized by the center head of manifested Spirit.

Water is symbolized by the blue clothing, and the stone with its water symbol.

Earth is symbolized by the wooden staff on which the napbag is tied and by the gnomes or Earth Faery allies.

Here, the seeker simply isn't aware of this knowledge and must be taught to see the primal elements of the land, and how to work with them.

Faery Lore

I have heard you calling, Dalua,
Dalua!
I have heard you on the hill,
By the pool-side still,
Where the lapwings shrill
Dalua . . . Dalua . . . Dalua!

What is it you call, Dalua,
Dalua!
When the rains fall,
When the mists crawl,
And the curlews call
Dalua . . . Dalua . . . Dalua!

I am the Fool, Dalua,
Dalua!
When men hear me, their eyes
Darken: the shadow in the skies
Droops: and the keening-woman cries
Dalua . . . Dalua . . . Dalua!

Dalua is one of the names of a mysterious being in the Celtic mythology, the Amadan-Dhu, the Dark Witless One, or Faery Fool. The following excerpt from Fiona MaCleod's *The Dominion of Dreams* (Duffield and Company, 1910) is a beautiful example of how the Faery Fool touches the soul:

"What with the dark and the rain and the whisky and the good words of Mhairi Bàn, my head's like a black boy," he muttered; "and the playing of that man there is like the way o' voices in the bog."

Then he heard without the wilderness in his ears. The air came faint but clear. It angered him. It was like a mocking voice, Perhaps this was because it was like a mocking voice. Perhaps because it was the old pipe-song. . . . [he] had never heard that playing before . . . .

Macara stopped and listened. It was sweet to hear. Was this a sudden magic that was played upon him? Had not the rain abruptly ceased, as a breath withdrawn? He stared confusedly: for sure, there was no rain, and moonlight lay upon the fern and upon a white birch that stood solitary in that white-green waste. The sprays of the birch were like a rain of pale shimmering gold. A bird slid along a topmost branch; blue, with breast like a white iris, and with wild-rose wings. Macara could see its eyes a-shine, two little starry flames. Song came from it, slow, broken, like water in a stony channel. With each note the years of Time ran laughing through ancient woods, and old age sighed across the world and sank into the earth, and the sea moaned with the burden of all moaning and all tears. The stars moved in a jocund measure; a player sat among them and played, the moon his footstool and the sun a flaming gem above his brows. The song was Youth.

Dan Macara stood. Dreams and visions ran past him, laughing, with starry eyes. . . .

Dalua stood by him, brooding darkly. . . . Many shadows stirred. Dalua lifted one. It was the shadow of a reed. He put it to his mouth and played upon it. . . .

It was years and years after that when I saw [Macara].

"How did this madness come upon him?" I asked; for I recalled him strong and proud.

"The Dark Fool, the Amadan-Dhu, touched him. No one knows any more than that. But that is a true thing.

He hated or feared nothing, save only shadows. These disquieted him, by the hearth side or upon the great lonely moors. He was quiet, and loved running water and the hill-wind. But, at times, the wailing of curlews threw him into a frenzy.

I asked him once why he was so sad. "I have heard," he said . . . and then stared idly at me; adding suddenly, as though remembering words spoken by another: "I'm always hearing the three ancientest cries: the cry of the curlew, an' the wind, an' the sighing of the sea."

He was ever witless, and loved wandering among the hills. No child feared him. He had a lost love in his face. At night, on the sighing moors, or on the glen-road, his eyes were like stars in a pool, but with a light more tender.

ᒣ

DRAOI GEBANN
The Druid

Meaning

Master of knowledge; the power of the primal world flows through you into this world; all awareness is awake within your soul; listen to the light of the patron within you, for she guides you to your destiny; hold the four magickal elements within your hands, but gently, knowing that they are not yours for the keeping but the caretaking. Use your powers wisely, for the Ancient Ones, not for personal satisfaction. The Initiate.

Card Description

A powerful druid stands within the boundaries of a stone circle. Two guardian trees rise in the background, their branches the frame for the rising full moon. Gebann is dressed in a feathered cloak, holding two of the four magickal tools: the wand and shield.

On a dolmen altar rests the same green napbag once carried by the seeker of knowledge. The remaining two magickal tools stand before the altar: the cauldron and sword.

Oghams, Alphabets, and Symbols

For border oghams, see The Border Oghams of the Ancient Ones Cards, page 250.

The Uinllean ogham appears five times on the shield, but in reverse. This symbolizes that the draoi's magick, his wisdom and strength, come from the OtherWorld. He is in touch with the ancestors, primal land, and Ancient Ones, of which he is one. The number five, reflected by the five reversed Uinllean ogham and by the five-pointed star, or pentagram, on the shield represents the synthesis of the draoi's knowledge; he lives by the five paths of law, which represents the cosmos. As a learned man he also knows Filidecht (philosophy or higher wisdom), and the five kinds of language: the language of the Femi, of separation, of the File, of Iarmberla, and the fifth kind of language known only to Chief Bards.

Five is the first number that was given only one form—the first four numerals were declined with feminine and masculine forms—thus combining or unifying the polarities. The vibration quality of the five is one of expansion, of awareness, which Gebann has achieved.

The five oghams and five-pointed star appearing on the face of the shield symbolizes that these qualities are grounded in the magickal element of earth (i.e., earth wisdom, primal land, ancestral wisdom, the synthesis of the knowledge learned in the Four Great Cities of the OtherWorld, and the application of such learning on earth).

The draoi holds the earth shield in his left hand as an indicator he is receptive to new teachings, and is in touch with the feminine polarity of life. Holding the magickal wand, the magickal tool of fire, and the symbol of power, in his right hand—raised to the Heavenly Realm—indicates that he is in full control of his personal powers and very connected to the power of the OtherWorld, thus the powers of the Ancient Ones flow through him. The masculine and feminine polarities are merged and balanced within.

The ultimate root of the word *Magic* is unknown, but approximately it is derived from the Magi, or priests of Chaldea and Media in pre-Aryan and pre-Semitic times, who were the great proponents of this system of thought so strangely mingled of superstition, philosophy, and scientific observation. The fundamental conception of magick is that of the Spiritual vitality of all nature. This Spiritual vitality was not, as in polytheism, conceived as separated from nature in distinct divine personalities. It was implicit and immanent in nature; obscure, undefined, invested with all the awfulness of a power whose limits and nature are enveloped in impenetrable mystery. In its remote origin it was doubtless, as many facts appear to support, associated with the cult of the dead, for death was looked on as the resumption into nature, and as the investment with vague and uncontrollable powers of a Spiritual force formerly embodied in the concrete, limited, manageable, and therefore less awful, form of a living human personality. Yet these powers were not altogether uncontrollable. The desire for control, as well as the suggestion of the means for achieving it, probably arose from the first rude practices of the art of healing. The first magicians were those who attained a special knowledge of healing or poisonous herbs; but "virtue" of some sort of being attributed to every natural object and phenomenon, a kind of magickal science—partly the child of true research, partly of poetic imagination, partly of priestcraft—would in time spring up, codified into rites and formulas, attached to special places and objects, and represented by symbols.[7]

Manannan Mac Lir, the Irish Sea God, was known to have a cloak of invisibility. Such a cloak is cited in many of the tales. In practical terms, what this term might imply is that the "natural" or everyday persona of the druid disappeared when the cloak for ritual and ceremony was donned, thus becoming the image of an OtherWorld Being. The feathered cloak is a sign that here is a holy person who works in attunement with the natural world, seeking his own continual Spiritual evolution (i.e., he is a perpetual seeker of knowledge even if, at this stage of development, he has become the master of knowledge).

The Undry (cauldron), the magickal tool of water, with the submerged tip of the magickal tool of air (the sword), further symbolizes that the draoi has not only achieved a balance of polarities of the feminine and masculine principles of the natural world and life, but has also achieved an inner balance and marriage of his own twin flames: the mind and heart, which sparks the presence of Spirit.

The seeker's napsack, laid open on the dolmen altar, contained the four magickal tools. As a symbol of the heart, the magickal bag (see the Crane Bag, page 373) is the holder of all symbols and fetishes that act as reminders that our true existence, our true power, comes from the gods.

The dolmen altar is a very ancient form of altar used by the druids in Ireland. The capstone is symbolic of the Lia Fail or Stone of Destiny brought by the De Dananns from the Great City of Falias. Used on an altar it indicates that the participants recognize that all magick is a reflection of the land and primal land in alignment, and when magick does not work it's because these two qualities were either out of attunement or the magician has no knowledge of the five paths of law.

The full moon is the light in darkness. She reminds the Draoi that his emotional security must always be felt. When insecurity is alive within our minds, our inner twin flames are not married or working in balance. The adept knows that emotional security can only be gained by marriage to one's Patron Goddess; for she *is* the heart of all life, and the provider of inner security.

Faery Lore

Gebann is the first noted draoi in Faery lore to arrive on the shore of Erin. Therefore, he represents the birth of the magickal ways in Faery Wicca. Once again, let us read the words of Fiona MaCleod to better understand the language of the magician:

It was at this hour, at a sundown such as this, that I saw him . . . . His mind dwelled almost wholly upon secret things: ancient mysteries, old myths, the forgotten gods and the power and influences starry and demoniacal, dreams, and the august revelation of eternal beauty . . . . he gave me four small objects, of which three were made of ivory and gold, and the fourth was a rounded stone of basalt double-sphered with gold.

I asked him what meaning they had, for I knew he gave them with meaning.

"Do you not know?" he said. One was the small image of a sword, the other of a spear, the third of a cup.

Then I knew that he had given me the symbols of the four quarters of the earth, and of all the worlds of the universe: the stone for the North, the sword for the East, the spear for the South, and the cup for the West.

"Hold the sword against the light that I may see it," he whispered; adding, after a while: "I am tired of all thoughts of glory and wonder, of power, and of love that divides." . . . He asked me to hold the little gold and ivory spear against the light. "I am tired," he said, "of all thoughts of dominion, of great kingdoms and empires that come and pass, or insatiable desires, and all that goes forth to smite and to conquer."

. . . I held before his dimmed eyes the little gold and ivory cup, white as milk in the pale gold of a rain-clear windy set. "I am tired," he said, "of all thoughts of dreams that outlive the grave, and of fearless eyes looking at the stars, and of old heroisms, and mystery, and the beauty of beauty." . . . he bade me lift the stone of basalt, though he could not see that which I held before his eyes. I saw the shadow in his closed eyelids become tremulous and pale blue, like faint, wind-shaken smoke.

When I put the stone on the marble by his side, not more still or white than that other silent thing which lay beside it, I knew that of the eternal symbols of which he has so often written in *The Book of the Opal*, one he had forever relinquished. With him, in that new passage, he had the spear, and the sword, and the little infinite cup that the tears of one heart might fill and yet not all the dews of the incalculable stars cause to overflow.

Among the impersonal episodic parts of *The Book of the Opal*, I found much diffuse and crude material, often luminous with living thought—the swimming thought of timeless imagination out of which an old-time romance of two worlds has been woven: two worlds, the one as the other remote from us now, though each in degrees to be recovered, if neither till after a deeper "sea-change" than any modern world has yet known.

Though the soul is the still-water in which each of us may dimly discern this "sea-change," Art, which is the symbolic language of the soul, is alone, now, the common mirror with which all may look. And Art, we must remember, is the continual recovery of a bewildered tradition, the tradition of Beauty and of Joy and of Youth, that like the Aztec word Ahecatl—which signifies the Wind, and the Breath, and the Soul—are but the three mortal names for one immortal Word.[8]

2

BANSAGART ARD BRIGID

The High Priestess

Meaning

You have arrived at the portal to the Garden of the Goddess. The Great Mother's daughter, her holy priestess and daughter, the Maiden Goddess must ask you of your worthiness—there is only one answer, which you must give from your heart. The wisdom and teachings of the Mysteries are beckoning to you to move deeper. Are you the student or the teacher?

Card Description

A priestess of Brigid stands before a portal, leading into the Garden of the Goddess. In the Garden we see the image of a red mare, flora, and a twisted tree. To either side of the portal and high priestess are curtains—one panel red and one panel blue—as well as two lantern torches held upright in two cauldrons. One candle and cauldron are black, while the other candle and cauldron are white.

The high priestess faces us. She wears the crown of the Moon God-dess upon her brow. In her hands she holds the Book of Life. She wears a black gown, richly embroidered with silver and purple Celtic knot work. The silver buckle on her girdle is that of a Full and Cres-cent Moon. Her long, wheat-colored hair flows freely except for two long braids framing her face. Her eyes are bottomless pits of black. Her facial expression is both stern and inviting. She is a woman in her prime; the beauty of youth still graces her, while the body of maturity envelops her with the aura of experience.

Oghams, Alphabets, and Symbols

For border oghams, see The Border Oghams of the Ancient Ones Cards on page 250.

On each lantern words are written in an ancient Gaelic alphabet (figure 5, page 23). These words are the only ones that the high priest-ess will ask each person seeking Her Mother—the Great Mother God-dess, seeking to enter the Garden of the Goddess, seeking to live in the Paradise on Earth. Each person's answer is recorded in the Book of Life, which the priestess holds open. Therefore, while she may already know the answer you will give, only you can give the correct answer, and there is only one answer.

The white candle and cauldron symbolize the daylight world, the conscious mind, the Lunar Realm. The black candle and cauldron symbolize the night light world, the subconscious mind, the Solar Realm. The high priestess dwells in perfect balance between the two worlds, thus she knows how to move betwixt and between at will. She, like the draoi, is a shaman whose learning encompasses the five paths of law.

The red curtain represents the life blood that flows from the Garden of the Goddess. The blue curtain represents the water of life that also flows from the Garden. The life blood is connected to the women's mysteries, in which every priest is learned and which is the power of every priestess. The water of life is the energy flowing from the Other-World into ours. To be attuned to the Ancient Ones, each aspirant must find this energy.

The twisted tree is the earth-binder of all magick performed by mortals, and an important line in the spellcraft rune spoken by Faery Wiccan practitioners. The red mare is the carrier of the soul, who seeks to commune with the Great Mother Goddess (see Carbad na an Morrigu Anand, page 288).

The Celtic knot work represents the Thread of Life. The human soul is thought to be a fragment of the Divine, which will ultimately return to its Divine Source. Through successive rebirths, the soul rids itself of its accumulated, inherited impurities until it finally achieves the goal of perfection. The interlaced, or latticed, knot work patterns, with their unbroken lines, symbolize the process of humankind's eternal Spiritual evolution. When the cord is unraveled, it leads us on.

Faery Lore

High Priestesses are known to be the voices of the Goddess; for in their deep meditation and trancing, they bring through the Oracle of the Great Mother Goddess. Hear now, the words of Her Soul:

The mortal gods move by the Immortal Will, and, therefore, I am here. The triumphant music of birds is a sign: the voice of Dana speaking in the air. The neighing of horses is a sign: the voice of Brigid speaking from the earth.

Can a spear divine the Eternal Will?

Do you know what the greatest thing in the world is? I have not told you before now. What I consider is the greatest thing in the world is the Divine Imagination. Mortals believe the greatest things to be Happiness and Commonsense.

The Divine Imagination may only be known through the thoughts of mortal creatures. A man has said Commonsense is the greatest thing in the world, and a woman has said Happiness are the greatest things in the world. These things are male and female, for Commonsense is Thought and Happiness is Emotion, and until they embrace in Love the will of Immensity cannot be fruitful. For, behold, there has been no marriage of humanity since time began. Men have but coupled with their own shadows. The desire that sprang from their heads they pursued, and no man has yet known the love of a woman. And women have mated with the shadows of their own hearts, thinking fondly that the arms of men were about them.

I saw my son dancing with an Idea, and I said to him, "With what do you dance, my son?" and he replied, "I make merry with the wife of my affection," and truly she was shaped as a woman is shaped, but it was an Idea he danced with and not a woman. And presently he went away to his labors, and then his Idea arose and her humanity came upon her so that she was clothed with beauty and terror, and she went apart and danced with the pervant of my son, and there was great joy of that dancing—for a person in the wrong place is an Idea and not a person.

Man is Thought and woman is Intuition, and they have never mated. There is a gulf between them and it is called Fear, and what they fear is that their strengths shall be taken from them and they may no longer be tyrants. The Eternal has made love blind, for it is not by science, but by intuition alone, that he may come to his beloved: but desire, which is science, has many eyes and sees so vastly that he passes his love in the press, saying there is no love, and he propagates miserably on his own delusions.

The finger tips are guided by Dana, but the demon looks through the eyes of all creatures so that they may wander in the errors of reason and justify themselves of their wanderings. The desire of a man shall be Beauty, but he has fashioned a slave in his mind and called it Virtue. The desire of a woman shall be Wisdom, but she has formed a beast in her blood and called it Courage: but the real virtue is courage, and the real courage is liberty, and the real liberty is wisdom, and Wisdom is the daughter of Thought and Intuition; and her names also are Innocence and Adoration and Happiness.

The world has all but forgotten me. In all my nation there is no remembrance of me. I, wandering on the hills of my country, am lonely indeed. I am the desolate goddess forbidden to utter my happy laughter. I hide the silver of my speech and the gold of my merriment. I live in the holes of the rocks and the dark caves of the sea. I weep in the morning because I may not laugh, and in the evening I go abroad and am not happy. Where I have kissed a bird has flown; where I have trod a flower has sprung. But Thought has snared my birds in his nets and sold them in the market-places.

Who will deliver me from Thought, from the base holiness of Intellect, the maker of chains and traps? Who will save me from the holy impurity of Emotion, whose daughters are Envy and Jealousy and Hatred, who plucks my flowers to ornament her lusts and my little leaves to shrivel on the breasts of infamy?

Lo, I am sealed in the caves of nonentity until the head and the heart shall come together in fruitfulness, until Thought has wept for Love, and Emotion has purified herself to meet her lover.

Tir na n'Og is the heart of a man and the head of a woman. Widely they are separated. Self-centered they stand, and between them the seas of space are flooding desolately. No voice can shout across those shores. No eye can bridge them, nor any desire bring them together until the blind god shall find them on the wavering stream—not as an arrow searches straightly from a bow, but gently, imperceptibly as a feather on the wind reaches the ground on a hundred starts; not with the compass and the chart, but by the breath of the Almighty which blows from all quarters without care and without ceasing.

Night and day it urges from the outside to the inside. It gathers ever to the center. From the far without to the deep within, trembling from the body to the soul until the head of a woman and the heart of a man are filled with the Divine Imagination. Hymen, Hymenæa! I sing to the ears that are stopped, the eyes that are sealed, and the minds that do not labor. Sweetly I sing on the hillside. The blind shall look within and not without; the deaf shall hearken to the murmur of their own veins, and be enchanted with the wisdom of sweetness; the thought-less shall think without effort as the lightning flashes, that the hand of Innocence may reach to the stars, that the feet of Adoration may dance to the Father of Joy, and the laugh of Happiness be answered by the Voice of Benediction.[9]

3

MÁTHAIR
BANDIA ÉIRÉ

The Mother

Goddess Éiré

Meaning

The wisdom of the feminine principle in life is at work in your life. Open to the fertility of the land and find abundance in your life. Allow creativity to flow through you. A call to return to nature. In quiet meditation, open to the stars above your head to receive the wisdom of Goddess. Align with your inner child and find bliss.

Card Description

Éiré, the Great Mother Goddess, who is the land of Ireland herself, rises up from the primal land. She holds in her arms, her sun-child. She wears a crown of seven stars upon her head, and a pearl necklace. She is gowned with the flora of the land. Her countenance is one of bliss. Her sun-child gazes intently upon us. His blue eyes hold an ancient wisdom, yet are the innocent eyes of a babe.

The Mother Goddess and sun-child sit before an ancient cairn located on Loughcrew—the witches' hill—in Co. Meath, Ireland. A circle of stone pillars ring the cairn. A red mare grazes on the grass in the background. The sky is full of white, fluffy clouds; it is a mild day.

Oghams, Alphabets, and Symbols

For border oghams, see The Border Oghams of the Ancient Ones Cards on page 250.

The red mare is the same depicted in the portal to the Garden of the Goddess in the Bansagart Ard Brigid and Grain Páiste cards (page 266 and 344, respectively). Here, the mare becomes the totem animal of the Great Mother Goddess, and has the ability to know the ways into the OtherWorld. The red mare is a good and faithful guide.

Loughcrew, traditionally known as Sliabh na gCailligh, the Witches Hills, is an area rich in Megalithic graves, stretching over three hills about a mile apart. There are about 30 passage graves dating from 3000 B.C.E. Some of these have spiral engravings. Legend says that the hills were formed when a *Cailleach,* or witch, let the stones fall from her apron as she was flying overhead.

The cairn is also a representation that "if that which you seek, you find not within your own heart, you will never find it without"; for the Great Mother Goddess has always been with us, and it is to Her, in the end, every apprentice returns.

The three Dragon's Eyes that appear on one of the standing stones circling the cairn represent the spiral dance that witches perform in sacred circles to demonstrate the concept of "As above, so below," mirroring the macrocosmic order of the heavens, the gyratory movement representing the whirling of the stars above the fixed earth. Winding in, the spiral dance establishes the still center within, approaching the heart of the universe, or the womb which will give birth. Winding out, the spiral dance births the Spirit back to its Divine Source of existence.

The seven-starred crown on Éiré's head shows that She is also the Great Weaver Goddess of the Cosmos, as well as the Earth Mother—her flora gown—as well as the UnderWorld Goddess, where Her feet stand firmly anchored. The cosmic consciousness of the Great Goddess is connected to the Seven Sisters, the Hyades or Pleiades star system, the Seven Sisters are represented on earth by a kernel of corn, another linking of the Great Mother to the land in Her role as the

Grain Goddess. In essence Eiré is All Goddesses, for all Goddesses are but One Goddess, who is called by many names: Eiré, Dana, Brigid, Demeter, Isis, Freya, Pelè, Laksmhi, and so on.

Pearls represent a connection to the Waters of Life, the magickal element of water, which is of a feminine nature, thereby imbuing the deeper meaning of the card to be one of Life (i.e., creativity, fertility) which the sun-child further demonstrates.

The sun-child is also an indicator that to enter the Garden of the Goddess and dwell in the presence of the Great Mother, one must seek to find their innocence and inner child (see Grain Páiste, page 344).

Faery Lore

When the Sons of Mil fought to take possession of Ireland, they had colloquy with the triune Goddess of the land, the last aspect of which was Eiré. The following excerpt from the *Lebor Gabála Erenn*, Vol. XLIV, Section VIII, gives the tale:

The sons of Mil had colloquy with Banba in Sliab Mis. Said Banba unto them: If it be to take Ireland ye have come, not right were the good fortune in which ye have come. It is by necessity, said Amorgen Gluingel, the poet. A gift from you to me then, said she. What gift? said they. That my name may be on this island, said she. What is thy name? said they. Banba, said she. Let it be a name for this island, said Amorgen.

They had colloquy with Fotla in Eblinne. She spake with them in like manner, and desired that her name should be upon the island. Said Amorgen: Let Fotla be a name upon this island.

They had colloquy with Eriu in Uisnech. She said unto them: Warriors, said she, welcome to you. Long have soothsayers had your coming. Yours shall be this island forever; and to the east of the world there shall not be a better island. No race shall there be, more numerous than yours. Good is that, said Amorgen; good is the prophecy. Not right were it to thank her, said Eber Donn, eldest of the sons of Mil; thank our gods and our own might. To thee 'tis equal, said Eriu; thou shalt have no profit of this island, nor shall thy progeny. A gift to me, ye sons of Mil, and ye children of Breogan, said she; that my name shall be on this island. It shall be its principal name, said Amorgen.

And Amorgen sang to the land, when the sons of Mil conquered:

I seek the land of Ireland,
Coursed be the fruitful sea,
Fruitful the ranked highland,
Ranked the showery wood,
Showery the river of cataracts,
Of cataracts the lake of pools,
Of pools the hill of a well,
Of a well of a people of assemblies,
Of assemblies of the king of Temair;
Temair, hill of peoples,
Peoples of the Sons of Mil,
Of Mil of ships, of barks;
The high ship Eriu,
Erin lofty, very green,
An incantation very cunning,
The great cunning of the wives of Bres,
Of bres, of the wives of Buaigne,
The mighty lady Eriu,
Erimón harried her,
Ir, Eber sought for her—
I seek the land of Ireland.

4

ATHAIR DIA DAGDA

The Father God

Meaning

Expansiveness is an opportunity; surrender to the call of duty; peace unto those who are balanced in their lives; the Noble Order of Tara may be speaking to you, calling you into Knighthood or Damehood as a protector of our Earth; the sound of destiny sings around you, what tune is heard: sorrow, joy, or the lulling tune of a lullaby.

Card Description

The Father God, or the Good God, Dagda, stands upon the Lia Fail—Stone of Destiny—on the Hill of Tara. He is dressed in royal attire: a purple cloak with gold braiding, a royal jerkin over a blue kilt embroidered with a golden Celtic knot work, red trousers, knee-high black boots, and a sheathed sword at his side.

His red hair appears to be lifting up, as if he were hanging upside down. Both arms are extended out from his sides, and his left leg is raised and bent at the knee so that his left foot rests against his right calf.

A patchwork landscape, in various shades of green, spreads out behind him. The sky is rosy, hinting that it is dawn.

Oghams, Alphabets, and Symbols

For border oghams, see The Border Oghams of the Ancient Ones Cards on page 250.

The ogham inscription on the Stone of Destiny identifies that the stone is a sacred talisman from the Great City Falias, which myth indicated screamed under every high king when stood on. The ogham Koad appears on the cuffs of the jerkin. The equivalent of Koad is that of Eadha, the Aspen tree. Koad signifies earth and is given the Bardic number of thirteen. Koad signifies the unity of all eight festivals of the traditional year. It can be described as the sacred grove, the location in which all things, hitherto separate, become connected together. At such a point, all things become clear.

The Celtic knot work embroidered on the kilt indicates that the Father God is connected to the Thread of Life, to the Great Weaver Goddess. To be the Father God, the Dagda occupies the conscious awareness of the dance of the soul's eternal Spiritual evolution, which is why he stands in perfect balance upon the Lia Fail.

The seasonal-colored belt buckle shows that Dagda is an Earth God, the Father to all life forms upon Eiré, and is the energy that turns the seasons one into the next.

The sword, which is yellow, symbolizes the mind or masculine energy. It is sheathed in a blue case, symbolizing the heart or feminine energy; the union of the two producing eternal peace.

The purple cloak indicates that his consciousness is Spiritual. The red jerkin and pants indicates that he is Spirit incarnate, while the blue kilt indicates that he is in touch with his heart.

The variegated landscape reflects the fertile qualities of the Father God, who is also the vegetation god.

Faery Lore

A curious little incident bearing on the power that the De Dananns could exercise by the spell of music may be inserted here. The flying Fomorians, it is told, had made prisoner the harper of the Dagda and carried him off with them. Lugh, the Dagda, and the warrior Ogma followed them, and came unknown into the banqueting-hall of the Fomorian camp. There they saw the harp hanging on the wall. The Dagda called to it, and immediately it flew into his hands, killing nine men of the Fomorians on its way. The Dagda's invocation of the harp is very singular, and not a little puzzling:

> "Come, apple-sweet murmurer," he cries, "come, four-angled frame of harmony, come, Summer, come, Winter, from the mouths of harps and bags and pipes."

The allusion to summer and winter suggests the practice in Indian music of allotting certain musical modes to the different seasons of the year (and even to different times of day), and also an Egyptian legend, in which the three strings of the lyre were supposed to answer respectively to the three seasons, spring, summer, and winter.

When the Dagda got possession of the harp, the tale goes on, he played on it the "three noble strains" that every great master of the harp should command, namely the Strain of Lament, which caused the hearers to weep; the Strain of Laughter, which made them merry; and the Strain of Slumber, or Lullaby, which plunged them all in a profound sleep. Under cover of that sleep the Danann champion stole out and escaped. It may be observed that throughout the whole of the legendary literature of Ireland, skill in music—the art whose influence most resembles that of a mysterious spell or gift of Faery—is the prerogative of the People of Dana and their descendants. Thus in the "Colloquy of the Ancients," a collection of tales made about the thirteenth or fourteenth century, St. Patrick is introduced to a minstrel, Cascorach, "a handsome, curly headed, dark-browed youth," who plays so sweet a strain that the saint and his retinue all fall asleep. Cascorach, we are told, was son of a minstrel of the Danann folk. St. Patrick's scribe, Brogan, remarks, "A good cast of thine art is that thou gavest us." "Good indeed it were," said Patrick, "but for a twang of the fairy spell that infests it; barring which nothing could more nearly resemble heaven's harmony." Some of the most beautiful of the antique Irish folk melodies, like the Coulin, are traditionally supposed to have been over-heard by mortal harpers at the revels of the Faery Folk.

The Dagda Mor was the father and chief of the People of Dana. A certain conception of vastness attaches to him and to his doings. In the Second Battle of Moytura, his blows sweep down whole ranks of the enemy, and his spear, when he trails it on the march, draws a furrow in the ground like the fosse which marks the nearing of a province. An element of grotesque humor is present in some of the records about this deity. When the Fomorians give him food on his visit to their camp, the porridge and milk are poured into a great pit in the ground, and he eats it with a spoon big enough, it was said, for a man and a woman to lie together in it. With this spoon he scrapes the pit, when the porridge is done, and shovels earth and gravel unconcernedly down his throat. We have already seen that, like all the Dananns, he is a master of music, as well as of other magickal endowments, and owns a harp that comes flying through the air at his call. The tendency to attribute life to inanimate things is apparent in the Homeric literature, but exercises a very great influence in the mythology of this country. The living, fiery spear of Lugh; the magick ship of Manannan; the sword of Conary Mor, which sang; Cu Chulainn's sword, which spoke; the Lia Fail, Stone of Destiny, which roared for joy beneath the feet of rightful kings; the waves of the ocean, roaring with rage and sorrow when such kings are in jeopardy; the waters of the Avon Dia, holding back for fear at the mighty duel between Cu Chulainn and Ferdia, are but a few out of many examples. A legend of later times tells how once, at the death of a great scholar, all the books in Ireland fell from their shelves upon the floor.

For the years that followed the coming of Dagda to Ireland, there was peace in all the lands of the north.

The tributary kings laid aside their swords: the spear and the arrow, save in the fray of the hunt, quenched no longer their red thirst. Every-where blue smoke ascended, from the great straths, from the shore-combs, from inland valleys, from the woodlands. The green corn grew to a yellow harvest: the aftermath was filled with peace, and without rumor of battles and dissensions. Winter, spring, summer; the white to the brown, the brown to the yellow, the yellow to the green, the green to the russet: each season came and went, orderly, glad, welcome.

In the forest townships and the great raths on the plains, the people grew slowly to the likeness of Dagda. The Ollamhs preached a life of peace and fair deeds; the poets sang of the great past, and of heroes, and of beautiful women, and of the passion of life, and in the songs of one and all was the beauty of dream.

Long, long afterward, this time was sung of as the golden age.

With longing eyes many a dreamer has turned upon it his backward gaze, fain of a day when men and women loved and had joy, in great peace, and to the charmed music of dream.[10]

5

TREORAÍ
The Guide

Meaning

When you are ready, the teacher will find you, but you must be willing to do your part to put yourself in the right place at the right time, to maximize the opportunity for such an attunement to transpire. You will know the true Guide by his or her works. When trusted without fear, the True Guide will lead you beyond the sphere of Lunar into the sphere of Solar. The answers are beneath the surface.

Card Description

A Druid and Arch-priestess, dressed in ceremonial garments, stand in greeting. The Druid wears the cloak of spades. He holds the priest's staff in his right hand. The Arch-priestess wears a red gown and a yellow vestment around her shoulders. Her left hand is extended forward.

Behind the pair rises Clonegal Castle, located in Eniscorthy, Ireland, home of the Fellowship of Isis. The Fellowship is dedicated to spreading the religion of all the Goddesses throughout this planet. The Gods are also venerated. The Goddess is seen as Deity, the Divine Mother of all beings, as well as the embodiment of Truth and Beauty. Hindus, Buddhists, Christians, including Catholics and Protestants, and Spiritualists have joined. From many countries, followers of the esoteric traditions have become members, including practitioners of Wicca, Qabalah, Rosicrucianism, Celtic Mysteries, and the Zen, Sufi and Tao paths. The revival of the ancient Nigerian religion is under way. Fellowship of Isis was purposely used to depict the true meaning of this card—traditionally called the Hierophant—as the Guide into the deeper teachings of the Mysteries.

Oghams, Alphabets, and Symbols

For border oghams, see The Border Oghams of the Ancient Ones Cards on page 250.

The spades are used to represent a shovel, a tool to be used in digging into the soil, in this case to be used to dig deeper into the mystery school of the Goddess.

The yellow vestment around the Arch-priestess symbolizes the inner radiant light to which a Guide, such as herself, can lead a seeker of knowledge.

Here, a man and a woman, combined, create the Guide. This is used to demonstrate that a true guide is balanced with the energy of life. With this balance, one knows how to wield personal power, symbolized by the priest's staff held in the right hand, as well as receive power from outside oneself, as symbolized by the Arch-priestess' extended left hand.

Every pilgrimage must begin on the earth, which is why the couple stands on the castle lawn. Every Guide will take the aspirant beyond the superficial structure of any school, organization, or religion—or in this case into the ex-"dungeon" of the Castle, now converted into the Temple of Isis.

Faery Lore

The following Manifesto is not only that of Fellowship of Isis, but representative of one which a true Guide would offer any seeker of knowledge in the mystery schools of Goddess:

Growing numbers of people are rediscovering their love for the Goddess. At first, this love may seem to be no more than an inner feeling. But soon it develops: it becomes a longing to help the Goddess actively in the manifestation of Her divine plan. Thus, one hears such inquiries as, "How can I get initiated into the Mysteries of the Goddess? How can I experience a closer communion with Her? Where are the nearest temples and devotees? How can I join the priesthood of the Goddess?" and many other questions.

The Fellowship of Isis has been founded to answer these needs. Membership provides a means of promoting a closer communion between the Goddess and each member, both singly and as part of a larger group. There is also a communion experienced with Deities, Spirit beings and all nature's offspring.

The Fellowship is organized on a democratic basis. All members have equal privileges within it, whether as a single member or part of an Iseum or Lyceum. Membership is free.

The Fellowship respects the freedom of conscience of each member. There are no vows required or commitments to secrecy. All Fellowship activities are optional and members are free to resign or rejoin at their own choice.

The Fellowship reverences all manifestations of Life. The Rites exclude any form of sacrifice, whether actual or symbolic. Nature is revered and conserved. The Noble Order of Tara concentrates on working for Goddess and Nature.

The Fellowship accepts religious toleration, and is not exclusionary. Members are free to maintain other religious allegiances. Membership is open to all of every religion, tradition, and race. Children, listed as "Children of Isis," are welcomed, subject to parental consent.

The Fellowship believes in a promotion of Love, Beauty and Abundance. No encouragement is given to asceticism.

The Fellowship seeks to develop friendliness, psychic gifts, happiness, and compassion for all life. The Druid Clan of Dana focuses on the development of telepathy, Spirit communion and awareness of other spheres of being.

The College of Isis has been revived after its suppression 1,500 years ago. Like Aset Shemsu, the Fellowship of Isis itself, it has always been alive in the Inner Planes. It is from these Inner Planes that its return has been inspired. As the College of Isis is part of the Fellowship, the ideals of the Manifesto also apply. The qualities of Goodness, Harmony and Wisdom are manifested through a multi-religious, multi-racial, and multi-cultural Fellowship that honors the good in all faiths.[11]

6

MUIRNEACH
DEIRDRE AND
NAOSIE
The Beloved

Meaning

Love is at once so great and so frail that there is perhaps no thought that can at the same time so appall and uplift us. And there is in love, at times, for some an unfathomable mystery. That which can lead to the stars can lead to the abyss. There is a limit set to mortal joy as well as to mortal suffering, and the flame may overleap itself in one as in the other. The most dreaded mystery of a love that is overwhelming is its death through its own flame.

Card Description

Two twisted trees have grown together, the branches of each joining in the middle. The branches have shaped into the faces of Deirdre and Naosie. On the trunk of each tree, ogham have been engraved—each is the name of the Beloved.

Dancing around the trunk is a troop of Faery, in their diminutive form as that of Earth fairies. Before the trees is an ancient pillar stone—the Guardian Stone—of true love.

Oghams, Alphabets, and Symbols

For border oghams, see The Border Oghams of the Ancient Ones Cards on page 250.

Both tree trunks are inscribed with ogham, designating the name of each tree in its connection to one of the Beloved. (For the myth of Deirdre and Naosie, see Ridire and Annir of Domhan, on pages 162 and 202, respectively.) On the right trunk, or the Naosie side, appears the Oir ogham. Traditionally, this ogham is associated with childbirth, being used magickally to ease the passage of the baby from the womb into the world. Here it is used to signify that love survives even death; for if love is that of the Beloved, it is an immortal love.

There are six Earth fairies dancing around the trunk of the trees. Six is also the number of this card. The symbolic meaning of the six is to show that the immortal souls of the Beloved are reunited in the OtherWorld as well as in the natural world—they are part of everything: the trees, the stones, the earth, the sky, the water—the Spirit of love lives on and on.

Deirdre and her Lover are perhaps the most famous of all Irish legends. The Guardian Stone is based on a carving on the Irish high cross of Castledermot and on a twentieth-century sculpture; its deeper meaning is best described by W. B. Yeats:

When my arms wrap you round I press
My heart upon thy loveliness
That has long faded from the world . . .

Faery Lore

But the years trampled his youth under foot. Sorrow breathed a gray change upon his hair, and a gray silence into his life; then dwelled with him as his comrade, looking out upon all things great and small, from his steadfast eyes. This sorrow, which was a grief too intimate to be thought of by him as either grief or sorrow, but had become the color and sound of life, was because of two things that were both mortal and immortal. The love of the woman in whose little, eager heart he had put his life, as one might with great joy lay the sacrifice on an altar, was one of these; the other was the beauty of her whom he loved, because it was so rare and wonderful in itself, and because it was to him the temporal and visible self of a beauty beyond mortal beauty and of a beauty beyond mortal change.

From the day he loved her, he saw a shadow draw nearer. In some strange, mysterious way life gave again what it took from her. When from too great weakness she could no more go out upon the heather, or stand under the mountain-ash by the brown rushing burn with its birch and fern-shadowed pools, or could no more gather flowers, or watch the wild roses glimmer with falling dew, or the stars gather one by one or in still companies out of dove-gray silences, Ian saw that the beauty of these things, so near and familiar, so remote and beyond all words, so finite alone, so infinite together—as a breath is at once a thing that dies, and is part of the one Breath that is life—had passed into her. There was not anything lost to her of the falling dew, of the loosened fragrances, of the flickering of leaf and fern, of the little radiant lives of flowers, of the still stars; these passed into her, and were a bloom upon her face, and a mystery in her eyes, and a light upon that which was comrade to these momentary breaths, and to that other Breath, wherein these were neither less nor greater than the shining constellations and the ancient, time-forgetting stars.

Great love had brought great sorrows: and it was not less great because in so large a part inarticulate. In her, he knew the highest. Life could give him no greater joy, if no deeper sorrow. He was grateful. And in his love she, for her part, forgot that youth was for her a flower that had to be relinquished while its bloom was still unfaded, while its fragrance was most sweet: that temporal beauty had dear mortal needs: and that the unfathomable silences wherein she was soon to sink were a cold bride-bed for desires so limited in hop and so vast in faith.

There are few who love thus. Theirs was that heroic love, not dependent upon those bittersweet claims and satieties which sustain lesser dreams; wherein faith was so absolute that neither knew there could be unfaithfulness, and love so deep that neither knew love's feet could stray.

They had great rewards. She left him, herself glad with august sureties, her memory without the least ignoble stain. And he: he had that for which the crowned and the laurelled have bowed their heads in intolerable, sad desire; and was more rich than misers who stare upon idle gold; and lit daily upon a secret altar a flame more great and wonderful than that which shines upon the brows of ancient cities, being more ancient than they.

To many of us these rapt passions are passions that cannot be, or that dwell only in the moonlit realms of the mind. That they should be possible among the humble is a reproach, and therefore belief halts.

But heroic love is not a dream. And though he was only a shepherd, Ivor M'Iain knew this: and when I write of him, I write of one whom I knew, and of what I know.

It was after his supreme loss that he was so seldom, and was yet so well loved, and often longed for.

But thereafter he dwelled more and more among the great solitudes, and dreamed dreams that could not be true for Ivor, but could be true for that which passed by that name, and through temporal eyes looked out upon the immortal things of beauty and desire.

Solitary, he tended his sheep day by day and week by week and month by month. He saw moons follow moons, and the sad march of the stars fill the nights, and knew vain, limitless desires; and from winter to spring, and from spring to winter, carried into these silences his patient heart, that little, infinite thing that God appalls with the terror of Eternity.[12]

7

CARBAD NA AN MORRIGU ANAND

The Chariot

Meaning

Moving forward by trusting that Spirit is your warrior. Call upon the Morrigu for protection on the astral realm; ride the red mare into your inner radiant light; find the way through the Plains.

Card Description

The Morrigan, whose true name is Anand, rides across Mag Muirthenme in her golden chariot drawn by the red mare. Her flaming red hair flares out about her head like solar flames. Her countenance is bright as fire, though her skin is alabaster white, with eyes dark and bottomless, crowned with flaming red eyebrows. She wears a red tartan cloak secured with a Tara brooch. Her dress is solid green. In her hands, she holds the Gae Bulga, the magickal spear of Lugh.

The golden chariot is inscribed with spirals: single, double, and a red Triple Spiral. It also bears the Luis ogham. The red mare wears a bridle of green, and a golden solar disc over its forehead.

Oghams, Alphabets, and Symbols

For border oghams, see The Border Oghams of the Ancient Ones Cards on page 250.

Luis is described as "delight of the eye" with regards to it being a red glare, and holds the additional meaning of a sheen or luster. Luis is connected to the Rowan, also known as the mountain ash, quicken, or quickbeam—a tree of life. Its round wattles, spread with newly flayed bull's hides, were used by the druids as a last extremity for compelling demons to answer difficult questions, hence the Irish proverbial expression "to go on the wattles of knowledge," meaning to do one's utmost to get information.

In ancient Ireland, fires of rowan were kindled by the Bards and Ollamhs of opposing armies and incantations spoken over them summoning the Fenian Heroes, or the Morrigu, to take part in the fight. Luis serves to protect its user against psychic attack and to develop the individual's powers of perception and prediction, all of which are under the domain of Morrigan.

Both single and double spirals were among the most sacred signs of Neolithic Europe. They appeared on megalithic monuments and temples all over the continent and the Celtic islands. Spiral oculi (double twists resembling eyes) appear prominently in places like the threshold stones at Newgrange.

The spiral is the cosmic symbol for the natural form of growth—a symbol of eternal life reminding us of the flow and movement of the cosmos. The whorls are the continuous creation and dissolution of the world; the passages between the spirals symbolized the divisions between life, death, and rebirth.

The apprentice would pass a spiral barrier into an inner sanctuary on their journey of the sacred dance through the labyrinth to the sacred realms beyond the center. The labyrinth creates and protects the still center, allowing entry to knowledge only in the correct way— initiation. Before the knowledge can be imparted, old preconceptions must be discarded and the traveler must again enter the preformal state of the earth-womb. At the center there is complete balance: the point where heaven and earth are joined.

The triple spiral is the symbol of the trinity. The power of three is well known in theories based on mathematics, philosophy, aesthetics, and physics. Throughout the Celtic countries, this power is found with threefold goddesses, such as the Morrigu—encompasses Badb, Neman, and Macha, the three Brigids, the three Mothers, with the male gods and heroes who often travel in three or are born at the same time as two others with the same name.

The three-spiraled Trinity from Newgrange is perhaps the best known symbol in all of Ireland, a symbol of great wisdom and antiquity. From a magickal point of view, the Trinity represents not only the triune of mind-body-soul, but also standing at the crossroads, resulting with a composite vision of past-present-future: being in the prophecy of Morrigan.

The Morrigan was an extraordinary goddess who appeared to embody all that is perverse and horrible among supernatural powers. She delighted in setting men at war, and fought among them herself, changing into many frightful shapes and often hovering above fighting armies in the aspect of a crow. She met Cu Chulainn once and proffered him her love in the guise of a human maid, as depicted in the tale that follows on page 291.

The red mare is also known as the "red mare of Macha." (See Fíorcheart Macha, page 294.) Here the red mare symbolizes The Great Mare or the Great Goddess, for the Celts' revered the Goddess as the embodiment of the equine imagery. In Irish legend, the white breakers of the ocean were described as the white mane of the Morrigan's head. If we ponder how the sea and horse draw a parallel in the Celts' mind, we may see a connection in the double use of the word *mare*. It means "sea" in Latin and Russian, and is the root of the English word "marine." At the same time it was used to designate a female horse. Both meanings of mare may have been derived from the same initial Indo-European source word, possibly the Sanskrit *mah*, meaning "mighty." This word may also be the foundation of the Goddess names: Morrigan and Morgan—the roots *gan*, *gin*, and *gen* meaning birth, as in *genesis* and *begin*.

Faery Lore

This tale, "The Colloquy of the Morrigan and Cu Chulainn," is taken from *The Ancient Irish Epic Tale, Táin Bó Cúalnge*, translated by Joseph Dunn, David Nutt, 1914.

Then Cu Chulainn saw draw near him a young woman with a dress of every color about her and her appearance most surpassing. "Who art thou?" Cu Chulainn asked. "Daughter of Buan ('the Eternal'), the king," she answered. "I am come to thee; I have loved thee for the high tales they tell of thee and have brought my treasures and cattle with me." "Not good is the time thou hast come. Is not our condition weakened through hunger? Not easy then would it be for me to foregather with a woman the while I am engaged in this struggle." "Herein I will come to thy help." "Not for the love of a woman did I take this in hand." "This then shall be thy lot," said she, "when I come against thee what time thou art contending with men: In the shape of an eel I will come beneath thy feet in the ford; so shalt thou fall." "More likely that, methinks, than daughter of a king! I will seize thee," said he, "in the fork of my toes till thy ribs are broken, and thou shalt remain in such sorry plight till there come my sentence of blessing on thee." "In the shape of a grey she-wolf will I drive the cattle on to the ford against thee." "I will cast a stone from my sling at thee, so shall it smash thine eye in thy head" (said he), "and thou wilt so remain maimed till my sentence of blessing come on thee." "I will attack thee," said she, "in the shape of a hornless red heifer at the head of the cattle, so that they will overwhelm thee on the waters and fords and pools and thou wilt not see me before thee." "I will," replied he, "fling a stone at thee that will break thy leg under thee, and thou wilt thus be lamed till my sentence of blessing come on thee." Therewith she went from him.

[The combat of Loch and Cu Chulainn on the Táin, and the slaying of Loch son of Mofemis, follow in the tale.] Then it was that the Morrigan daughter of Aed Ernmas came from the fairy dwellings to destroy Cu Chulainn. For she had threatened on the Cattle-raid of Regomain that she would come to undo Cu Chulainn what time he would be in sore distress when engaged in battle and combat with a goodly warrior, with Loch, in the course of the Cattle-spoil of Cualnge. Thither then the Morrigan came in the shape of a white hornless, red-eared heifer, with fifty heifers about her and a chain of silvered bronze between each two of the heifers. She bursts upon the pools and fords at the head of the cattle. It was then that Cu Chulainn said, "I cannot see the fords for the waters." The women came with their strange sorcery, and constrained Cu Chulainn by geasa and by inviolable bonds to check the heifer for them lest she should escape from him without harm. Cu Chulainn made an unerring cast from his sling-stick at her, so that he shattered one of the Morrigan's eyes.

Now when the men met on the ford and began to fight and to struggle, and when each of them was about to strike the other, the Morrigan came thither in the shape of a slippery, black eel down the stream. Then she came on the linn and she coiled three folds and twists around the two feet and the thighs and forks of Cu Chulainn, till he was lying on his back athwart the ford and his limbs in the air.

While Cu Chulainn was busied freeing himself and before he was able to rise, Loch wounded him crosswise through the breast, so that the spear went through him and the ford was gore-red with his blood . . . .

The Morrigan next came in the form of a rough, grey-red bitch-wolf with wide open jaws and she bit Cu Chulainn in the arm and drove the cattle against him westwards, and Cu Chulainn made a cast of his little javelin at her, strongly, vehemently, so that it shattered one eye in her head. During this space of time, whether long or short, while Cu Chulainn was engaged in freeing himself, Loch wounded him through the loins. Thereupon Cu Chulainn lain chanted a lay.

Then did Cu Chulainn to the Morrigan the three things he had threatened her on the Cattle-raid of Regomain, and his anger arose within him and he wounded Loch with the Gae Bulga (the Barbed spear), so that it passed through his heart in his breast . . . .

(The Healing Of The Morrigan:) Great weariness came over Cu Chulainn after that night, and a great thirst, after his exhaustion. Then it was that the Morrigan, daughter of Ernmas, came from the fairy dwellings, in the guise of an old hag, with wasted knees, long-legged, blind and lame, engaged in milking a tawny, three-teated milch cow before the eyes of Cu Chulainn. And for this reason she came in this fashion, that she might have redress from Cu Chulainn. For none whom Cu Chulainn ever wounded recovered there-from without himself aided in the healing. Cu Chulainn, maddened with thirst, begged her for a milking. She gave him a miling of one of these tests and straightway Cu Chulainn drank it. "May this be a cure in time for me, old crone," quote Cu Chulainn, "and the blessing of gods and of non-gods upon thee!" said he; and one of the queen's eyes became whole thereby. He begged the miling of another teat. She milked the cow's second teat and gave it to him and he drank it and said, "May she straightway be sound that gave it." Then her head was healed so that it was whole. He begged a third drink of the hag. She milked the cow's third teat and gave him the miling of the teat and he drank it. "A blessing on thee of gods and of non-gods, O woman! Good is the help and succor thou gavest me." And her leg was made whole thereby. Now these were their gods, the mighty folk: and these were their non-gods the folk of husbandry. And the queen was healed forthwith. "Well, Cu Chulainn, thou saidst to me," spake the Morrigan, "I should not get healing nor succor from thee forever." "Had I known it was thou," Cu Chulainn made answer, "I would never have healed thee." Or, it may be Drong Conculainn (Cu Chulainn's Throng) on Tarthesc is the name of this tale in the Reaving of the Kine of Cualnge.

Then it was she alighted in the form of a royston crow one bramble that grows over Grelach Dolair (the Stamping-ground of Dolar) in Mag Murthemne. "Ominous is the appearance of a bird in this place above all," quote Cu Chulainn. Hence cometh Sgé nah Einchi (Crow's Bramble) as a name of Murthemne.

8

FÍORCHEART
MACHA

Poetical Justice

Meaning

Karmic destiny; divine compassion is required to endure the trials and tribulations in which you may find yourself involved; the three fates hold the scales of justice—the power to control the end result is not within your hands; give birth to new pathways; deliver that which is just and fair, being mindful of the law of love.

Card Description

Macha, while in the last stages of pregnancy, runs her last race to her death. As she reaches the finish line, her water bursts, and she goes into labor.

Behind her the crowd jeers on a male racer, except for one young boy, who hesitates. Off to the right of Macha stand the ghostly forms of three women in mourning, wearing white. Their eyes are closed and their blood-red lips are parted with the keening ululation. The center woman holds scales.

Oghams, Alphabets, Symbols

For border oghams, see The Border Oghams of the Ancient Ones Cards on page 250.

The name Macha literally means "mighty." In the Irish *Noinden Ulad*, Macha is symbolized by a white horse, symbol of life, suggesting a relationship to the Celtic Mare goddess known in Europe as Epona, and in Wales as Rhiannon.

Two sites in Ireland's county of Ulster still bear the name of Macha, one an ancient capital in Ulster known as Emain Macha, literally Twins of Macha; the other, Ard Macha, is the present-day city of Armagh.

Macha is also a name that appears in different guises and in different times in Irish mythology. Sometimes she is related as a human woman, marrying named individuals and giving birth to identifiable people. Her essential origins, however, lie deeper: Macha is a mystical Spiritual entity, one of the three aspects of the Goddess of war and destruction, the others are Badb and Morrigan. As such, Macha was an inspiration to warriors in battle—heads cut off in battle were called "Macha's Acorns." One of the chambers at Emain Macha was used as a storehouse for the display of enemies' heads. The religion of Macha's people was a warrior cult of war and death.

Faery Lore

One story tells of the origin of Emain Macha:

One day a mysterious Macha arrived in the bed of one Crunniuc Mac Agnomain, a local Ulster chieftain. She became his wife, and pregnant by him. One day, whilst racing horses, Crunniuc told the king that his wife, pregnant as she was, could outrun the king's horses and every male runner. Under threat, Macha was forced to take part in a race. At the end of the field she gave birth to twins, this place then named Emain Macha, a phrase which can be translated as "Macha's Twins." While Macha gave birth she screamed and she then said that all who heard this scream would suffer pangs of childbirth in times of Ulster's dangers. Women, boys, and Cu Chulainn were to be immune from this curse. After saying this, Macha died.

The curse, known as the Cess Noinden Ulad, has links to the primitive Couvade, practiced by Basques and southern Europeans until recent times. In this, after childbirth, it is men who take to their beds in sickness for a few days. The origins of all this lie in religions where the female menstrual cycle and the phases of the moon played a part in religious beliefs. In its mystical origins, Emhain Macha belongs to this cultural system.[13]

Like all myths, the story is open to several interpretations. Perhaps the story symbolizes the last pagan appeal to true motherhood as the basis for public social ethics, and a curse on the patriarchal age that had dawned.

The Goddess was effectively saying that although you may develop sophisticated doctrines of rebirth, although you have taken to yourselves the right of life and death, although your efforts might seem logical and plausible in the light of patriarchal culture, your efforts are doomed to failure as long as they are based on the subordination of women. Speaking the language of peace and common good on the one hand; on the other, you are calling the troops to war against women and the earth.

Irish mythology points to the early preeminence of goddesses. As agriculture and many of the arts were first in the hands of women, goddesses of fertility and culture preceded gods and still held their place when gods were evolved. Even war goddesses are prominent in Ireland. Celtic gods and heroes are often called after their mothers, not their fathers, and women loom largely in the tales of Irish colonization, while in many legends they play a most important part. Goddesses give their names to divine groups, and even where gods are prominent, their actions are free, their personalities still clearly defined. The supremacy of the divine women of Irish tradition is once more seen in the fact that they woo and win heroes, while their capacity for love, their passion, their eternal youthfulness and beauty are suggestive of their early character as goddesses of ever-springing fertility.[14]

9

DÍTHREABHACH
ARIAS
The Holy Man

Meaning

The time for deep thinking is at hand. The choice to develop one's Spirituality, thereby encouraging the soul's continual evolution, has nothing to do with religion, or dogma, but true belief that there is something grander than oneself, and that one's consciousness is only a part of a greater mind. Attune to the stars above your head and draw the starlight down through your inner stars, into the stars inside the earth. Open to the voice of ancient wisdom.

Card Description

The cloaked figure who appeared in the suit of Aer and Tine, stands before a raging fire. Both arms are raised aloft, and in his left hand, he holds a wand, igniting with magickal fire. He is drawing down the starlight from the star Venus, which shines brightest of all. The starlight spirals down through his wand to the land below. In the background rises a stone oratory, and next to it rests a pillar stone.

Oghams, Alphabets, and Symbols

For border oghams, see The Border Oghams of the Ancient Ones Cards on page 250.

The stone pillar has a hole going through its top-center; this links the stone to the Gift of Faery card, The Holy Stone (page 378). Meditation on the meaning of the Holy Stone card will aid in deeper meaning to the stone pillar in the Holy Man Card.

The planet Venus, depicted here as a Star, is very significant, for here we see it as the Light-bringer, or the Messenger. Drawing down the Starlight was an ancient rite practiced by Faery-Faith Holy Men; one which directly tied into the ancient teachings dealing with the Regulation of the World, or the creation of the world. The Regulation of the World contains three points of action, and specifically dealt with the second regulation:

The second was of all that moved under the dominion of time; it comprises sun, moon, and planets and is called Mundus.

The idea expressed deals with constellations, which in turn create within time the "World of the Planets." This system of time as seen through the constellations was known as "Time in Night," a system of time based on the movement of the constellations through the seamanly observation of the stars for practical voyaging purposes, or in this case the astronomical observation of the stars by the Holy Man for prophesying purposes. Such a system shows minds trained in thought. Each planet and sphere had its defined place and precise name. The night of the stars shaped earth through the pole's circling, which created the "Triple Dial of the Sun," a microcosm of the earth's system, dividing the day into three parts.[15] Holy Men knew that at twilight the world entered into the realm of ancient wisdom, when the Time in Night would tell exactly where we are in the great order of the universe.

Understanding that the sun, moon, and planets were there before us and before earth, and would be after, was an important wisdom. The second regulation of the world is more closely connected to the first: Dana, that which is not created; Annwyn, the outermost from God, not abyss but outer darkness.[16]

The midnight cloak worn by the Holy Man is associated with invisibility, allowing the Holy Man to blend into the heavens, thus becoming part of something grander then himself. Later, when the worship and practices of the old religion crept farther and farther into the wilderness and oak groves due to the encroaching religion of the Catholics or Protestants, such a cloak would help the wearer blend into the colors of the forest, or in this case the blackness of night.

Faery Lore

To the lonely cloghan on the bluffs of Dingle Peninsula the clans people sometimes came for advice on subjects too recondite for even those extremes of elucidation, the parish priest and the tavern. These people were always well received, and their perplexities were attended to instantly, for the Holy Man liked being wise and they were not ashamed to put their learning to the proof, nor was he, as so many wise people are, fearful lest he should become poor or less respected by giving away his knowledge. These were favorite maxims with him:

> You must be fit to give before you can be fit to receive.
>
> Knowledge becomes lumber in a week, therefore, get rid of it.
>
> The box must be emptied before it can be refilled.
>
> Refilling is progress.
>
> A sword, a spade, and a thought should never be allowed to rust.
>
> The greatest of all virtues is curiosity, and the end of all desire is wisdom.
>
> Time is the tick of a clock.
>
> Good and evil are two peas in the one pod.
>
> To understand the theory which underlies all things is not sufficient.
>
> Theory is but the preparation for practice.
>
> Wisdom may not be the end of everything.
>
> Goodness and kindliness are, perhaps, beyond wisdom.
>
> Wisdom is the oldest of all things.
>
> Wisdom is all head and no heart.

Chaos is the first condition.

Order is the first law.

Continuity is the first reflection.

Quietude is the first happiness.

The toxin generates the anti-toxin.

The end lies concealed in the beginning.

All bodies grow around a skeleton.

Life is a petticoat about death.

Washing is an extraordinary custom. We are washed both on coming into the world and on going out of it, and we take no pleasure from the first washing nor any profit from the last.

Habit is continuity of action, it is a most detestable thing and is very difficult to get away from.

A proverb will run where a writ will not, and the follies of our fore-fathers are of greater importance to us than is the well-being of our posterity.

There are exceptions to every rule.

Here is insight into the way an Irish Holy Man's mind might work: 'The human body is an aggregation of flesh and sinew, around a central bony structure. The use of clothing is primarily to protect this organism from rain and cold, and it may not be regarded as the banner of morality without danger to this fundamental premise. If a person does not desire to be so protected who will quarrel with an honorable liberty? Decency is not clothing but Mind. Morality is behavior. Virtue is thought

I have often fancied, that the effect of clothing on mind must be very considerable, and that it must have a modifying rather than an expanding effect, or, even, an intensifying as against an exuberant effect. With clothing the whole environment is immediately affected. The air, which is our proper medium, is only filtered to our bodies in an abated and niggardly fashion which can scarcely be as beneficial as the generous and unintermitted elemental play. The question naturally arises whether clothing is as unknown to nature as we have fancied? Viewed as a protective measure against atmospheric rigor we find that many creatures grow, by their own central impulse, some kind of exterior panoply which may be regarded as their proper clothing. Bears, cats, dogs, mice, sheep and beavers are wrap din fur, hair, fell, fleece or pelt, so these creatures cannot by any means be regarded as being naked. Crabs, cockroaches, snails and cockles have ordered around them a crusty habiliment, wherein their original nakedness is only to be discovered by force, and other creatures have similarly provided themselves with some species of covering. Clothing, therefore, is not an art, but an instinct, and the fact that man is born naked and does not grow his clothing upon himself from within but collects it from various distant and haphazard sources is not any reason to call this necessity an instinct for decency. These, you will admit, are weighty reflections and worthy of consideration before we proceed to the wide and thorny subject of moral and immoral action.[17]

At the Threshold of the Lunar Cycle and the Path of the Moon

Ancient Ones Cards 10 through 20

The Path of the Moon

Circles or wheels mark turning points in initiatory processes. Situated at points in space and time where the clockwise solar sphere reverses its turning to lead into the counter-clockwise lunar sphere, the cards arrive at the center of the infinity sign, the still point of the turning worlds. This is the very point that ancient civilizations identified with any mystical center.

The path of the sun expanded outward toward learning and adapting, as well as understanding how to manipulate the material world; yet nearly every intelligent individual turns inward at some point, whether at mid-life or in Spiritual question, asking what it all means, striving for new insights, or even preparing for the inevitability of death.

The path of the moon is the descent — perhaps the most important part of the psychic journey. Beyond the threshold represented by the Roth Grian card lie the real meanings of life and death, locked in the graphic language of the lunar sphere or the unconscious.

Now the Cuardaitheoir, the Neophyte, prepares for the ordeals of Initiation into Spiritual rebirth through alchemical transmutation. On the path of the moon the neophyte endures death and resurrection and faces the horned God and receives the Waters of Life from Dana. The successful accomplishment of this Initiation is depicted by the symbolic "lightning struck Tower." From this ordeal, we realize that the Cuardaitheoir has been initiated through the opening of his or her Crown Center at the top of the head by the Fire in the Head or inner Radiant Power.

The newly awakened one returns precipitously to Mother Earth. The Apotheosis of the initiate is signaled by the enjoyment of the spheres of moon, sun, and stars. The Beatific Vision is given whereby the Two Goddesses of Sun and Moon are seen Unveiled. The Máthair Bandia Eiré has shed her Crown and Robes and is revealed as the illuminated Love Goddess—Réalta Dana—and above her is the constellation of Taurus, with the seven stars of the Hyades, with the Red Eye of the Bull, Aldebaran. She is the Source and pours forth the Waters of Life.

10

ROTH GRIAN

The Sun Wheel

Meaning

The door to the UnderWorld has opened. Travel down into the roots of the Tree of Life, to sojourn into the new world—the ancient world—of Faery. Awareness must now turn inward. Attention need now be given to your inner self. Who are you? From where have you come? To where are you going? These are the questions for which answers may be found in the realm of Tir na n'Og. You stand on the threshold that leads into the darkest part of your soul, but should you willingly travel there, you will find the greatest light—the inner radiant fire, the Solar Fire, of your Spirit.

Card Description

We stand at the entrance into an ancient cairn located at Loughcrew, Co. Meath, Ireland, stretching over three hills about a mile apart, also known as Carnbane. There are about thirty passage graves dating from 3000 B.C.E. Cairn T has been shown to be a calendar, the outer alignments giving a reading for each day of the year.

Inside Cairn T are three compartments, one to either side—depicted in the illustration as dark openings—and one compartment located straight back, which can be seen from the entrance. A sun wheel carving is on the back wall. Each spoke of the sun wheel contains an ogham appropriate to its corresponding time of year. The sun wheel is like a door that is slightly open, and a golden light shines out.

Oghams, Alphabets, and Symbols

For border oghams, see The Border Oghams of the Ancient Ones Cards on page 250; however, all of the border oghams are also found on the Sun Wheel.

Heliolatry, or sun worship, was a common practice among the Celts, judging by the abundance of solar motifs, although there is little direct evidence of a sun cult in the myths and sagas. There are references to obvious sun deities such as Mac Gréine (son of the sun), who was the husband of Eire, who gave her name to Ireland. The god Bilé was known as "the shining one," and his feast on Beltaine (May 1) was obviously connected with a sun cult at one time. On Mount Callan, near Ennis, a sun altar stands where the Beltaine festival was celebrated on midsummer's day down to 1895. Near Macroom is a standing stone called "stone of the sun," while Seathrún Céitinn claimed that many of the dolmens associated with Gráinne were, in fact, originally connected with Gréine the sun. Among the various sun references in Irish, we have Giolla Gréine, whose mother was a sunbeam.

Beginning at the top of the sun wheel, the first ogham is Ailm, the Station of the Winter Solstice, December 21, Season of Rebirth and the Time of Repose.

Moving sunwise or deosil, the second ogham is Luis, which marks the quickening of the year, the coming of spring, representing the important Celtic feast of Oimlec, or Imbolc, the day of Brigid, also called Lady's Day, on February 2.

The third ogham is Ohn, the Station of Spring Equinox, March 21, Season of Spring and the Time of Birth. The fourth ogham, Saille, is the sacred moon month of the goddess, containing her wedding day to the god—La Baal Tinne, or May Day, May 1.

The ogham at the bottom of the sun wheel is Ur, Station of the Summer Solstice, June 21, Season of Summer and the Time of Growth. The sixth ogham is Tinne, containing the Great Festival of Lughnasadh, August 1.

The seventh ogham, halfway up the left side of the sun wheel, is Eadha, Station of the Autumnal Equinox, September 21, Season of Autumn and the Time of Decline. The final and eighth ogham is Ngetal, containing the festival of the dead, or Samhain, October 31, marking the ending of the Celtic year.

Faery Lore

All myths constructed by a primitive people are symbols, and if we can discover what it is that they symbolize we have a valuable clue to the Spiritual character, and sometimes even to the history, of the people from whom they sprang. The meaning of the Danann myth as it appears in the Bardic literature, though it has undergone much distortion before it reached us, is perfectly clear. The Dananns represent the Celtic reverence for science, poetry, and artistic skill, blended, of course, with the earlier conception of the divinity of the powers of Light. In their combat with the Firbolgs the victory of the intellect over dullness and ignorance is plainly portrayed—the comparison of the heavy, blunt weapon of the Firbolgs with the light and penetrating spears of the People of Dana is an indication that it is impossible to mistake. Again, in their struggle with a far more powerful and dangerous enemy, the Fomorians, we see the combat of the powers of Light with evil of a more positive kind than that represented by the Firbolgs. The Fomorians stand not for mere dullness or stupidity, but for the forces of tyranny, cruelty, and greed—for moral rather than for intellectual darkness.

But the myth of the struggle of the Dananns with the sons of Miled is more difficult to interpret. How does it come that the lords of light and beauty, wielding all the powers of thought (represented by magic and sorcery), succumbed to a human race, and were dispossessed by them of their hard-won inheritance? What is the meaning of this shrinking of their powers which at once took place when the Milesians came on the scene? The Milesians were not on the side of the powers of darkness. They were guided by Amorgen, a clear embodiment of the idea of poetry and thought. They were regarded with the utmost veneration, and the dominant families of Ireland all traced their descent to them. Was the Kingdom of Light, then, divided against itself? Or, if not, to what conception in the Irish mind are we to trace the myth of the Milesian invasion and victory?

We can suppose that the Milesian myth originated at a much later time than the others, and was, in its main features, the product of Christian influences. The People of Dana were in possession of the country, but they were pagan divinities—they could not stand for the progenitors of a Christian Ireland. They had somehow or other to be gotten rid of, and a race of less embarrassing antecedents substituted for them. So the Milesians were fetched from the region that is modern Spain and endowed with the main characteristics, only more humanized, of the People of Dana. But the latter, in contradistinction to the usual attitude of early Christianity, are treated very tenderly in the story of their overthrow. One of them has the honor of giving her name to the island, the brutality of one of the conquerors toward them is punished with death, and while dispossessed of the lordship of the soil they still enjoy life in the fair world, which by their magic art they have made invisible to mortals. They are no longer gods, but they are more than human, and frequent instances occur in which they are shown as coming forth from their fairy world, being embraced in the Christian fold, and entering into heavenly bliss. The strange and beautiful tale of the Transformation of the Children of Lir is one such example, as is the Tale of Ethné; these, taken together with numerous other legendary incidents that might be quoted, illustrate well the attitude of the early Celtic Christians—in Ireland, at least—towards the divinities of the older faith.[18]

What this infers to the meaning of the Sun Wheel card is that the wheels of life will swing from one extreme to the other. To get back to the source, or origin, one must enter the UnderWorld of any current religion or civilization to understand what has been denigrated beneath it; for therein lies the ancient wisdom, the ancient ways, the sometimes, but not always, lost and forgotten memories.

ㄱ

RÚNDAIGNE
BANBA
Strength of Will

Meaning

The Mother Goddess' love will lead you into the UnderWorld of your soul. She will guide you to your inner radiant light, where you will tame the wild beast within yourself, thereby enacting a psychic healing and imbuing you with inner strength. Don't be afraid to face your fears.

Card Description

Banba stands by a Holy Well located in the Sliev Mis range. She wears a blue gown, edged with gold, and has long, golden hair. The cavern, containing the well, is built into the side of a hill.

Two Celtic dogs are painted on the stone face of the well. The one closest to Banba has its jowls open, and Banba rests her hand just above his open mouth. On top of the well is a burning candle.

Before the well is the stream from the mountains that feeds into the well. Scattered about the area are small piles of stones. In the background is a Guardian tree; red votive offerings dangle from the branches.

Overhead, a Full Moon shines brightly, illuminating the landscape as if it were day. The sky reflects the typical Celtic twilight.

Oghams, Alphabets, and Symbols

For border oghams, see The Border Oghams of the Ancient Ones Cards on page 250.

The Irish Book of Invasions alludes to Banba as one of the three eponymous goddesses of Ireland, the other two being Érié and Fotla. Banba has been used over the centuries as one of the symbols for "Mother Ireland." She is one of the three goddesses who each exact from the Sons of Mil the promise that the island will bear her name. Banba was the wife of Mac Cuill, a member of the Tuatha De Danann.[19] Banba represents the sovereignty and Spirit of Ireland.

The strongest belief in Ireland is a belief in the curative power of the Holy Wells that are scattered about the country, fountains of health and healing that at one time were either blessed by one of the Irish goddesses, or by which some goddess had dwelt in the far-off ancient times, or, in the more current history, some saint had either blessed or had dwelt by.

Two aspects of wells caused them to be endowed with sanctity. One involves underground forces, whereby wells were perceived as a means of communicating with the UnderWorld, as a link between the upper and lower worlds. The second concerns water symbolism. Thus, wells represent similar symbolism to that of pits, but with the additional dimension of water.

Insular stories link wells with hazel trees, sacred salmon, and the UnderWorld. In a legend of the Irish hero Finn, he acquires wisdom from an OtherWorld well. Wells were still regarded as holy in Christian times.

The veneration of water, in the form of rivers and wells, was dominant in ancient Celtic society. Like many aspects of the landscape, with which the Celts felt at one, wells were formed by the deities, and each well had its own indwelling Spirit.

Those who did not observe the taboos connected with wells, even though they be deities themselves, could be in trouble. The Well of Segais rose up and drowned Boann, and the path it made chasing her became the Boyne. In medieval times, as reflected in certain legends, the Spirits of the wells were still there. Indeed, veneration at wells could not be stamped out by the new Christian religion. Therefore, it was adapted to it. Pope Gregory, writing in A.D. 601, told the missionaries of the church not to destroy the pre-Christian sites of worship, but to bless them and convert them from "the worship of devils to the service of the true God." Therefore, throughout the Celtic lands, Holy Wells that were once the sites of pagan veneration still survive.

Because water is the symbol of the gateway into the Land of Faery, divination by water scrying was used. It is best to water scry during the Full Moon outdoors near a Holy Well.

Whenever a whitethorn or an ash tree, such as in this card, shadows the place, the well is held to be peculiarly sacred; and on leaving, having first drunk of the water, a pilgrim would tie a votive offering to the branches—generally a colored handkerchief, a bright red strip cut from a garment, or a ribbon tied around a lock of the pilgrim's own hair. These offerings were never removed; they would remain for years fluttering in the wind and the rain. They are signs and tokens of gratitude to the Patron of the Well.

The candle flame atop the well symbolizes the inner light one will find if they willingly enter into the UnderWorld of their soul.

Animals and birds were considered sacred and were often used to represent the Ancient Ones. Shapeshifting was a common attribute of the Celtic goddesses and gods. These semi-mythological characters, who adopted the form of an animal, were soon turned into art.

Zoomorphic and anthropomorphic ornaments are symbols that show us that nothing is as it first appears. Often, such artwork looks like a beautiful mosaic of miscellaneous design and color until, upon closer examination, one identifies a head, or a tail, or a plant, all interwoven with each other. These intricate patterns first appeared in Bronze Age art of Ireland. Artisans fashioned them into a complicated contortion of bodies, but they kept the motif logical and conforming with nature.

In both Classical and Celtic mythology and religion, dogs possessed composite symbolism in which the animals could represent hunting, healing, and death. The significance of the hunt speaks for itself, but healing symbolism is derived from the belief that the saliva of the animal contains curative properties. The death role may come from observation of the dog's carrion habits.

In the archaeology of Celtic religion, dogs are featured in two distinct ways: in the iconography they appear as companions of many different divinities; and dogs were buried with a specific set of rituals, attesting, perhaps, their chthonic symbolism.

As hunting companions, dogs have the dual role of aggressive fighter and guardian of their masters, and it is as protectors that the creatures frequently appear in the iconography.

On this card, the dogs accompany an Irish Mother goddess. They possess a combined healing and UnderWorld role. In their Under-World role they are the wild beast within ourselves that must be tamed, and in their healing role, they symbolize our own ability to restore balance and harmony to our psyche after venturing into the UnderWorld of our soul.

At many of the ancient wells in Ireland, quantities of beautiful white stones were found that glittered in the sun. They were highly esteemed and valued as pieces of star dust that had fallen to earth upon the arrival of the Tuatha De Danann. These white stones were used to build many of the prayer monuments found throughout the country. The stones represent a keen link to the Land of Faery and have instantly thinned the veil between this world and that, so instantly that the soft, exquisite music of the Faery has been known to rise from the water of many of the wells. When a pilgrim is so favored by the Faery as to receive such an intimate connection, that person is warned to remain quiet and humble, for any loud noise, such as the clapping of hands or joyous laughter, will instantly still the music and cause the stone cairn to fall.

Faery Lore

"There are seven Wells of Peace. Four you found long since, blind dreamer; and of one you had the sweet, cool water a brief while ago; and the other is where your hour waits; and the seventh is under the rainbow."

"The Wells of Peace," he muttered, "which I have dreamed of—which I have dreamed of through tears and longing, and old, familiar pain, and sorrow too deep for words."

"Even so, poet and dreamer, you too have been blind, for all your seeing eyes and wonder-woven brain and passionate dreams," said the nymph of the well.

"Tell me! What are the four Wells of Peace I have already passed and drunken of and not known?"

"They are called 'Love,' 'Beauty,' 'Dream,' and 'Endurance.'"

The pilgrim bowed his head. Tears dimmed his eyes.

"Art," he whispered, "art, bitter, bitter waters were those that I drank in that fourth Well of Peace. For I knew not the waters were sweet, then., And even now, even now, my heart faints at that shadowy well."

"It is the Well of Strength, and its waters rise out of that of Love, which you found so passing sweet."

"And what is that of which I drank a brief while ago?"

"It was in the Glen of the Willows. You felt its cool breath when you turned and went back to that poor, outcast woman, and saw her sorrow, and looked into the eyes of the little one. And you drank of it when you gave the woman peace. It is the well where the Son of God sits forever, dreaming His dream. It is called 'Compassion.'"

And so, the man thought, he had been at the Well of Peace that is called Compassion, and not known it.

"Tell me, Art, what are the sixth and seventh?"

"The sixth is where your hour waits. It is the Well of Rest; deep, deep sleep; deep, deep rest; balm for the weary brain, the weary heart, the Spirit that hath had weariness for comrade and loneliness as a bride. It is a small well that, and shunned of men, for its portals are those of the grave, and the soft breath of it steals up through brown earth and the ancient, dreadful quiet of the UnderWorld."

"And the seventh? That which is under the rainbow in the West?"

"My man, you know the old, ancient tales. Once, years ago, I heard you tell that of Ulad the Lonely. Do you remember what was the word on the lips of his dream when, after long years, he saw her again when both met at last under the rainbow?"

"Ay, for sure. It was the word of triumph, of joy, the whisper of peace: "There is but one love.""

"When you hear that, and from the lips of her whom you have loved and love, then you shall be standing by the Seventh Well."

They spoke no more, but moved slowly onward through the dusk. The sound of the sea deepened. The inland breadth rose, as on a vast wing, but waned, and passed like perishing smoke against the starry regions in the gulfs above.

When the moon sank behind the ridge-set mountains, and darkness oozed out of every thicket and shadowy place, and drowned the black green boughs and branches in a massed obscurity, the man turned.

His quest was over . . . or just beginning. Not beyond those crested hills, nor by the running wave on the shore, whose voice filled the night as though it were the dark whorl of a mighty shell: not there, nor in this nor that far place, were the Wells of Peace.

Love, Beauty, Dream, Endurance, Compassion, Rest, Love Fulfilled; for sure the Wells of Peace were not far from home.[20]

12

CROCHADÓIR AMORGEN

The Hangman

Meaning

Consider marrying yourself to the Earth Mother, or becoming her lover. In doing so, you will develop a more intimate relationship with the natural world. This will bring forth the power of abundance. The natural world shall then come alive and you will see the magick of the earth shining up from the soil, illuminating rocks and trees, as the aura of the vital life force in the universe. Magick is change; no need to sacrifice anything—sacrifice implies martyrdom or victimhood, extremes of emotion. Change, however, is the recognition that mind and heart are aligned with Spirit; thus, reprioritizing is initiated willingly. Magick can become a daily occurrence.

Card Description

An ancient oak tree frames the left side of the card, with three stepping pegs in the shape of Uinllean ogham, but upside down. Hanging by one foot, from one of the tree's branches, is a dolly. Directly beneath the dolly, the Celtic or Milesian Bard, Amorgen, wearing a blue cloak, is kneeling. Amorgen, son of Mil, was a warrior and poet who pronounced the first judgment in Ireland and decided that Eremon should be the first Milesian king of the country. Three poems are accredited to him. The first is his famous and extraordinary incantation to Ireland (following on page 316), in which he subsumes everything into his own being. The philosophical outlook of this poem parallels the Hindu concepts in the *Bhagavadgita*.

A second Amorgen appears in Irish myth in the person of the father of Conall Cearnach and foster father to the poet Athairne. He also is a poet, and during Bricriu's Feast he boasts of his valor, wisdom, fortune, and eloquence.

Here, Amorgen is the Milesian bard. He holds the shaft of his sword, he has stuck the blade into the land. Behind him are freshly harvested fields of haystacks. The sky is a clear blue—a beautiful summer day.

The Milesians were considered to be the fifth wave of invaders of Ireland. With them, we have the beginning of the Celtic race in Ireland.

The idea that Celtica was ever inhabited by a single pure and homogeneous race must be dismissed. The true Celts were a tall, fair race, warlike and masterful, whose place of origin (as far as can be traced) was somewhere around the sources of the Danube. They spread their dominion both by conquest and by peaceful infiltration over Mid-Europe, Gaul, Spain, and the British Islands—among which is Ireland. They did not exterminate the original prehistoric inhabitants of these regions—paleolithic and neolithic races, dolmen-builders, and workers in bronze—but they imposed on them their language, their arts, and their traditions, taking, no doubt, a good deal from them in return, especially, in the important matter of religion. Among these races the true Celts formed an aristocratic and ruling caste. In that capacity they stood, alike in Gaul, in Spain, in Britain, and in Ireland, in the forefront of armed opposition to foreign invasion. They bore the worst brunt of war, of confiscations, and of banishment. They never lacked valor, but they were not strong enough or united enough to prevail, and they perished in far greater proportion than the earlier populations whom they had subjugated. But they also disappeared by mingling their blood with these inhabitants, whom they impregnated with many of their own noble and virile qualities. Hence it comes that the characteristics of the peoples called Celtic in the present day, and who carry on the Celtic tradition and language, are in some respects quite different from those of the Celts of classical history and the Celts who produced the literature and art of ancient Ireland, and in others so strikingly similar. To take a physical characteristic alone, the more Celtic districts of the British Islands are at present marked by darkness of complexion, hair, etc. They are not very dark, but they are darker than the rest of the kingdom. But the true Celts were certainly fair. Even the Irish Celts of the twelfth century are described by Giraldus Cambrensis as a fair race.[21]

Oghams, Alphabets, and Symbols

For border oghams, see The Border Oghams of the Ancient Ones Cards on page 250.

The reversed Uinllean represents the ancient wisdom of the Celts, brought to Ireland in the form of magick (the three stepping pegs on the tree), in the form of religion. The nature of this religion of magick was a potent element in the formation of the body of myths and legends which come from Celtic Ireland.

The religious, philosophic, and scientific culture superintended by the Druids is spoken of by Caesar with much respect. "They discuss and impart to the youth," he wrote, "many things respecting the stars and their motions, respecting the extent of the universe and of our earth, respecting the nature of things, respecting the power and the majesty of the immortal gods" (bk. vi 14).

The teachings of the Druids were an area of interest to many scholars. But the Druids, though well acquainted with letters, strictly forbade the committal of their doctrines to writing; an extremely sagacious provision, for not only did they surround their teaching with an atmosphere of mystery that exercises so potent a spell over the human mind, but they ensured that it could never be effectively controverted.

We, however, distinguish five distinct factors in the religious and intellectual culture of Celtic lands as we find them prior to the influx of classical or Christian influences. First, there is a mass of popular superstitions and of magickal observances, possibly including human sacrifice. These varied from place to place, centering as they did largely on local features regarded as embodiments or vehicles of divine or diabolic power.

Second, there was certainly a thoughtful and philosophic creed in existence, having as its central object of worship the Sun as an emblem of divine power and constancy, and as its central doctrine the immortality of the soul.

Third, there was a worship of personified deities, conceived as representing natural forces, or as guardians of social laws. Fourth, the Romans were deeply impressed with the existence among the Druids of a body of teaching of a quasi-scientific nature about natural phenomena and the constitution of the universe, the details of which we unfortunately know little. Last, there is the prevalence of a sacerdotal organization, which administered the system of religious and secular learning and literature, which carefully confined this learning to a privileged caste, and which, by virtue of its intellectual supremacy and of the atmosphere of religious awe with which it was surrounded, became the sovereign power, social, political, and religious, in every Celtic country.[22]

The hanged dolly represents the Ancient Ones, who willingly sacrificed their domain, Ireland, to the Celts, or mortals, as their intellectual evolution began to separate them from the gods. This connection—that humankind must remain connected to the Spirit of land, for therein the Ancient Ones dwelled—was retained by the magickal religion of the Druids, as represented by Amorgen's pledge of sovereignty to Érié, or the Goddess of the land.

The freshly harvested haystacks symbolize the abundance the gods of the land will continue to give humans as long as this connection is maintained.

Amorgen's deep blue cloak shows that one must be deeply connected through spiritual emotion to the Earth Mother to be able to see, know, and receive the natural abundance of the gods.

Faery Lore

As he set his right foot upon Ireland, Amorgen Glúingel s. Mil spoke this poem:

I am Wind on Sea,
I am Ocean-wave,
I am Roar of Sea,
I am Bull of Seven Flights,
I am Vulture on Cliff,

I am Dewdrop,
I am Fairest of Flowers,
I am Boar for Boldness,
I am Salmon in Pool,
I am Lake on Plain,
I am a Mountain in a Man,
I am a Word of Skill,
I am the Point of a Weapon (that poureth forth combat),
I am God who fashioneth Fire for a Head.
    [i.e. a giver of inspiration.]
Who smootheth the ruggedness of a mountain?
Who is He who announceth the ages of the Moon?
And who, the place where falleth the sunset?
Who calleth the cattle from the House of Tethys?
On whom do the cattle of Tethys smile?
    [i.e. the stars rising out of the sea.]
Who is the troop, who the god who fashioneth edges in a
    fortress of gangrene?
Enchantments about a spear? Enchantments of Wind[23]

Item Amorgen cecinit—

A fishful sea!
A fruitful land!
An outburst of fish!
Fish under wave,
In streams (as) of birds,
A rough sea!

A white hail
With hundreds of salmon,
Of broad whales!
A harbour-song—
"An outburst of fish,
A fishful sea!"

At the end of three days and three nights thereafter the Sons of Mil broke the battle of Sliab Mis against demons and Fomoraig, that is, against the Tuatha De Danann. (For the colloquy with Banba, Fotla, and Érié, see Máthair Bandia Érié card on page 271.)

The sons of Mil and of Bregon went on, until they were in Druim Chain, that is, Temair. The three kings of Ireland—Mac Cúill, Mac Cécht, and Mac Gréine—were there. They pronounced judgment against the sons of Mil that they should have the island to the end of three days, free from assault, from assembly of battle, or from giving of hostages; for they were assured that they (the invaders) would not return, because druids would make spells behind them, so that they should not be able to come again. We shall adjudge it, said Mac Cúill s. Cermat, as Amorgen your own judge shall pronounce to you; for if he should give a false judgment, he [*aliter*, you] would die at our hands. Give the judgment, Amorgen, said Eber Donn. I pronounce it; said Amorgen. Let this island be left to them. How far shall we go? said Eber. Past just nine waves, said Amorgen. This is the first judgment given Ireland. Amorgen cecinit—

Men, seeking a possession!
Over nine great green-shouldered waves,
Ye shall not go, unless with powerful gods!
Be it settled swiftly! Be battle permitted!

I adjust the possession
Of the land to which ye have come;
If ye like it, adjudge the right,
If ye like it not, adjudge it not—
I say it not to you, except with your good will.[24]

13

BEAN SIDHE
CAILLEACH

The Banshee Crone

Meaning

The cycles of life are spinning around you. Do not fear the soul's transformation. Be open to the change and see it as an opportunity rather than a disillusionment. The keening voice of the wind may foretell of distant death—but the summer must die into autumn and autumn into winter and winter will eventually rebirth into spring, for that is the way of nature.

Card Description

A Bean Sidhe washes bloody garments in a stream. Her white hair seems to be standing on end. She has blue skin and fiery red eyes. Her mouth is wide open with keening. A gray cloak covers her green gown. The landscape around the Bean Sidhe is gray and dismal. The sky is stormy, angry, purple. The trees are bare.

In the foreground stands the Crone Goddess, who holds a purple sphere in her hands. She wears a black gown, trimmed with purple, and a Triple Goddess priestess band across her brow. On her right hand she wears a ring on her pointer finger. Autumn leaves are in her hair. Like the Bean Sidhe, but not as fiery, the Crone's eyes are a purple-red.

Oghams, Alphabets, and Symbols

For border oghams, see The Border Oghams of the Ancient Ones Cards on page 250.

The Triple Goddess sign—new crescent, full moon, waning crescent—symbolizes the three phases of life: birth, death, and rebirth, reminding us that to be born in this physical incarnation means to one day surrender the physical body back to the elemental world.

The color purple is prominent in this card. In ancient Irish the color purple is called *huath* or terrible, and considered the forbidden color of the hag. Huath is also the sixth character of the ogham alphabet connected to the moon month from May 13 to June 9. As an ogham of the UnderWorld, Huath has the healing properties of balancing the blood, nerves, and Spirit. The hawthorn or whitethorn is this ogham's tree. The destruction of an ancient hawthorn tree in Ireland was considered to be extremely unlucky; thus, huath is an unlucky ogham.

Magickally, by working with hawthorn or calling upon the Hag such as the Cailleach, one can become protected against all ills, for you are invoking the power of the UnderWorld.

The Crone is the Goddess of the UnderWorld in Irish tradition, and is connected with the Transmigration of the Soul. The purple sphere she holds in her hands represents the transmutation that the soul undergoes from lifetime to lifetime.

The transmigration of the soul is a basic pre-Christian belief among the ancient Celts. Souls migrated from the Land of the Living to the Land of the Dead and vice versa. They also migrated through various births. Not only could people be reborn as other people, they could go through various changes. Fintan survived the Deluge by changing into a salmon.

Many ancient writers assert that the Celtic idea of immortality embodied the Oriental conception of the transmigration of souls, and to account for this the hypothesis was invented that they had learned the doctrine from Pythagoras, who represented it in classical antiquity. Thus Diodorus:

> Among them the doctrine of Pythagoras prevails, according to which the souls of men are immortal, and after a fixed term recommence to live, taking upon themselves a new body.

Now traces of this doctrine certainly appear in Irish legend. Thus the Irish chieftain, Mongan, who is a historical personage whose death is recorded about A.D. 625, is said to have made a wager as to the place of death of a king named Fothad, slain in a battle with the mythical hero Finn Mac Cumhal in the third century. He proves his case by summoning to his aid a revenant from the OtherWorld, Keelta, who was the actual slayer of Fothad, and who describes correctly where the tomb is to be found and what its contents were. He begins this tale by saying to Monga, "We were with thee," and then, turning to the assembly, he continues: "We were with Finn, coming from Alba. . . ."

"Hush," says Mongan, "it is wrong of thee to reveal a secret." The secret is, of course, that Mongan was a reincarnation of Finn.[25] But the evidence on the whole shows that the Celts did not hold this doctrine at all in the same way as Pythagoras and the Orientals did. Transmigration was not, with them, part of the order of things. It might happen, but in general it did not; the new body assumed by the dead clothed them in another, not in this world, and so far as we can learn from any ancient authority, there does not appear to have been any idea of moral retribution connected with this form of the future life. It was not so much an article of faith as an idea that haunted the imagination, and that, as Mongan's caution indicates, ought not to be brought into clear light.

In the vernacular literature, life after death in the happy Other-World, rebirth, and regeneration are important belief systems that run as a strong thread through the mythology. Manannan was associated with rebirth; and there is frequently confusion as to which events belong to the world of earth and which belong to the supernatural OtherWorld.

Faery Lore

Popularly known in English as *banshee,* the term literally means "woman of the hills," or, in modern usage, "women of the fairies." After the Ancient Ones went underground and were transformed, in popular thought, to fairies, the banshee became a female fairy attached to a particular family; she warned of approaching death by giving an eerie wail.

Many have seen her as she goes wailing and clapping her hands. The keen, the funeral cry of the peasantry, is said to be an imitation of her cry. When more than one banshee is present, and they wail and sing in chorus, it is for the death of some holy or great one. An omen that sometimes accompanies the banshee is the *coiste-bodhar,* the coach-a-bower, an immense black coach mounted by a coffin and drawn by headless horses driven by a dullahan. It will go rumbling to your door, and if you open it, a basin of blood will be thrown in your face. These headless phantoms are found in places other than Ireland. In 1807, two of the sentries stationed outside St. James Park died of fright. A headless woman, the upper part of her body naked, used to pass at midnight and scale the railings. After a time, the sentries were no longer stationed at the haunted spot. In Norway, the heads of corpses were cut off to make their ghosts feeble. Thus came into existence the Dullahans, perhaps; unless, indeed, they are descended from that Irish giant who swam across the Channel with his head in his teeth.[26]

A Lamentation: for the Death of Sir Maurice Fitzgerald, Knight of Kerry, who was killed in Flanders, 1642.

> *There was lifted up one voice of woe,*
> *   One lament of more than mortal grief,*
> *Though the wide South to and fro,*
> *   For a fallen-Chief.*
> *In the dead of night that cry thrilled through me,*
> *   I looked out upon the midnight air!*
> *My own soul was all as gloomy,*
> *   As I knelt in prayer.*
>
> *O'er Loch Gur, that night, once-twice-yea, thrice-*
> *   Passed a wail of anguish for the Brave*
> *The half curled into ice*
> *   Its moon-mirroring wave.*

Then uprose a many-toned wild hymn in
  Choral swell from Ogra's dark ravine,
And Mogeely's Phantom Women
  Mourned the Geraldine!

Far on Cara Mona's emerald plains
  Shrieks and sighs were blended many hours,
And Fermoy in fitful strains
  Answered from her towers.
Youghal, Keenalmeaky, Eemokilly,
  Mourned in concert, and their piercing keen
Woke to wondering life the stilly
  Glens of Inchiqueen.

From Loughmoe to yellow Dunanore
  There was fear; the traders of Tralee
Gathered up their golden store,
  And prepared to flee;
For, in ship and hall from night till morning,
  Showed the first faint beamings of the sun,
All the foreigners heard the warning
  Of the Dreaded One!

"This," they spake, "portendeth death to us,
  If we fly not swiftly from our fate!"
Self-conceited idiots! thus
  Ravingly to prate!
Not for base-born higgling Saxon trucksters
  Ring laments like those by shore and sea!
Not for churls with souls like hucksters
  Waileth our Banshee!

For the high Milesian race alone
  Ever flows the music of her woe!
For slain heir to bygone throne,
  And for Chief laid low!
Hark! . . . Again, methinks, I hear her weeping
  Yonder! Is she near me now, as then?
Or was but the night-wind sweeping
  Down the hollow glen?27

14

UISCE
COISRIC̄THE
The Holy Waters

Meaning

The holy waters of healing can wash away the past of pain; give your-self to the opportunity of true love; hold back no longer; find the com-patible; release what only exists in agitation; while you are being asked to trust, this does not imply blind faith, but rather faith in the law of the Goddess, which is Love.

Card Description

The high priestess of Brigid (see Bansagart Ard Brigid, page 266) is veiled. Over the white veil she wears a crescent moon diadem. From two chalices, she pours the holy waters into the healing water already contained in the hollow of a bullaun stone.

Behind rises the Teltown mound,[28] where trial marriages were per-formed in pagan Ireland. A canopy, surrounded by a Faery Ring of flowers, designate the place of union.

Oghams, Alphabets, and Symbols

For border oghams, see The Border Oghams of the Ancient Ones Cards on page 250.

Teltown, named after Tailtiu, wife of Eochaid Mac Eirce, king of Ireland, is perhaps one of the more important symbols in this card. Teltown was anciently an assembly center. Tailtiu had organized the clearing of the forest of Cill Cuan that was formerly here, and her dying request had been that games would be held every year to commemorate her. These were held from earliest times until around A.D. 1770. Revived in the twentieth century, they are currently in abeyance again. The games at Teltown were held around the First of August, that being the Feast of Lughnasa (Lugh was Tailtiu's foster son). The ancient assembly was known as Aonach Tailten.

In another context, Amorgen, the Milesian, is said to have fought against the Tuatha De Danann here in 500 B.C.E. Banba, Queen of the De Danann, was slain at this battle by Caicher. Also slain were her sister Érié, and Fotla, killed by Eaden, a Milesian chieftain.

At a later date it is recorded that in A.D. 944 King Congalach and his warriors saw a ship floating by in the air high above. They saw one of the crew cast a dart at a salmon that was also floating by. The dart fell to the ground and the crewman was held by Congalach's men but when the "king of the ship" appeared they let him go. The ship and crew disappeared.[29]

Bullaun stones, or basin-stones, were associated with numerous ritual sites, including wells. Some of the larger bullauns were certainly mortars, and very similar "knocking stones" were used until recent times for preparing barley meal by pounding the grain with a beetle or maul. Old specimens, more especially when the basins are sunk in an outcrop of rock, are frequently found to hold water, and they are then regarded as wells, the water being held efficacious as a cure for warts, fertility, or other maladies. That such rock-basins have magick powers is illustrated by the following reference to a site at Clonegal Castle, Eniscorthy, Ireland. In the back of the castle a bullaun, such as depicted in this card, does exist, and its water has been commented as curing cancer.

The pouring and mingling of the waters symbolizes that when true love is joined together, such love is no longer separate. Think on this:

unlike vinegar and oil, which must be kept in a state of agitation to remain blended, water and water, when poured together, blends so completely that one can never identify water "A" from water "B"; that is as relationships ought to be.

Faery Lore

Come to my life that is already yours, and at one with you:
Come to my blood that leaps because of you,
Come to my heart that holds you. . .
Come to my heart that holds you as the green earth clasps and
*   holds the sunlight,*
Come to me! Come to me. . . .

And, too, why does the common familiar bow that is set in the heavens thrill us in each new apparition as though it were a sudden stairway to all lost or dreamed-of Edens? . . . A rainbow rises with vast, unbroken sweep, a skyey flower fed from the innumerous hues of sunset woven this way and that on the looms of the sea. And I know that I have never seen a rainbow before, and of all that I may see I may never see another again as I have seen this. Yet it is a rainbow as others are, and have been and will be for all time past and to come (see Breithiúnas, page 348).

One hears everywhere that passion is but dissatisfied desire, that love is but a fever. So, too, as I have heard, the moles, which can see in twilight and amid the earthly glooms they inhabit, cannot see the stars even as shining points upon the branches of the trees, nor these moving branches even, nor their wind-lifted shadows.

Their love did not diminish, but grew, through tragic circumstances. As endurance became harder—for love deepened and passion became as the bird of prey that God sets famished in the wilderness, while the little and great things of common life came in upon this love like a tide—it seemed to each that they only withdrew the more into that which was for them not the most great thing in life, but life.

When, at last, the end came—a tragic, an almost incredible end, perhaps, for love did not change, passion was not slain, but translated to a starry dream, and every sweet and lovely intercourse was there still—the suffering was too great to be borne. Yet neither death nor tragic mischance came with veiled healing.

Love can come, not in his mortal but in his immortal guise: as a Spirit of flame. There is no alchemy of life which can change that tameless and fierce thing, that power more intense than fire, that creature whose breath consumes what death only silences.

Love is more great than we conceive, and Death is the keeper of unknown redemption.[30]

15

AIBHIRSEOIR
CERNUNNOS
The Old One

Meaning

Which god do you follow? Perhaps one or the other. Perhaps both. Perhaps neither. Be aware of your own desires. Find the innocence within your heart. Reunite with the fecundity of nature. Merge with the law of Love. There is peace. Open yourself to it and find the blessings of the Ancient Ones.

Card Description

The Celtic Horned God, Cernunnos, sits in the forefront, in traditional portrayal. Behind him rises the figure of Christ. To either side of the gods are pillars bearing inscriptions in ancient Gaelic alphabet. The pillar to the left of the gods bears the cross, while the pillar to the right of the gods bears the chalice.

Oghams, Alphabets, and Symbols

For border oghams, see The Border Oghams of the Ancient Ones Cards on page 250. See figure 5, page 23, for the Gaelic inscriptions.

The name Cernunnos means "horned" or "peaked one." On a monument dedicated by Parisian sailors in the reign of Tiberius, the name is inscribed above the head and shoulders of a balding, bearded, elderly god wearing antlers, with a torc, or neck ring, hanging from each one. In addition to the antlers, the god has the ears of a stag. Although the association of name and antlered image occurs only on this one monument, Cernunnos has served to identify numerous other images of an antlered deity that occur before and during the Romano-Celtic period in the Celtic world.

Cernunnos is remarkable in that, unlike most Celtic divinities, he appears in the pre-Roman, free Celtic period. The earliest recorded manifestation is on a fourth century B.C.E. rock carving at Paspardo in Camonica Valley in North Italy, where an antlered god bears a torc on each arm and is accompanied by a ram-horned snake and a small ithy-phallic being. On the Gundestrup Cauldron, which could date as early as the fourth to third century B.C.E., Cernunnos appears cross-legged, with two twisted torcs and antlers. He is accompanied by a stag, a ram-horned snake and other creatures.

Cernunnos is one of the most striking examples of a semi-zoomor-phic Celtic god, perhaps one of those beings who regularly underwent transmogrification or shape-shifting from human to animal form, which is mentioned frequently in myth. His close affinity with his for-est companion, the stag, is demonstrated by his adoption of antlers, and sometimes cervine ears or hooves. His other intimate associate is the snake, frequently ram-horned, which wraps itself around his body and, at Cirencester, actually merges with the image of the god himself. The snake was a symbol of renewal or regeneration; the stag, a wood-land animal, fast and aggressive in its sexuality. In many of his images, Cernunnos displays a role as god of abundance and fertility, with cor-nucopia, fruit, bowls of grain or money.

Above all, Cernunnos is lord of animals. In addition to his stag and snake, he is sometimes depicted in company with many differ-ent species of beast, wild and domesticated, all enhancing his sym-bolism as a god of wild and tamed nature, fecundity, and a Noah-like beneficence. His intimate rapport with the animal world is displayed above all by his image, whereby he is both man/god and beast.

In the *Faery Wicca* card, Cernunnos wears the torc around his neck. Torcs are Celtic neck rings indicative of high status when worn by individuals; they are frequently depicted around the necks of Celtic divinities. It is possible that the torc possessed intrinsic magickal and religious significance. He also holds up both his hands, making the Blessing of the Horned God, symbolizing the horns of balance, the right-hand path of the masculine and the left-hand path of the feminine, the marriage of polarities.

A gold chalice is held aloft by the pillar to the right of Cernunnos. This chalice symbolizes the "Holy Grail," which is considered to be the cup that Jesus drank out of at the Last Supper. The quest for it is featured prominently in the Arthurian saga, and is really not connected to Irish mythology. However, the origin of the idea of a quest for this magickal vessel lies in the original Celtic idea of the cauldron of abundance. This is the quest for the lost feminine (i.e., the Goddess), for to find the "grail" means to bring fertility back to the land. Here, the grail represents the fecundity connected to Cernunnos, as a god of the old religion, who becomes the devil of a new religion.

The Christos represents this new religion, in this case Christianity. In all his benevolent teachings, Christ never condemned the ancient traditions or Spiritual ways, but rather sought to become harmonized with them, by searching one's heart to attain to the highest law—the law of Love. Jesus stands with both hands raised in the hand signal known as the Blessing of Peace.

The pillar holding aloft the cross is representative of the Christian religion, here symbolized by the sword used by the crusaders to force the new religion on believers of different faiths.

Faery Lore

. . . King of the Tree of Life with its flowers, the space around which noble hosts were ranged, its crest and its showers on every side spread over the fields and plains of Heaven.

On it sits a glorious flock of birds and sings perfect songs of purest grace; without withering (with choice bounty rather) of fruit and of leaves.

Lovely is the flock of birds which keeps it, on every bright and goodly bird a hundred feathers; and without sin, with pure brilliance, they sing a hundred tunes for every feather. . . (Irish author, unknown; 988 C.E.).

While the children were playing with the rabbits an ancient, stalwart he-goat came prancing through the bracken. He was an old acquaintance of theirs, and he enjoyed lying beside them to have his forehead scratched with a piece of sharp stick. His forehead was hard as rock and the hair grew there as sparse as grass does on a wall, or rather the way moss grows on a wall—it was a mat instead of a crop. His horns were long and very sharp, and brilliantly polished. On this day the he-goat had two chains around his neck—one was made of buttercups and the other was made of daisies, and the children wonder to each other who it was that could have woven these so carefully. They asked the he-goat this question, but he only looked at them and did not say a word. The children liked examining this goat's eyes; they were very big, and of the queerest light-gray color. They had a strange, steadfast look and had also at times a look of queer, deep intelligence, and at other times they had a fatherly and benevolent expression, and at other times again, especially when he looked sidewards, they had a mischievous, light and airy, daring, mocking, inviting and terrifying look; but he always looked brave and unconcerned. When the he-goat's forehead had been scratched as much as he desired he arose from between the children and went pacing away lightly through the wood. The children ran after him and each caught hold of one of his horns, and he ambled and reared between them while they danced along on his either side singing snatches of bird songs, and scraps of old tunes which the Thin Woman of Inis Magrath had learned among the people of the Shee.

In a little time they came to Gort na cloca Mora, but here the he-goat did not stop. They went past the big tree of the Leprechauns, through a broken part of the hedge and into another rough field. The sun was shining gloriously. There was scarcely a wind at all to stir the harsh grasses. Far and near was silence and warmth, an immense, cheerful peace. Across the sky a few light clouds sailed gently on a blue so vast that the eye failed before that horizon. A few bees sounded their deep chant, and now and again a wasp rasped hastily on his journey. Other than these, there was no sound of any kind. So peaceful, innocent and safe did everything appear that it might have been the childhood of the world as it was of the morning.[31]

16

AN CLOGÁS
The Round Tower

Meaning

Free yourself from false pretense; take the risk of flying rather than falling; an enlightenment is at hand, one that will cause a paradigm shift in your thinking; don't lose heart; face the encroaching change.

Card Description

A figure stands at the top of a round tower, a portion of the side of stone crumbled away. The figure is preparing to launch himself from the tower. Appearing on his back is the iridescent outline of wings. At his feet lies a sword, with a crown circling the blade, and a broken chalice. The sky is stormy and hostile. Lightning flashes in the distance. Below, the land is boggy.

Oghams, Alphabets, and Symbols

For border oghams, see The Border Oghams of the Ancient Ones Cards on page 250.

Lakes and marshes were active foci of prehistoric European ritual, especially during the Celtic phase. It is not always easy to separate lakes from bogs because what is marshland in the present may originally have been a lake, when associated with Celtic ritual. Sometimes, though, it is possible to associate bogs with ritual activity. As was the case with lakes and rivers, bogs received offerings of rich and prestigious material, especially metalwork. Bogs possess the particular property of being dangerous and treacherous, with the ambiguity of seeming innocuous, like firm ground. Their ability to suck in and engulf the unwary who strayed into them must have given rise to the perception of bogs as possessing lives of their own with a perhaps malignant, supernatural power residing within them. These spirits had to be appeased and propitiated by means of gifts, both animate and inanimate. Many Irish cauldrons have been found deliberately deposited in marshy ground.

Round Towers were built as places of protection for fighting off invaders. Here, the round tower is breaking apart, and furthermore, seems to be built on "shaky" ground, such as bog land.

The Celts venerated all natural phenomena, acknowledging the behavior of the weather and storms as evidence of the supernatural power of the gods. Wherever the ground was hit by a thunderbolt was thereafter held sacred.

The broken chalice implies that mind and heart are at risk of being separated; the feminine principle in life is at risk of disappearing beneath the bogs forever to remain a hidden mystery of the past. The crown joined with the sword indicates that heads of state are inclined to rule by force rather than reason.

The jumping figure with the sprouting wings is symbolic of the Spirit of the true heart freeing itself from the atrocities that can and usually are produced when the heart is missing from power.

Faery Lore

It has broken us, it has crushed us, it has drowned us, O King of the star-bright Kingdom; the wind has consumed us as twigs are consumed by crimson fire from Heaven.

Cold is the night in the Great Moor, the rain pours down, no trifle; a roar in which the clean wind rejoices howls over the sheltering tower.

The choice earth has not covered, there will not come to the towers of Tara, Ireland of the many fields has not enfolded a man like the pure gentle Mael Mhuru.

There has not drunk bravely of death, there has not reached the fellowship of the dead, the cultivated earth has not closed over a sage more wonderful than he.[32]

Without embarking on a description of these ancient and graceful architectural objects, it may properly be asked, "Do they throw any light upon the question of religion in Ireland?"

The first inquiry will be as to the age of Round Towers in Ireland. If, as some authorities declare, they date from Christian times, they may be regarded as silent, so far as prior heathenism is concerned. If, however, as others contend, their structure and arrangement indicate a period of greater antiquity, they may tell a tale of pagan symbolism.

As writers of the twelfth century assure us that there were then no stone churches in Ireland, these buildings must, if Christian, have been raised since the Norman conquest of that island. Yet, as Marcus Keane informs us, "more than eight of the supposed sites of towers are associated with the names of fifth and sixth century saints, or of ancient divinities."

One has affirmed that a celebrated tower was built by the devil in one night. To this, Latocnaye says, "If the devil built it, he is a good mason." Others may still ask, "Who erected the rest?" While over a hundred are known to us now, their number must have been much greater formerly, if, as that ancient chronicle, the *Ulster Annals*, declares, seventy-five fell in the great Irish earthquake of 448.

We have been told that they were fire towers, belfries, watch towers, granaries, sepulchers, forts, hermit dwellings, purgatorial pillars, phallic objects of worship, astronomical marks, depositories of Buddhist relics, Baal fireplaces, observatories, sanctuaries of the sacred fire, Freemason lodges, and the like. They were Pagan and Christian, built long before Christ, or a thousand years after.

H. O'Brien, on the Round Towers, held that they were built by the Tuatha De Danann, and "were specifically constructed for a twofold purpose of worshipping the Sun and Moon, as the authors of generation and vegetable heat. I do deny that the Round Towers of Ireland were fire receptacles [but] in honor of that sanctifying principle of nature, emanating, as was supposed, from the Sun, under the denomination of Sol, Phoebus, Apollo, Abad, or Budh, etc.; and from the Moon, under the epithets of Luna, Diana, Juno, Astarte, Venus, Babia, or Batsee, etc."

Another authority compared the Irish towers to buildings found in India. He states, "Those temples were usually round, and some of them were raised to a great height. The lower part of an Irish Round Tower might have answered very well for a temple; that is, a place in which was an altar, on which the sacred fire was preserved, while the middle floors could have served as habitations for the persons employed in watching it. The highest part of the tower was an observatory, intended for celestial observations, as I think evidently appears from the four windows being placed opposite to the four cardinal points."

Simply said: no one knows.

17

RÉALTA DANA

Dana's Star

Meaning

Attune to the Stars above your head and align them to the stars within your body. Hear the sphere of melodies. Receive the wisdom and grace of Dana. Divine Love is waiting to flow through your crown, to illuminate you. Fear not the enlightenment of illumination.

Card Description

The elusive Star Goddess appears. Her hair is as the solar flames of the sun. Her diadem is made up of seven stars, the hyades. The blue-green sphere of earth is seen through her body. Yet she stands with one foot on solid land and one foot in a flowing stream.

Oghams, Alphabets, and Symbols

For border oghams, see The Border Oghams of the Ancient Ones Cards on page 250. The symbolism of this card is very simple, for here we see the cosmic consciousness of Dana manifesting into the material world and universe. She is the comet, the planets, the stars. She is the earth, the waters, the grass, the trees, the stones. She is all.

As Olivia Robertson instructs: "The Deities have Their own Bodies of varying colored radiations, stronger and more beautiful than anything we can imagine. Yet we and all other beings partake in Their Glory because we are all born of the Cosmic Mother. We project our shadow selves into incarnation in order to learn through experience. We develop discrimination and will power through choosing the good, and rejecting the evil."[33]

Faery Lore

"The Star of Beauty"

It dwells not in the skies,
My Star of Beauty!
'Twas made of her sighs,
Her tears and agonies,
The fire in her eyes,
My Star of Beauty!

Lovely and delicate,
My Star of Beauty!
How could she master Fate,
Although she gave back hate
Great as my love was great,
My Star of Beauty!

I loved, she hated, well,
My Star of Beauty!
Soon, soon the passing bell:
She rose, and I fell:
Soft shines in deeps of hell

My Star of Beauty![34]

An Oracle: *"Star Attunement"*

If you would find Me, look within yourself. Within you is space and time and all the stars that are. There is no star within My being that echoes not some hope, some dream, within each creature held within My Self. There is no distance in Me, no separation: am I not the Void of Space? All moves with perfect accord within My blackness: and in My manifestation is there Light.

Feel no fear. My life is eternal and so therefore are you! All that are, that shall be, are my children. When you think—you reflect My thoughts; and when you feel, you know the beating of My heart. The breath of Life is Mine and through this you live. Yet each of you is unique: if you were not so, you would not exist! Not one flower is like another. For in Me is perfect Origin. Show forth My grace in your ideas and work, in individual peculiarity. For why should I hold in My embrace so many stars, if only one would do. Laugh! I am too great for solemnity: too mighty for analysis—yet none of My children may be belittled. In My laughter is heard the happy music of the constellations.[35]

18

SEANCHAILLEACH
GEALACH CNOC
Old Witch
Moon Hill

Meaning

The dark night of soul is upon you. Time to re-evaluate your inner-most beliefs and come to terms with those that no longer resonate for you. In doing so, you find your inner light, a soft, gentle light not unlike that of the full moon light. The primeval witch is resurfacing. Awaken to ancient memories. Discover the mystery that is you.

Card Description

A black-gowned priestess stands in a stone circle outside an ancient cairn on Loughcrew. Her arms are raised to the Full Moon, as she enacts the ritual of Drawing Down The Moon. Overhead, the sky is alive with twilight.

Oghams, Alphabets, and Symbols

For border oghams, see The Border Oghams of the Ancient Ones Cards on page 250.

On the stone circle in which the priestess stands is found the symbol of the halo, which was considered to be carved on rock at a particular known latitude. From this, sometimes the season of the year, or even the time of day, that the design was copied from the skies can be discovered.

Halos around the sun (or moon) merely indicate the existence of ice crystals floating in the atmosphere. Occasionally even these days conditions favor ice crystal formation with accompanying halos that range from the simple to the complex. The suggestion being made is that a continuing ice crystal veil covered much of the earth during a long period following the last glacial epoch. Climatically, this ice crystal veil acted to ameliorate the weather. The seas were calm. Winds were low. Storms were virtually non-existent. This "canopy" of ice crystal clouds created much speculation upon ancient peoples, and was used to lead the investigation toward logical, and possibly insightful, conclusions.

The open first question regarding the ice crystal veil was—where is it now? And if one couldn't find it, when did it leave? Asked another way, when were halos last being observed and recorded? The answer varied:

- Boyne Valley (Ireland) halos were being recorded about 3300 B.C.E.
- Chinese voyages to Europe via a northern sea passage may have occurred about 2250 B.C.E.
- Stonehenge and Callanish were in use about 2000 B.C.E.
- The Swiss Lake villages were flooded about 1800 B.C.E.
- Halo patterns were copied by Egyptian artists about 1400 B.C.E.
- Celtic burials show halo patterns as late as 600 B.C.E.
- Vikings used Dragon boats for raids and voyages, C.E. 900.
- Chinese halo patterns are displayed on a dragon crown dating about C.E. 1100.
- Scientific halo drawings were being made in Europe about C.E. 1600.

The tenuous thread that ties these various presumed events together is the ice crystal veil that produced halos that are recorded in various ways by various people at various times. Considered as a scientific hypothesis, the evidence that exists at the moment can then be evaluated.

In considering this, there are two forms that are commonly found at megalithic sites in Ireland. One example shows a broken 220 degree halo. From the geometry of the "break" in the halo, we can deduce that the sun was precisely 18 degrees above the horizon at the time the drawing was made.

The second example shows two concentric halos, likely 220 and 460 degrees, respectively. Again, from the geometry of the "break" in the outer halo, we can deduce that the sun was approximately 34 degrees above the horizon when the drawing was made.

While there are a number of possible dates, directions, and times of day for some latitudes in Ireland, the first example (single broken halo) would occur at noon on December 21, looking due south. Does the outer double halo, outer ring broken, indicate noon on June 21? Not actually, for the sun would be well up in the skies. At latitude 530 N, the lower ring would be about 14 degrees above the horizon. So the broken double halo may represent an earlier date in the year, if the south-looking surmise is correct. Alternatively, the direction could be either westerly or easterly during the summer.

One of the powers portrayed or represented by the full moon is that of divination. The goddess Brigid is portrayed as learned in poetry and in divination and thus seems to become the patron goddess of divination. The Irish myths and sagas are full of prophecy and divination.

While most Irish mythology is filled with the veneration of the Sun Gods and Goddesses, and emphasis is placed on the solar year, there are obscure references made to the lunar magickal workings of the female Druids. However, no writings can be found on such practices, which lends itself to the understanding that lunar magick and ceremony was, perhaps, considered the most powerful of all Druidic magick and thus kept hidden. The only remnants found of such possible magick are the fifteen lunar oghams.[36]

Faery Lore

Greeting to you, gem of the night!
Beauty of the skies, gem of the night!
Mother of the stars, gem of the night!
Foster-child of the sun, gem of the night!
Majesty of the stars, gem of the night![37]

Though the Celtic cults of sun and sky are well attested, there is, by contrast, little evidence for the veneration of the moon. This is curious, for it is the major nocturnal luminary and is visibly very prominent in its changing form. Pliny (*Natural History XVI*, 95) alludes to a druidical rite concerned with bull sacrifice and mistletoe, which took place on the sixth day of the moon. He further states that the druids regarded the moon as a great healer.

The Druids attached more importance to the moon than to the sun, though this is often misunderstood because they did not celebrate any nocturnal ceremonies; all their services are said to have taken place in daylight. However, there were festivals on the day of the new moon, on the sixth day of the moon, and on the day of the full moon.

Also, a strong connection to the lunar mysteries exists through the Bardic ogham alphabet, as represented through the thirteen moon ogham, of which two moon months are assigned a second ogham and which account for the original fifteen ogham in the alphabet. Lunar magick has, even if obscurely, been linked to the cult of Macha (see Fíorcheart Macha, page 294).

To the Irish, the moon was but a form of the sun. At the Lucaid-lamh-fada, or festival of love, from August 1 to August 16, games were held in honor of the sun and moon.

At Inismore, or Church Island, in Sligo, in a rock near the door of the church, is a cavity called Our Lady's Bed, into which pregnant women going at full moon, and turning thrice round, with the repetition of certain prayers, fancied that they would then not die in childbirth.

Dr. Tomas De Bhaldraithe, the compiler of the modern Irish/English dictionary, contends that the moon bore a proper name, the name of a god, or more likely, a goddess, which was made a taboo name by the druids—never to be spoken or written by people. William Camden noted, in the reign of Elizabeth, that the Irish would kneel facing a new moon and recite the Lord's Prayer, indicating a remnant of pre-Christian worship. Only euphemisms were allowed, however, to refer to the moon. Today, *gealach* (brightness) is the popularly used word to name the moon. Other words exist as well—Old Irish contains *ésca* (*aesca*) and this word still survives in Manx as *eayst* but nowhere else. It is interesting to note that the word *éicse* was the word for wisdom, knowledge, poetry, and divination. It is, perhaps, interesting that the word seems so close to *éicse*, another form of *ésca*, which doubles not only for moon, but also for water.

19

GRAIN PÁISTE
The Sun Child

Meaning

You need to stand up for yourself by voicing your truth. The innocence of Spirit is required for you to dwell in paradise. Brightest of Blessings are upon you. Good health. The Gift of the Gods. Shine like the sun.

Card Description

A young child, dressed all in red, sits astride the back of a red mare, on a purple blanket edged with golden cord, bearing the Ailm ogham. The red mare is guiding the child deeper into the Garden of the Goddess, lush with flora. In the blue sky, a brilliant rising sun shines.

Oghams, Alphabets, and Symbols

For border oghams, see The Border Oghams of the Ancient Ones Cards on page 250.

On the horse blanket is the Ailm ogham; the Station of the Winter Solstice; Season of Rebirth. The elm tree is assigned Ailm. Elm has its station on the first day of the new solar year, the birthday of the Divine Child, also known as the extra day of the winter solstice. Ailm represents the god-like strength that one needs to rise above adversity, like the elm tree, to create a viewpoint from a higher level: the god-like capabilities of healing and perception of future trends.

Once again, the red mare is representing the Great Goddess, who is the Divine Mother of the Sun Child. The blue-eyed child dressed in red symbolizes the Spirit of the gods manifest. As a mortal child we are being reminded of the theme that frequently occurs in Irish mythology, that of reincarnation. Not only the gods could be born again or pass through different stages of existence, but mortals could also participate in this complex process. One of the most interesting reincarnation cycles is that of the swineherds Fruich and Nár, who go through various changes to emerge, in their final forms, as Finnbhenach and Donn, the two massive bulls who have their final clash in the closing stages of the *Táin Bó Cuailgne*.

Horse and child united signify that total peace and harmony can only be attained when Goddess and God reign side by side—only then can one enter Paradise.

The sun and Sun god are represented very simplistically, first by the sun and second by the child. The Celts perceived the presence of divine forces in all aspects of nature. One of the most important venerated natural phenomena was the sun, seen as a life giver, promoter of fertility and healing.

In Ireland, the Sun god was both masculine and feminine. Lugh was solar, as was the Insular goddess, Érié—in one legend, she is associated with a golden goblet, which symbolizes the sun:

Greeting to you, sun of the seasons, as you travel the skies on high, with your strong steps on the wing of the heights; you are the happy mother of the stars.

You sink down in the perilous ocean without harm and without hurt, you rise up on the quiet wave like a young queen in flower.

The circle of prosperity—symbolized by the sun—seems to be a survival of a Druidical ritual. The daily course of the sun, bringing about the alternation of light and darkness and the succession of the seasons, was the most immediate example of the natural order of the universe. In old Irish, the universe was seen as something circular and the words for universe, *cruinne* and *roth*, signified that concept. The circle of the universe served as the modus operandi for prosperity and increase, both spiritually and physically. To imitate the course of the sun, to go right-handed, was to perform a ritual to bring beneficial results.

Fire was carried deosil, or righthand-wise, around houses, corn, cattle, or people to ensure a beneficial result. In the early days of Christianity, it was recorded that women, after child bearing, would have a similar circle of fire inscribed around them and then around their infants before they were allowed Christian baptism. Similar processions of moving deosil around healing wells, sacred stones, cairns, or churches have also been noted and among Celtic fishermen one began a journey by sea by rowing the boat "sunwise," up until recent times.

Faery Lore

Lugh has already been described. He has more distinctly solar attributes than any other Celtic deity; and, as we know, his worship was spread widely over Continental Celtica. In the tale of the Quest of the Sons of Tureen, we are told that Lugh approached the Fomorians from the west. Then Bres, son of Balor, arose and said, "I wonder that the sun is rising in the west today, and in the east every other day." "Would it were so," said his Druids. "Why, what else but the sun is it?" said Bres. "It is the radiance of the face of Lugh of the Long Arm," they replied.

Lugh was the father, by the Milesian maiden Dectera, of Cu Chulainn, the most heroic figure in Irish legend, in whose story there is evidently a strong element of the solar myth.

The Irish sun gods, naturally enough, fought successfully in summer, and the Bards give many illustrations of their weakness in winter. Sun heroes were not precisely deities, as they were able to go down into the UnderWorld. Oengus, the young sun, whose foster father was Mider, King of the Faery, was the protector of the Dawn goddess Etain, whom he discreetly kept in a glass grainan or sun bower, where he sustained her being most delicately on the fragrance and bloom of flowers. His father was the great god Dagda.

Sun gods usually have golden hair, and are given to shooting off arrows (sunbeams). As a rule, they are not brought up by their mothers;

one, in fact, was first discovered in a pigsty. They grow very rapidly, are helpers and friends of humankind, but are engaged everywhere in ceaseless conflicts with the gods or demons of darkness.

The Irish sun gods had chariots. They indulged in the pleasures of the chase, and of fighting, but were more given to the pursuit of Erin's fairest daughters. Occasionally they made improper acquaintance with darker beings, and were led into trouble in that way.

Grian was the appellation of the sun, and Carneach for the priest of the solar deity. It has been affirmed by an Erse scholar that the Irish Coté worshipped the sun under forty different names. Dal-greine, or sun standard, was the banner of the reputed Fingal. Dagda was an Apollo, or the sun. He was also the god of fire.

Samhain, literally servant, is derived from *Sam*, the sun; so, samhan, like the sun. As the Irish Pluto, he is guardian of the dead. As such, he would receive the prayers for souls on Hallow Eve. The name of Bal-Sab proves that *Bal*, *Bel*, or *Beal* is the same as the Irish Samhan. Bal is the personification of the sacred fire become visible. The year, the work of Samhan, the Sun, was known as the Harmony of Beal. Samhan was that idol which the King of Ireland adored after the name of head of all the gods. Bel is also the sun in Irish. Bel-ain were wells sacred to the sun. The Irish vernal equinox was Aiche Baal tinne, the night of Baal's fire. The sun's circuit was Bel-ain, or Bel's ring. A cycle of the sun, or an anniversary, was Aonach (pronounced Enoch); and it is singular that we are told that the days of Enoch were 365 years.

Griann, Greine, Grianan, and Greienham have relations to the sun. The hill Grianan Calry is a sunny spot. The word *Grange* is from Griann. There is a Grianoir in Wexford Bay. The Grange, near Drogheda, is a huge cone of stones, piled in honor of the sun. Greane, of Ossory, was formerly Grian Airbh. As Graine, the word occurs in a feminine form. The beautiful story of Diarmaid, or Dermot, and Graine is clearly a solar myth. The runaway pair, pursued by the irate husband Finn Mac Cull, for a whole year, changed their resting place every night. One bard sings of "Diarmaid with a fiery face." The last Danann sovereign was Mac Grene. The cromlech on a hill of Kilkenny is known as the Sleigh-Grian, hill of the sun. The women's quarter of the dwelling was the Grianan, so called from its brightness. The cromlech at Castle Mary, near Cloyne, is Carrig-Croath, Rock of the Sun.

20

BREITHIÚNAS

The Judgment

Meaning

A grain of wheat is reaped in silence. The Teacher gives knowledge: the student through meditation receives what is given, and by inner understanding transmutes knowledge into wisdom. What was true is forever the truth, but knowledge manifests in different ways in the course of cycles. Look into the past and you will know the future, for the future lies buried in the past. The past through action in the present, brings about the future.

Card Description

In perhaps the most ominous card of the deck, we meet a gruesome scene depicting the Burning Times, in which three women are found in various stages of inquisition.

The woman to the left has been stripped and put in the block. There she awaits her torture. The woman to the right, now clothed, is on the stretching bed, in the process of torture. The central figure, the woman tied to the stake, has been found guilty and condemned to burn at the stake.

The flames of the fire rise into the sky, becoming the red mane of the Great Mother Goddess' hair. In Her agony, she keens for her tortured and murdered daughters. From Her mouth come two rainbows; above them Her Triple Sign. Seven yellow stars dance in Her etheric body above the three women.

Oghams, Alphabets, Symbols

For border oghams, see The Border Oghams of the Ancient Ones Cards on page 250.

The symbology of the European Burning Times is evident in this card and is used here to exalt the horrific judgments once used by absolute power in an age of unreason and insanity. Witchcraft was a rarity in Ireland, and the dealings with it were really very few compared to the scourge that flashed through England and the Continent. The Irish had their own superstitious beliefs and did believe in the cunning ones and the power of the Faery. Dealings with the unseen were not originally regarded as an offense against the laws of the Catholic Church, God, or man, and had the auspices of custom and antiquity.

However, in time the inquisition crossed the channel and hit Ireland. Faery-Faith practitioners were then stigmatized as heretics and associates of the Church's evil god, Satan, held no role in the Faery-Faith beliefs. The Protestants who dwelled in Ireland soon acted similarly to the Roman Catholic Church because of the Holy Writ, which contained the grim command "Thou shalt not suffer a witch to live."

We are reminded here not to forget the ancestors who died for their belief in the natural world, the Old One, and most importantly, for Goddess.

The Great Mother Goddess is portrayed in the act of keening. Her keening brought forth Her Triple Sign: the waxing crescent, full moon, waning crescent, and the double rainbow. Her Triple Sign represents the moon's phases, indicating that She will always be present and not far away. All one need do is gaze upon Her luminous face to reconnect with Her soul. The double rainbow is a sign of Her covenant. While She did not stand in the way of human will and choice, She reminds us that true glory is found in the natural world, and no matter how hard some humans try to sever another human's connection and commitment to the supernatural, She was in the beginning, and She will be in the end.

The seven stars found scattered in Her luminescent body are there to remind us of Her wisdom. If one meditates on the heavenly seven sisters, pleideas, or the hyades, Her wisdom will flow down into their crown chakra, illuminating the stars within the physical body.

The fire flame is symbolic of the Ordeal by Fire. Purification by fire for body and soul, and assimilation thereby to the purest essence of the universe, were the fundamental ideas of a creed—the infallible means of the highest and most acceptable apotheosis. From the earliest of time, the sun has been the object of human adoration. But the common flame itself, being destructive, yet beneficial, while ever mounting upward as if disdaining earth contact, became with most races of humankind a religious emblem.

The sanctity of Irish places for fire was notorious. The ancient lighting of fires was attended with solemn ceremonies. Ireland had her perpetual fire at Kildare, known as Brigid's Flame. The Daughters of the Fire were Inghean au dagha, and as fire-keepers they were Breochwidh. Even after Brigid was turned into a saint, her nuns maintained a constant flame in Kildare, until the Archbishop of Dublin, in 1220, shocked at this revival of fire worship, under the mask of Christianity, ordered the Kildare fire to be extinguished. It was, however, relighted, and duly maintained, until the suppression of the nunnery in the reign of Henry VIII. As an old poet sang:

The bright lamp that shone in Kildare's holy fane,
And burned through long ages of darkness and stain.

The Brigid's Flame has been restored in the late twentieth century, by the Brigideen sisters at Kildare today. The Goddess is still alive. Brigid once again takes Her place of honor.

Faery Lore

A word must be said here about the ancient laws, for this is a card giving testimony to judgment. The earliest form of law, known as the Geis (*geasa*—a prohibition or taboo),was the prime power placed in the hands of the Druids, both male and female, to give authority to their edicts.

Druids could pronounce the *glam dicín* or the *geis* to assert their authority. The geis was primarily a prohibition placed on a particular person and since it influenced the whole fate of that person it was not imposed lightly. Anyone transgressing a geis was exposed to the rejection of their society and placed outside the social order. Transgression could bring shame and outlawry and could also bring a painful death. The power of the geis was above human and divine jurisdiction and brushed aside all previous rulings, establishing a new order through the wishes of the person controlling it.

When Setanta was given the name Cu Chulainn (Hound of Culann) he was also given a geis never to eat the flesh of a dog. Trapped by his enemies, he broke the geis and this inevitably led to his death. Fergus Mac Roth's geis was the prohibition never to refuse an invitation to a feast and on this fact turned the tragedy of the fate of the sons of Usna. Conaire Mór was subjected to a whole series of complicated and independent geasa.

The glam dicín, like the geis, was only invoked by Druids and was a satirical incantation, directed against a particular person, which imposed an obligation. In short, it was a curse, which could be pronounced for infringement of divine or human laws, treason, or murder. Its pronouncement was feared as its victims had put upon them a sense of shame, sickness and death. The person subjected to the glam dicín was rejected by all levels of Celtic society.

Another method of exerting authority, available to all members of society, was the ritual fast—the *troscad*. As a legal form of redressing a grievance, this act emerged in the Brehon law system. The troscad was the means of compelling justice and establishing one's rights. Under law, the person wishing to compel justice had to notify the person they were complaining against and then would sit before their door and remain without food until the wrong-doer accepted the administration or arbitration of justice. "He who disregards the faster shall not be dealt with by God nor man . . . he forfeits his legal rights to anything according to the decision of the Brehon."

The troscad is referred to in the Irish sagas as well as laws, and when Christianity displaced the pagan religion, the troscad continued. We find St. Caimin fasting against Guaire the Hospitable, St. Ronan fasting against Diarmaid, even St. Patrick himself fasting against several persons to compel them to justice. Some people even fasted against the saints themselves to get them to give justice, and wives fasted against their erring husbands.

It is fascinating, as well as sad, that in the long centuries of England's sorry relationship with Ireland, the Irish have continued a tradition of the troscad, which has become the political hunger strike. One of the most notable Irish political hunger strikes was that of the Lord Mayor of Cork, Terence MacSwiney, also an elected Member of Parliament, who was arrested by the English administration in Cork City Hall and forcibly removed from Ireland to London's Brixton Prison. He died in Brixton on October 24, 1920, on the seventy-fourth day of his hunger strike. The troscad was never entered into lightly and always with full knowledge of the seriousness of the final intent.

In ancient times, the troscad was an effective means of someone of lesser social position compelling justice from someone of higher social position. Thus, Druids could fast against a king, even a man or woman in the lower order of society could fast against their chieftain.

At the Sacred Center—
Betwixt and Between

Ancient Ones Card 21

The Stillness of Center

As the Honorable Olivia Robertson, Arch-priestess of the Fellowship of Isis, tells us:

> The glory of Magic is that the Practitioner may attain co-creation with the Deities. The Magic Wand is the paint-brush, the Magic Circle is the canvas, and the pigments are living rays. The forms conjured may through Invocation become animated: and causes imagined within the mind may produce effects on many levels through the law of Octaves.[38]

Here is the understanding of the stillness of center wherein we find the final Ancient Ones Card—Fíodóir Bandia, the Great Weaver Goddess unveiled—once the Goddess-Hierophant robed in priestly attire. Now she stands forth naked as the invitation to an alternate reality.

Finally, the successful Initiate takes on the role of the Draoi, as an enchantress or magician, and is ready to guide a new Cuardaitheoir who quests for initiation, who will, along the way if she or he is lucky, receive one or more of the Gifts of Faery, which presents the neophyte with a new skill and symbol for deeper meditation as a magickal lesson from the Ancient Ones.

21

FÍODÓIR BANDIA

The Weaver Goddess

Meaning

The eye of the Great Weaver Goddess is found in our hearts; it sees everything that is perceptible in its right form, place, time, cause, and purpose—this is also known as our conscience. Study the counsel of other wise ones. In doing so you will come to know the saying of wisdom: "Take as an answer, I know, and I do not know, and try to understand it. One who possesses wisdom, will correct themselves, and will not stand in need of another."

Card Description

The Great Weaver Goddess stands among the stars and planets of the universe. She holds a distaff in her left hand; a loose thread weaves about her. She wears the exalted Star Crown, with crescent moons on either side. Around her neck is the five-pointed star—The Star of Knowledge. Both of her upper arms are tattooed with waves of spirals.

In each of the four directions, the seasonal ogham borders are illuminated with colored light. Behind the Goddess a rift appears in the material of the universe. This rift becomes a doorway, slightly open, an iridescent light—an OtherWorldly light—shines out from it.

Oghams, Alphabets, and Symbols

For border oghams, see The Border Oghams of the Ancient Ones Cards on page 250.

In this card, however, each of the seasonal ogham are illuminated with colored light. Ailm is illuminated with yellow light. Ohn is illuminated with red light. Ur is illuminated with blue light, and Eadha is illuminated with green light.

Yellow is symbolic of the east, spring, air. Yet, it is illuminating the Station of Winter. What this demonstrates is the connectedness between the directions, seasons, elements, etc. The north will guide us to the east. The winter will become the spring. Earth supports the air.

Red is symbolic of south, summer, fire. Yet, it is illuminating the Station of Spring, demonstrating that the east will guide us to the south. The spring will become summer. The air supports fire.

Blue is symbolic of west, autumn, water. Here it illuminates the south, summer, fire, continuing the connectedness that the other two have demonstrated: south will lead to the west, summer becomes autumn, fire supports water.

Finally, green is symbolic of north, winter, earth. Green illuminating the west demonstrates: west leads to north, autumn becomes winter, water supports earth.

The Star Crown indicates that the Weaver Goddess is also the Queen of Heaven. She is every Goddess—the star goddess, the moon goddess, the earth goddess, and so on—holding the distaff shows that she weaves the web of life. The thread becomes symbolic of the mother's umbilical cord. From this cord the baby is nourished.

The Star of Knowledge represents created matter, the world as we know it, consisting of the four elements, the fifth—ether—being the unifying element. The blue wave of spiral tattoos connect Her to the life-giving waters, of which the planet and our bodies are based on, as well as representing that She is the beginning and the end; She is the Three Circles of Existence; She is the All.

The doorway in the universe reminds us that ours is not the only universe. There are hundreds of millions of universes, some of which are located in alternate realities, and quite possibly paralleling, as well as overlapping, ours. She *is* the threshold into them all.

Faery Lore

I came from the Great World having my beginning in Annwn. With the particles of light, which are the smallest of all small things, did I make all corporal things, imbued with life. Yet one particle of light is the greatest of all great things, being no less than material for all materiality that can be understood and perceived as within the grasp of My power. And in every particle there is a place whole commensurate with Me, for there is not and cannot be less than I Am in every particle of light and I Am in every particle; nevertheless, I Am only one in number. On that account, every light is one, and nothing is one in perfect co-existence but what cannot be two, either in or out of itself. I created all corporal things in the twinkling of an eye, when existence and life, light and vision occurred.

I made the world with three substances: fire; nature; and finiteness. These were the three instrumentalities I used in making the world: will, wisdom, and love. My three principal occupations are: to enlighten the darkness; to give a body to nonentity; and to animate the dead. These three things I cannot be: unskillful, unjust, and unmerciful. These are the three principal temperaments of life: strength, vigor, and perception. These are the three principal properties of life: temper, motion, and light.

Truth is the sciences of wisdom preserved in memory by conscience. Justice is the art and office of conscience, regulated by reason, understanding and wisdom, considering and acting accordingly. The soul is My breath in your carnal bodies. Life is My Love.[39]

Spreads for Spiritual Development Using the Ancient Ones Cards

In this section we shall work with the Ancient Ones Cards when performing a reading, and in one case the four Ace Cards of the Element Cards will also be used. The followings spreads will focus on Spiritual evolution through gleaning information to enlighten our station in this current incarnation.

Two spreads are presented below, the Circles of Existence and the Tree of Trees. Both were designed for the individual who is leading a Spiritual life or is actively undergoing an apprenticeship in the Wiccan mysteries.

As discussed earlier, the Ancient Ones Cards can be used shamanically as meditational aides to guide one into deeper levels of inner knowing and health simply by contemplating the symbology of each card.

When performing the Ancient Ones spreads, a significator card can be utilized to anchor the querent's energy into the foundation of the reading, and is encouraged to be worked with here as a useful tool.

Circles of Existence Spread

This is a most challenging spread, for it is performed only once in your lifetime, which means you must be willing to accept the information received and dedicate the remainder of your life to remaining open to the experience of the lesson and the energy connected to your Spirit's state of evolution for this incarnation.

To perform this spread you will need one coin, crystal or a die to use for tossing. I do encourage you to perform this reading in sacred space at either a Full Moon or the Samhain Sabbat to receive optimum communication with divinity.

Figure 18, page 358, shows the twenty-two Ancient Ones Cards, including the Crann na Beatha Card and four Aces of the Element Cards laid out in the Circles of Existence symbol.

The circle layouts are as follows:

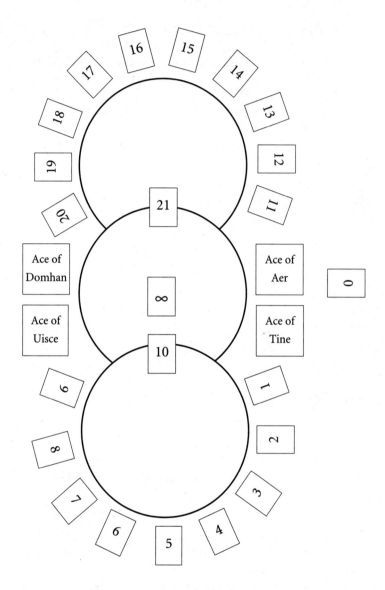

FIGURE 18. *Circles of Existence Spread.*

Top Circle: Circle of Ceugant represents infinity, the realm where there is neither animate nor inanimate, except Dana. This is Birth or Cosmos, also connected to the Heavenly Realm. The Ancient Ones Cards 11 through 21 are found here.

Middle Circle: Circle of Abred represents rebirth, the realm of Death and Rebirth. This circle is connected to the Plains. Here the four Aces of the Element Cards and the 00 Crann na Beatha Card are found.

Bottom Circle: Circle of Gwynvyd represents white life or the Circle of Perfection, the realm of absolute knowledge gained through experience. The UnderWorld is connected to Gwynvyd. Here the Ancient Ones Cards 1 through 10 are found.

You'll notice that the 0 Cuardaitheoir Card is placed outside the Three Circles, on the right side just before the Middle Circle. This card represents you or the querent. If desired, you could place your significator beneath the Cuardaitheoir Card. However, when you're ready to comprehend what stage of the evolutionary ladder you're operating on during this incarnation, you place yourself in front of the Cuardaitheoir Card, becoming the Seeker. Position yourself so that when you hold your arm out, your hand is directly over the Middle Circle.

Hold the dice, coin, or crystal in your hands. Close your eyes and focus all of your attention onto the reading. Connect with your Sacred Self. Connect with Deity. Pray to receive the knowledge of your evolutionary station in which you are living and learning this life. When you feel motivated to learn this truth, keeping eyes closed, hold your arm out. Your hand is directly over the Circles of Existence. Gently move your hand left-right-left-right, in a rocking motion.

As this motion becomes natural, continue to pray to Deity. Continue in this frame of mind until Deity opens your fingers, allowing the dice, coin, or crystal to fall—this will happen automatically. When this happens, open your eyes and see which Ancient Ones Card has been identified as your station.

Be very aware of the card before and after your card, because this card tells you two things:

- the card preceding yours indicates the focus of your past life, while,

- the card following yours indicates the karma which you will take with you when you leave this incarnation.

The Ancient Ones Card that is identified becomes your personal card, one which needs to be worked with for the rest of your living days.

Note that the dice, coin, or crystal must be touching only one card. If the dice, coin, or crystal falls between two cards or is not touching any card, then repeat the process. Repeat only three times. If no card has been identified on the third attempt, Deity is informing you that you are not quite ready to know this information. Accept this reality, and try again at another time.

The Tree of Trees Spread

Work this spread with only the Ancient Ones cards. After shuffling the cards, place a card in each of the positions. Interpret the cards accordingly (figure 19, page 362).

Position 1: This is the level of awareness from which you are operating at this time.

Position 2: This is the center of your Being at this time.

Position 3: This represents your understanding of the most exalted or Heavenly divinity of Great Weaver Goddess.

Position 4: This represents your understanding of the most exalted or Heavenly divinity of Bith or Cosmos.

Position 5: This represents the most pure reflection of Form or Feminine energy connected to Sacred Self.

Position 6: This represents the most pure reflection of Force or Masculine energy connected to Sacred Self.

Position 7: This is the level of connection to the Great Weaver Goddess you are capable of having at this time.

Position 8: This is the level of connection to Bith or Cosmos you are capable of having at this time.

Position 9: This is the manner in which the Great Weaver Goddess speaks to you if you are connected to Her.

Position 10: This is the manner in which Bith or Cosmos speaks to you if you are connected to Him.

Position 11: This represents the new understanding of nature your warrior Spirit is capable of learning through the guidance of the Great Weaver Goddess and Bith at this time.

Position 12: This represents the understanding of balance your warrior Spirit is capable of achieving through the guidance of the Great Weaver Goddess and Bith at this time.

Position 13: This represents the inner mysteries which your warrior Spirit is capable of learning through the guidance of the Great Weaver Goddess and Bith at this time.

Position 14: This represents the inner strength your warrior Spirit must achieve in order to undergo initiation by the Great Weaver Goddess and Bith at this time.

Position 15: This represents the Spirit Challenge the Morrigu is bringing to you.

Position 16: This represents the Spirit Challenge Lugh is bringing to you.

Position 17: This is the emotional balance needed to successfully undergo the Spirit Challenges.

Position 18: This is the mental balance needed to successfully undergo the Spirit Challenges.

Position 19: This represents an important message from the Faery Queen, which will aid you in your Spiritual deepening at this time.

Position 20: This represents an important message from the Faery King, which will aid you in your Spiritual deepening at this time.

Position 21: This represents an insight from your past life which you are awakening to in this life. This knowledge will allow you a deeper understanding into the lessons, challenges, and messages in this reading.

Position 22: This represents a glimpse of your future life which you can awaken to in this life. This knowledge can aid you in the integration process of the lessons, challenges, and messages in this reading.

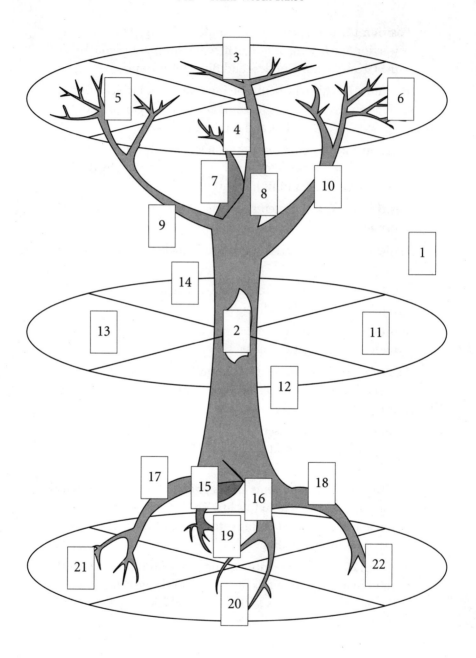

FIGURE 19. *Tree of Trees Spread.*

Part Four
Integration

Tuatha De Danann

LXV

68. *Though I should be reckoning the very pure kings*
    over the land of the assaults of mighty deeds,
    though I be relating tales of princess of Temair
    it will make me joyful and worthy of praise. . . .

71. *Though they be high kings of the . . . world,*
    with poet-power and with treasures,
    they are dead after the time of its youth,
    with pride and with trappings.

72. *Though these be the tales published*
    to people of the world of generations,
    their truth is known with witnesses
    according to rules and catalogues.

73. *The elders enumerated to the saints*
    before the scholars of the world of fortresses:
    as it was woven and verified
    it was written upon their knees. . . .

75. *Finntan saw it, who was the greatest,*
    it was for his love with which he would relate
    Tuan son of Cairell of hundreds,
    so that Findia came to him.

76. *Findia the very great, from whom it is known,*
    and Colum by whom it is composed,
    they are the persons to whom it will be traced,
    it is not concealed from every author.

77. *The authors of Ireland stitched it together,*
    they made mention of learning that they forsook not;
    the rule of every saying which they uttered,
    let them not neglect, and let them hear.

78. *Eochu ua Flainn the man of caution*
    who guards the clans of every assembly-place,
    to heaven is the shout which he sends forth
    according to the choice of youth and age.

> —*Lebor Gabala Erenn*
> Vol. XLI, Part IV, Sec. VII

Putting It All Together

When you are ready to weave all the cards together, your journey into the Land of Faery is ready to begin. This is the time when the Gift of Faery Cards become very important.

The Four Gift of Faery Cards

The Gift of Faery Cards have many uses, aside from their base meaning as described below. When used in conjunction with the lessons provided in the *Faery Wicca* book series, the Gift of Faery Cards would be worked with in the following ways.

Area of Perception

One of the four Gift of Faery Cards can be pulled to indicate the level of perception you are operating in. The Cards would be used as follows:

The Apple Branch Card represents the area of Thinking.

The Crane Bag Card represents the area of Willing.

The Hazel Wand Card represents the area of Feeling.

The Holy Stone Card represents the Apprentices.

Thinking is connected to the Mythological Cycle, the Tuatha de Danann. If the Apple Branch Card is pulled, your journey will take you into the Heavenly Realm.

Willing is connected to the Ulster Cycle, the Warrior Clans and Heroric Faery. If the Crane Bag Card is pulled, your journey will take you into the Plains.

Feeling is connected to the Fenian Cycle, the fianna and Medieval Faery. If the Hazel Wand Card is pulled, your journey will take you into the UnderWorld.

The Apprentice is connected to the now, Faery Wicca and the Faery Allies. If the Holy Stone Card is pulled, your journey will begin your apprenticeship in our world.

The Faery Fetch and Spiritual Benefactor

The Gift of Faery Cards can also be used to link you with a Faery Fetch.

The Apple Branch Card is linked to Beauty.

The Crane Bag Card is linked to Strength.

The Hazel Wand Card is linked to Ugliness.

The Holy Stone Card symbolizes the Spiritual Benefactor.

When working with the Gift of Faery Cards in this manner, it would be wise to perform a tarot reading, keeping in mind that your Fetch or Spiritual Benefactor has something to communicate to you.

Element Fairy Allies

The Gift of Faery Cards may also represent an Element fairy ally.

The Apple Branch Card is connected to the Air fairy ally.

The Crane Bag Card is connected to the Fire fairy ally.

The Hazel Wand Card is connected to the Water fairy ally.

The Holy Stone Card is connected to the Earth fairy ally.

When a Gift of Faery Card represents an Element fairy ally, the time has come to connect with this ally and learn from it.[1]

The Four Great Cities

Each Gift of Faery Card is related to one of the Four Great Cities, and, likewise, to one of the four De Danann treasures.

Card	City	Treasure
Apple Branch	Gorias	Dividing Sword
Crane Bag	Findias	Gae Bulga
Hazel Wand	Muirias	Undry
Holy Stone	Falias	Lia Fail

When worked with in this manner, special attention would then be given to the Element Suit connected to the city or treasure. A journey to the city would be greatly beneficial as provided in *Faery Wicca, Book Two*, for added insight into the message of the card.

OtherWorld Beings Found in the Great Cities

Finally, when the Gift of Faery cards are associated to a Great City it may very well be a token invitation from the OtherWorld Being encountered in the city.

The Apple Branch Card is connected to the Faery Guardian.

The Crane Bag Card is connected the Faery Companion.

The Hazel Wand Card is connected to the Faery Guide.

The Holy Stone Card is connected to the Faery Ally.

Faery Guardian will provide aid in gaining entrance into locked realms, as well as provide protection and a sense of security when journeying into the OtherWorld.

Faery Companion will help one move between elemental realms, as well as help the OtherWorld traveler overcome any sense of loneliness encountered during a journey.

Faery Guide will help one overcome obstacles encountered in the OtherWorld, as well as provide direction, when asked, during a journey.

Faery Ally will help one understand symbols, codes, or puzzles that may be encountered when traveling in the OtherWorld.

With these additional correspondences for the Gift of Faery cards one can easily incorporate their meaning into any tarot spread reading, which allows the four Gift of Faery cards to become a necessary and integral part of the *Faery Wicca Tarot*.

Let us review each Gift of Faery Card for further depth of meaning.

Gorías

THE APPLE BRANCH

Meaning

Entrance into the Land of Faery has now been granted to you. As you begin your journey therein, it will be important to be on guard for your own intentions imposed on self to overcome unrealistic goals. Self-sabotage can be easily realigned and turned into success, when the golden apples of Gorias are eaten. Meditate on the Star of Knowledge by cutting a golden apple in half, horizontally. The wisdom of the Great Weaver Goddess shall then flow into your crown, illuminating your mind and heart with clarity.

Card Description

This is the First Gift of Faery Card, one that is connected with the ancient teachings of Gorias. On a yellow background, there is a budding apple branch. To the bottom right are three golden apples.

Faery Lore

The apple branch is known to be the key into the Land of Faery; it is given to favored mortals by the Faery Queen. One of the best examples of lore is connected to the Voyage of Bran:

. . . When they were all gathered together in the palace, they saw a woman in a strange dress in the middle of the hall. Then she sang fifty verses to Bran (half of which are given here), while the company listened to them, and they all saw the woman:

"Here is a branch from the apple tree of Emhain, like those that are familiar; twigs of white silver on it, and crystal fringes with flowers.

There is an island far away, around which the seahorses glisten, flowing on their white course against its shining shore; four pillars support it.

It is a delight to the eye, the plain which the hosts frequent in triumphant ranks; coracle races against chariot in the plain south of Findargad.

Pillars of white bronze are under it, shining through eons of beauty, a lovely land through the ages of the world, on which many flowers rain down.

There is a huge tree there with blossom, on which the birds call at the hours; it is their custom that they all call together in concert every hour.

Colors of every hue gleam throughout the soft familiar fields; ranged round the music, they are ever joyful in the plain south of Argadnél.

Weeping and treachery are unknown in the pleasant familiar land; there is no fierce harsh sound there, but sweet music striking the ear.

Without sorrow, without grief, without death, without any sickness, without weakness, that is the character of Emhain; such a marvel is rare.

Loveliness of a wondrous land, whose aspects are beautiful, whose view is fair, excellent, without a trace of mist.

Then if one see Airgtech, on which dragon stones and crystals rain down, the sea makes the wave wash against the land, with crystal tresses from its mane.

Riches, treasures of every color are in Cíuin, have they not been found? Listening to sweet music, drinking choicest wine.

Golden chariots across the plain of the sea rising with the tide to the sun; chariots of silver in Magh Moy, and of bronze without blemish.

Horses of golden yellow there on the meadow, other horses of purple colour; other noble horses beyond them, of the colour of the all-blue sky.

There comes at sunrise a fair man who lights up the level lands, he resides over the bright plain against which the sea washes, he stirs the ocean so that it becomes blood.

There comes a host across the clear sea, to the land they display their rowing; then they row to the bright stone from which a hundred songs arise.

Through the long ages it sings to the host a melody which is not sad; the music swells up in choruses of hundreds, they do not expect decay or death.

Emhnae of many shapes, beside the sea, whether it is near or whether it is far, where there are many thousands of motley-dressed women; the pure sea surrounds it.

If one has heard the sound of the music, the song of the little birds from Imchíuin, a troop of women comes from the hill to the playing-field where it is.

Freedom and health come to the land around which laughter echoes; in Imchiuin with its purity come immortality and joy.

Through the perpetual good weather silver rains on the lands; a very white cliff under the glare of the sea, over which its heat spreads from the sun.

The host rides across Magh Moy, a lovely sport which is not weakly; in the many-coloured land with great splendor they do not expect decay or death.

Listening to music in the night, and going to Ildathach the many-colored land, a brilliance with clear splendor from which the white cloud glistens.

There are three times fifty distant islands in the ocean to the west of us; each of them is twice or three times larger than Ireland . . . . My words are not for all of you, though their great wonders have been told; from among the throng of the world let Bran listen to the wisdom expounded to him.

Do not sink upon a bed of sloth, do not let your bewilderment overwhelm you; begin a voyage across the clear sea, to find if you may reach the Land of Women."

Then the woman went from them, and they did not know where she went, and she took her branch with her.[2]

This is an invitation to visit the Land of Faery. In this song, she describes the many different lands that one can journey to, but as she indicates, the invitation is not for all, only for the few who are visited by the Faery and given the apple branch.

The three golden apples are connected to the story of Conn-Eda, known as the "Golden Apples of Lough Erne." In the story Conn is married to the Good Queen Eda. During their reign, all the lands were fertile and there was abundance—a sign that Conn was married to the goddess of the land. They had a son, whom they named Conn-Eda, after both his parents because the druids foretold at his birth that he would inherit the good qualities of both.

Eventually the Queen died, plunging her spouse, son, and all her people into a depth of grief and sorrow from which it was difficult to relieve them. After a year and a day of mourning, Conn took a new queen. But no matter how many children she gave Conn, it was clear Conn-Eda was his favorite son and the darling of the people. Eventually the new queen grew jealous. She consulted a henwife (enchantress). The henwife put a spell on a chess board, instructing the queen to invite Conn-Eda to a game, which the queen would win, and to wage as the prize that whoever won a game would be at liberty to impose whatever geis the winner pleased on the loser. When the queen won she was to bid the prince, under the penalty either to go into exile, or procure for her, within the space of a year and a day, the three golden apples that grew in the garden—which was an impossible task.

The queen won the game and imposed her geis on the prince. Who set out upon his task, but before so doing, he consulted his druid, who divined that the geis was intended for the prince's destruction. The Arch-Druid then gave him special instructions to follow. After some difficulty, but following the druid's instructions, he won the three golden apples by winning the favor of the guardians of the apples.

Upon returning, the queen was so upset that she threw herself from a tower and was instantly dashed to pieces. Conn-Eda planted the three golden apples in his garden, and instantly, a great tree bearing similar fruit sprang up. This tree caused all the district to produce an exuberance of crops and fruits so that it became as fertile and plentiful as the dominions of the Firbolgs, in consequence of the extraordinary powers possessed by the golden fruit. His reign was long, prosperous, and celebrated among the old people for the great abundance of corn, fruit, milk, fowl, and fish that prevailed during this happy reign. It was after the name Conn-Eda the province of Connaucht, or Conneda, or Connacht, was so called.

This myth symbolizes the overcoming of one's adversities that can and often is imposed upon them by their shadow self, which is usually an attempt to sabotage one's own success. When backed by the favor of the Faery Queen, all odds can be overcome.

Findias

THE CRANE BAG

Meaning

There is great protection being offered you from the Hag of the Temple. To receive this protection you must first willingly shape-change or metamorphose any ill-natured behavior within yourself, recognizing that self is not always the center of attention, or the center of the universe for that matter. Life does not always revolve around us, and we must curb our desire in thinking it does. A code of ethics is being taught, and true magick is the result.

Card Description

The green Crane bag, with a golden drawstring and black raven feather is set on a red background. Around the middle panel of the bag, in an ancient Irish alphabet, a word is beaded in red. A crescent moon and three stars appear on the top portion of the bag. On the lower portion of the bag are three symbols: white herringbone design, a red triple spiral, and a white and black spiral.

This is the Second Gift of Faery Card, one that is connected with the ancient teachings of Findias.

Faery Lore

I have a question for thee, Caoilte, man of the interchanged weapons: to whom did the good Crane bag belong that Cumhall son of Tréanmhór had?

A crane that belonged to gentle Manannan—it was a treasure of power with many virtues—from its skin, strange thing to prize—from it was made the Crane bag.

Tell us what was the crane, my Caoilte of many exploits, or, tell us, man, why its skin was put about the treasures.

Aoife, daughter of dear Dealbhaoth, sweetheart of Ilbhreac of many beauties—both she and Iuchra of comely hue fell in love with the man.

Iuchra, enraged, beguiled Aoife to come swimming, it was no happy visit: when she drove her fiercely forth in the form of a crane over the moor lands.

Aoife then demanded of the beautiful daughter of Abhartach: "How long am I to be in this form, woman, beautiful breast-white Iuchra?"

"The term I will fix will not be short for thee, Aoife of the slow-glancing eyes: thou shalt be two hundred white years in the noble house of Manannan.

"Thou shalt be always in that house with everyone mocking thee, a crane that does not visit every land: thou shalt not reach any land.

"A good vessel of treasures will be made of thy skin—no small event: its name shall be—I do not lie—in distant times the Crane-bag."

Manannan made this of the skin when she died: afterwards in truth it held every precious thing he had.

The shirt of Manannan and his knife, and Goibhne's girdle, altogether: a smith's hook from the fierce man: were treasures that the Crane-bag held.

The King of Scotland's shears full sure, and the King of Lochlainn's helmet, these were in it to be told of, and the bones of Asal's swine.

A girdle of the great whale's back was in the shapely Crane bag: I will tell thee without harm, it used to be carried in it.

When the sea was full, its treasures were visible in its middle: when the fierce sea was in ebb, the Crane bag in turn was empty.

There thou hast it, noble Oisin, how this thing itself was made: and now I shall tell its faring, its happenings.

Long time the Crane bag belonged to heroic Lugh Long-arm: till at last the king was slain by the sons of Cearmaid Honey-mouth.

To them next the Crane-bag belonged after him, till the three, though active, fell by the great sons of Mile.

Manannan came without weariness, carried off the Crane-bag again: he showed it to no man till the time of Conaire came.

Comely Conaire slept on the side of Tara of the plains: when the cunning well-made man awoke, the Crane bag was found about his neck.[3]

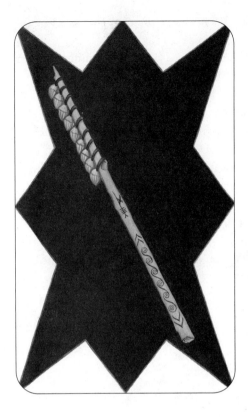

Muirias

THE HAZEL WAND

Meaning

The Tree of Life will and can materialize before you. When it does, climb the Spindal of Necessity, the shaman's ladder, either up or down. When you come to the doorway, don't be afraid to experience the mystic union of creation of the universe. If you hear the sound of bells, the Faery are calling you to remember them, to commune with them. The musical branch heralds the approach of a Faery co-walker, who can become your guide.

Card Description

This Third Gift of Faery Card is connected with the ancient teachings of Muirias. On a blue background is a hazel branch—the tree of wisdom and great inspiration—with nine hazel nuts attached to its male end. The female end is decorated with blue chevrons and connected spirals.

Faery Lore

Manannan, as a god-messenger from the invisible realm bearing the apple branch of silver, is externally, though not in other ways, like Hermes, the god-messenger from the realm of the gods bearing his wand of two intertwined serpents. In modern fairy lore this divine branch or wand is the magic wand of fairies; or where messengers like old men guide mortals to an UnderWorld, it is a staff or cane with which they strike the rock hiding the secret entrance.

The Druidic wand, *slat an draoichta* (rod of the Druid) such as the musical branch, was carried by the bards. They made their wands of divination from the yew tree; and like the ancient priests of Egypt, Greece, and Rome, they are believed to have controlled spirits, fairies, daemons, elementals, and ghosts while making such divinations. It will help us to understand how closely the ancient symbols have affected our own life and age—though we have forgotten their relation with the OtherWorld—by offering a few examples, beginning with the ancient Irish bards who were associated with the Druids. A wand in the form of a symbolic branch, like a little spike or crescent with gently tinkling bells upon it, was borne by them; and in the piece called *Mesca Ular* or *Inebriety of the Ultonians* it is said of the chief bard of Ulster, Sencha, that in the midst of a bloody fray he "waved the peaceful branch of Sencha, and all the men of Ulster were silent, quiet." In *Agallamh an dá Shuadh* or the "Dialogue of the two Sages," the mystic symbol used by gods, fairies, magicians, and by all initiates who know the mystery of life and death, is thus described as a Druid symbol: "Neidhe" (young bard who aspired to succeed his father as chief poet of Ulster), "'made his journey with a silver branch over him. The Anradhs, or poets of the second order, carried a silver branch, but the Ollamhs, or chief poets, carried a branch of gold; all other poets bore a branch of bronze."

Modern and ancient parallels are worldwide, among the most civilized as among the least civilized peoples, and in civil or religious life among ourselves. Thus, it was with a magick rod that Moses struck the rock and pure water gushed forth, and he raised the same rod and the Red Sea opened; kings hold their scepters no less than Neptune his trident; popes and bishops have their crosiers; in the Roman Church there are little wand-like objects used to perform benedictions; high civil officials have their mace of office; and all the world over there are the wands of magicians and of medicinemen and women.[4]

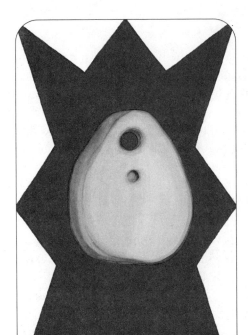

Falías

THE HOLY STONE

Meaning

If you are to attain to greatness, you must learn to speak to the Ancient Ones with poetic measure. Find the beauty in all that you see. Poetic art is in a person's body; for it is in their soul, and the soul is in the body.

Card Description

The final Gift of Faery card is connected to the ancient teachings from the realm of Falias. On a hunter-green background is a Holy stone, containing a cup design.

Faery Lore

The "hole"y stone was considered to be a stone placed on earth by the Tuatha De Danann. Such stones are usually small, no larger than the palm of the hand, with a perfectly round hole naturally bored through the stone. This stone, however, contains the symbol of the cup, like the cauldron of inspiration—as based on Amorgen's *Song of the Three Cauldrons*:

My own cauldron, cauldron of warming,
God-given from the mysterious elements;
ennobled is each belly from which pours forth the oral utterance.
Amorgen White-knee am I,
blue tattooed shank and beard of grey.
My cauldron of warming serves up
multiplicity of forms
and many-coloured verse.
Not equally does God distribute
gifts to each person:
but some inclined, some prone, some supine,
some empty, some half-full,
some full of knowledge like Eber and Donn,
creating their verse
with innumerable chantings,
in masculine, feminine, and neuter,
in signs denoting double consonants,
long vowels and short vowels;
thus is its function metrically declared,
by the votary of this cauldron.
I sing of the cauldron of knowledge,
whence the law of each art is dispensed,
which gives boundless treasure,
which magnifies each artist in general,
which gives each person its gift.[5]

Major Tarot Spreads
Using All the Cards

When using all eighty-three cards of the *Faery Wicca Tarot*, the messages received through divination will take you deeper into the spiritual forces and essence of all things visible and invisible. You will gain deeper insight into your spiritual evolution and develop a keen understanding of Little Self, ego, which will naturally deepen the connection between Sacred Self and the Great Weaver Goddess, She Who Weaves the Web of Life, or any Deity form with which one desires communion.

As already seen in the three previous sections, and as will be seen in this section, powerful spreads have been specially designed to reflect the ancient mystery teachings, and to enlighten our station in this current incarnation and spirit evolution, such as the Key Pattern and Circles of Existence spreads already discussed (pages 230 and 358), and the As Above-So Below Spread presented on page 383.

The Spirit Lesson spread will overview the querent's life at present, and for making changes the Choices spread will look at the pros and cons of each opportunity. The Wheel of the Year spread will present a pathway into the immediate future, and for individuals who are leading spiritual lives and actively undergoing apprenticeships, a shamanic meditation spread has already been provided to assist deepening.

The Spirit Lesson Spread

This spread helps define the spiritual lessons one is undergoing, highlighting areas you might need to give your attention (figure 20, page 381). Do not work with a significator in this spread. After shuffling the cards, cut the deck into three stacks. Close your eyes and focus on your female energy; your intuitive wisdom, the nurturer, caretaker, creative intelligence. When you feel connected, open your eyes and choose one stack. Pull one card from the stack and place it in the first position—your female energy.

Repeat the process, this time focusing on your male energy; your linear intellect, the protector, provider, builder, active wisdom. Choose one of the remaining two stacks and pull one card from the stack for position 2—your male energy.

Repeat the process by focusing on your sacred self; your connection to divinity, divine love, divine truth, divine wisdom, divine

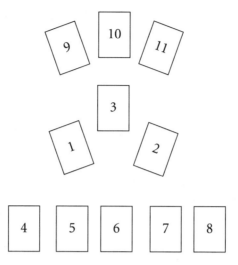

FIGURE 20. *Spirit Lesson Spread.*

understanding. Choose one card from the remaining stack for position 3—your sacred self.

Shuffle the cards together, cut once to the lesson you are currently
working on. Take the top five cards and place in positions 4, 5, 6, 7,
and 8.

Shuffle the remaining cards together, cut once to discover the Spirit
Challenge you are currently undergoing. Take the top three cards and
place in positions 9, 10, and 11.

Interpret the cards accordingly.

The Wheel of the Year Spread

This spread can be performed at any point in the year. I've found it to
be a great birthday reading. The major focus of each season will be
highlighted (figure 21, page 382). A Significator is useful in this spread.

> **Position 1:** This is the core energy for the year, representing the
> current season you are in. For the sake of clarity in explaining
> this spread, I will use the season of spring as the current season
> in this example.
>
> **Position 2:** This is the transition energy from spring into summer.
>
> **First Triad—Positions 3, 4, and 5:** This triad represents the sea-
> son of summer.

Position 6: This is the transition energy from summer into autumn.

Second Triad—Positions 7, 8, and 9: This triad represents the season of autumn.

Position 10: This is the transition energy from autumn into winter.

Third Triad—Positions 11, 12, and 13: This triad represents the season of winter.

Position 14: This is the transition energy from winter into spring.

Fourth Triad—Positions 15, 16, and 17: This triad represents the season of spring.

Position 18: This represents the energy that will become the core for the following year.

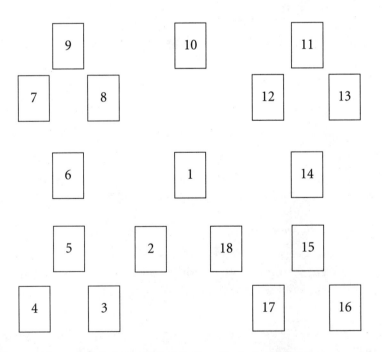

FIGURE 21. *Wheel of the Year (Projection) Spread.*

As Above-So Below Spread

This spread can be used to gain deeper understanding into information you might have received during a meditation or other journey work (figure 22). A Significator card is useful in this reading.

Shuffle the cards and focus on the unclear factor—such as a symbol—you are trying to gain clarity on. Draw cards for positions 1, 2, 3, and 4. Interpret the cards accordingly.

Shuffle the remaining cards and focus on how you might consciously integrate this clarity into your life. Draw cards for positions 5, 6, 7, and 8. Interpret the cards accordingly.

Shuffle the remaining cards and focus on a direction that was given to you by Deity or an OtherWorld Being with regards to the unclear factor. Draw cards for positions 9, 10, 11, and 12. See if these cards support the previous positions.

Finally, shuffle the remaining cards and focus on what you are being asked to learn by enacting this direction. Draw cards for positions 13, 14, 15, and 16. Interpret the cards accordingly.

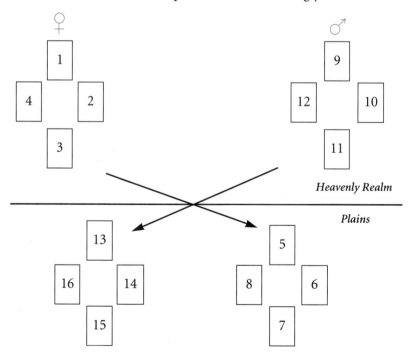

FIGURE 22. *As Above-So Below Spread.*

Choices Spread

When you find yourself in a situation where a decision must be made, this spread will provide insight. Lay the cards out in the order shown in figure 23, page 385. A significator card is useful here.

Group A

Card 1: Represents the querent's nature of the situation.

Card 2: Represents the querent's personality.

Card 3: Represents the nature of the circumstances.

Group B

Cards 4, 8, and 12: These cards represent the potential future events and influences in the direction the querent's life will naturally take unless changes are employed.

Group C

Cards 5, 9, and 13: These cards represent the alternative course of action querent may choose.

Group D

Cards 6, 10, and 14: These cards represent the psychological basis and implications of the situation to assist the querent in making the correct decision.

Group E

Cards 7, 11, and 15: These cards represent the forces at work that are beyond the querent's control or destiny; karma—querent must be able to adapt and learn from them.

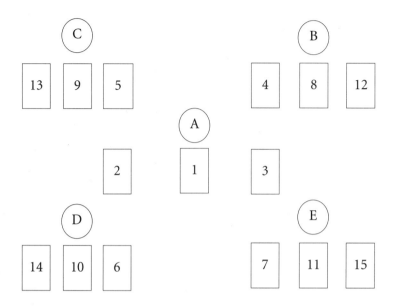

FIGURE 23. *Choices Spread.*

Know Thy Self

No matter what our spiritual orientation or our religious philosophies may be, Deity has a Divine Plan. Whether we can ever know the full extent of such a Plan, we can do our best to open our hearts to receiving an essence of such divinity. This Divinity can be brought to conscious awareness through the art of divination. Divination is experienced whenever tarot readings are endeavored. Tarot readings help us understand our lives, the cards can be used as a tool for personal transformation.

My wish is that you see and recognize such a tool in the *Faery Wicca Tarot*, and eagerly study each card to gain deeper insight for Self. On your spiritual journey: "May the Road Always Rise Up To Greet You! Deep Peace and Blessings Be! Slan Agát."

Seasoning Ritual for the Faery Wicca Tarot Cards

Energizing Your Tarot Deck as a Tool of Spiritual Transformation

When preparing to season the *Faery Wicca Tarot* Cards, it will be important to decide how you intend to use the cards—for yourself only, for other people, or for yourself and other people.

Gather together the following items: a special scarf, pouch, or wooden box in which the cards will be stored; a smudge stick or cleansing incense such as the one listed in *Faery Wicca, Book Two*, page 228; a white candle; and crushed lepidolite for its spiritual vibration (optional).

When you're ready, smudge yourself and the cards or burn the cleansing incense. Light the candle. Sprinkle lepidolite over your hands. Pick up your cards and begin shuffling them while chanting: "Domhan, Aer, Tine, Uisce," over and over, in any order. You are enacting the creation process itself: the mixing and ordering of the elements of the universe, while invoking the Elemental Spirits of which humans themselves are composed. Water creates the bloodstream, fire is our vital heat, earth is our flesh, and air is our breath.

When the cards feel right, bring them to your lips while toning "Ma"—the sound of Creation. By doing this, you are imposing order on primal chaos by forming the elements out of the Great Mother's magick syllables joined together by the Mother's syllable of "intelligence."

Hold the cards to your heart, and pray to your Deity, asking that the cards be blessed for use in the manner you've chosen as your intent above, as a tool for spiritual transformation. Blow your breath of Spirit upon the cards and recite:

Thou art water,
Thou art earth,
Thou art fire,
Thou are air,
Thou art the void and
Thou art the Supreme Divinity.

Bring your cards once more to your lips and kiss them. Blessed Be! Your cards are now seasoned and ready for use.

As a cartomancer (diviner by cards) remember that each time you work with the cards you are enacting the oldest theory applied to them: The mystic power of Great Weaver Goddess guides the shuffling and dealing of the cards so that the resulting layout will yield a meaningful message when *properly* interpreted.

Endnotes

Introduction
1. *Lebor Gabala Erenn*, Vol. XLI, Sec. VII, v. 306, p. 109.
2. Olivia Robertson, *Gaea: Initiations of the Earth*, Cesara Press.

Part One
1. For further information on oghams, refer to Kisma Stepanich, *Faery Wicca, Book One*, Llewellyn Publications, 1994, and Stepanich, *Faery Wicca, Book Two*, Llewellyn Publications, 1995.
2. Refer to Stepanich, *Faery Wicca, Book One* and *Faery Wicca, Book Two* for information on the Lunar, Solar, and Stellar Realms.

Part Two
1. T. W. Rolleston, *Celtic*, Senate, 1994 and Lady Gregory, *Gods and Fighting Men* Colin Smythe Ltd., 1976.
2. Cross and Slover, *Ancient Irish Tales*, Henry Holt and Company, Inc., 1936, and Rolleston, *Celtic*.
3. Stepanich, *Faery Wicca, Book One*; Gregory, *Gods and Figting Men*; and Rolleston, *Celtic*.
4. Rolleston, *Celtic*.
5. Gregory, *Gods and Fighting Men*
6. "The Voyage of Bran, Son of Febal, To the Land of the Living" Alfred Nutt, ed., London: published by David Nutt in the Strand, 1895.
7. Cross and Slover, *Ancient Irish Tales*. Cross and Slover have taken this tale from an eighth century manuscript. Although they do not give the manuscipt title, I believe that it is *Lebor na hUidre*, familiarly known as *The Book of the Dun Cow*, which was compiled in the monastery of Clonmacnoise in the twelfth century. Today, we know this book as *Táin Bó Cuailnge*, eleventh century.
8. Stepanich, *Faery Wicca Book One*, and O'Faolain, *Irish Sagas and Folk Tales* Oxford University Press, 1954.
9. Now Lusk, a village on the coast a few miles north of Dublin.
10. Cross and Slover, *Ancient Irish Tales*. Cross and Slover have taken this tale from an eighth century manuscript. Although they do not give the manuscipt title, I believe that it is *Lebor na hUidre*, familiarly known as *The Book of the Dun Cow*, which was compiled in the monastery of Clonmacnoise in the twelfth century. Today, we know this book as *Táin Bó Cuailnge*, eleventh century.
11. For more information, see the Gift of the Faery card: The Apple Branch, page 368.

12. Cross and Slover, *Ancient Irish Tales*. Cross and Slover reprinted this tale from the eleventh century manuscript *The Colloquy of the Old Men*.
13. McGarry, *Great Folk Tales of Old Ireland*. Bell Publishing Company, 1922.
14. A *cumal* was the unit of value in Celtic Ireland. It is meant to be the price of a woman slave.
15. Rolleston, *Celtic*. Rolleston has taken this tale, verbatim, from *Táin Bó Cuailnge*, eleventh century.
16. Squire, *Celtic Myth and Legend*.
17. Rolleston, *Celtic*. Rolleston has taken this tale, verbatim, from *Táin Bó Cuailnge*, eleventh century.
18. *Lebor Gabála Erenn*, vol. XLIV, part V, and De Jubainville, *Cycle Mythologique Irlandais*, vol. ii. Paris: n.p., 1884.

Part Three

1. For more information on the Transmigration of Souls, refer to Stepanich, *Faery Wicca, Book One* and *Book Two*.
2. Note that the cards of each companion group will add up to the number 20, which breaks down into a 2; the vibration of partnership: right-hand path + left-hand path, male and female, god and goddess, matter/spirit, reason/inspiration, conscious/subconscious, that when joined creates a perfect union that functions forever inseaparably.
3. For more information on Celtic Numerology refer to Stepanich, *Faery Wicca, Book One*.
4. W. B. Yeats, source unknown.
5. In *The Lives of the Irish Saints*, eleventh century manuscript.
6. Dames, *Mythic Ireland*, Thames and Hudson, 1992.
7. Rolleston, *Celtic*.
8. Macleod, *The Book of the Opal*, Duffield and Company, 1895.
9. Stephens, *The Crock of Gold*, The Macmillan Company, 1913.
10. Macleod, *The Dominion of Dreams*, Duffield and Company, 1895.
11. Robertson, *The Handbook of The Fellowship of Isis*, Cesara Publications, 1980.
12. Macleod, *The Dominion of Dreams*.
13. Kennedy and Smyth, *Irish Mythology, Visiting The Places*, Morrigan Books, 1989.
14. Ellis, *The Druids*, William B. Eermans Publishing Company, 1994.
15. Refer to *Faery Wicca, Book Two*.
16. Refer to *Faery Wicca, Book One*, for a study on the Three Circles of Existence.
17. Stephens, *The Crock of Gold*.
18. Rolleston, *Celtic*.
19. Mac Cuill means Son of the Hazel, or whose god was the hazel or whose

god was the sea. He represented the primoridal water element.

20. Sharp, *Under The Dark Star*, Stone and Kimball, 1895.
21. Rolleston, *Celtic*.
22. Rolleston, *Celtic*.
23. This is the apparent sense of the words of the concluding lines, but we can only conjecture that they refer to spells for the healing of poisoned wounds, and for securing favourable winds—both of which become necessities in the course of the Milesian invasion.
24. *Lebor Cabála Erenn*, Vol. XLIV, Part V.
25. De Jubainville, "Irish Mythological Cycle," p. 191.
26. Yeats, *Irish Fairy and Folk Tales*.
27. From the Irish, by Clarence Mangan.
28. As of September 1997, the Teltown mound was unfortunately plowed under by a new landowner.
29. To many, this tale is that of the sighting of a UFO, and intercourse with aliens.
30. Macleod, *The Domionion of Dreams*.
31. Stephens, *The Crock of Gold*.
32. Jackson, *A Celtic Miscellany*, Routledge and Kegan Paul, 1951.
33. Robertson, *Sybil: Oracles of the Goddess*, Cesara Publications, n.d.
34. Macleod, *The Dominion of Dreams*.
35. Robertson, *Sybil*.
36. Based on the author's own magickal practices and research on the lunar oghams, she is currently working on a forthcoming book dealing with this subject matter.
37. A traditional Gaelic folk prayer.
38. I would like to acknowledge Olivia Robertson's *Urania: Ceremonial Magic of the Goddess*, who so eloquently deals with the lessons of the neophyte through the major arcana of the tarot.
39. *Barddas*, Longman and Co., 1862 (Ed.).

Part Four

1. Refer to Stepanich, *Faery Wicca, Book One* for the Faery Ally Journeys.
2. Irish, author unknown, seventh–eighth century original.
3. *Duanaire Fionn (The Book fo the Lays of Fionn)*, edited and translated by Eoin Macneill. David Nutt, London, 1908.
4. Evans-Wentz, *The Fairy Faith in Celtic Countries*, Oxford University Press, 1911.
5. Matthews, *The Encycloapedia of Celtic Wisom: A Celtic Shaman's Sourcebook*.

Bibliography

Bhreathnach, Edel. *Tara*. Dublin: Stationary Office, 1995.

Bonwick, James. *Irish Druids and Old Irish Religions*. Dorset Press, 1986.

Campbell, Florence. *Your Days Are Numbered*. DeVorse and Company, 1931.

Cicero, Chic, and Sandra Tabatha Cicero. *The New Golden Dawn Tarot*. Llewellyn, 1991.

Cross and Slover. *Ancient Irish Tales*, Henry Holt and Company, Inc. 1936.

Cyr, Donald (ed.). *Celtic Secrets*. Stonehenge Viewpoint, 1980.

Dames, Michael. *Mythic Ireland*. Thames and Hudson, 1992.

Duanaire Fionn (The Book of the Lays of Fionn), ed. and trans. by Eoin Macneill, David Nutt, London, 1908.

Eakins, Pamela, Ph.D. *Tarot of the Spirit*. Samuel Weiser, Inc., 1992.

Ellis, Peter Berresford. *Dictionary of Celtic Mythology*. ABC-CLIO, Inc., 1992.

———. *The Druids*. William B. Eerdmans Publishing Company, 1994.

Evans-Wentz, W. Y. *The Fairy Faith In Celtic Countries*. Oxford University Press, 1911.

Green, Miranda. *Dictionary of Celtic Myth and Legend*. Thames and Hudson, 1992.

Jackson, Kenneth Hurlstone. *A Celtic Miscellany*. Routledge and Kegan Paul, 1951.

Javane, Faith and Dusty Bunker. *Numerology and The Divine Triangle*. Whitford Press, 1979.

Kennedy and Smyth. *Irish Mythology, Visiting The Places*, Morrigan Books, 1989.

Lady Gregory. *Gods and Fighting Men*. John Murray, 1904.

Edited and Translated by R.A. Stewart MacAlister. *Lebor Gabála Erenn*, 5 Vols. The Educational Company of Ireland, Ltd., 1941.

Logan, Patrick. *The Holy Wells of Ireland*. Colin Smythe Limited, 1980.

Macleod, Fionna (William Sharp). The Book of the Opal. Duffield and Company, 1895.

————. *The Dominion of Dreams*. Duffield and Company, 1895.

Matthews, John and Caitlin. *The Encyclopaedia of Celtic Wisdom: A Celtic Shaman's Sourcebook*. Element Books Ltd., 1994.

————. *The Celtic Reader*. Aquarian/Thorsons, 1991.

McMann, Jean. *Loughcrew: The Cairns*. After Hours Books, 1993.

McGarry, Mary. *Great Folk Tales of Old Ireland*. Bell Publishing Co., 1922.

O'Faolain, Eileen. *Irish Sagas and Folk-Tales*. Oxford University Press, 1954.

Roberts, Jack. *The Sacred Mythological Centres of Ireland*. Bandia Design, 1996.

Robertson, Olivia. *Urania: Ceremonial Magic of the Goddess*. Cesara Publications, 1983.

————. *Sybil: Oracles of the Goddess*. Cesara Publications, 1989.

————. *The Handbook of The Fellowship of Isis*, Cesara Publications, no date.

Rolleston, T. W. *Celtic*, Senate, 1994.

Sharp, William (Fionna Macleod). *Under The Dark Star*, Stone and Kimball, 1895.

Squire, Charles. *Celtic Myth and Legend*. Newcastle Publishing Co., Inc., 1975.

Stepanich, Kisma. *Faery Wicca, Book One*. Llewellyn Publications, 1994.

————. *Faery Wicca, Book Two*. Llewellyn Publications, 1995.

Stephens, James. *The Crock of Gold*. New York: The Macmillan Company, 1913.

The Táin Bó Cualnge, The Ancient Irish Epic Tale. Translated by Joseph Dunn. London: David Nutt, 1914.

Thomas, N. L. *Irish Symbols of 3500 B.C.* Mercier Press, 1988.

Wang, Robert. *The Qabalistic Tarot*. Samuel Weiser, Inc., 1983.

Yeats, W. B. *Irish Fairy and Folk Tales*. London: Walter Scott, 1893.

Index

☽ LOOK FOR THE CRESCENT MOON

Llewellyn publishes hundreds of books on your favorite subjects! To get these exciting books, including the ones on the following pages, check your local bookstore or order them directly from Llewellyn.

ORDER BY PHONE

- Call toll-free within the U.S. and Canada, 1-800-THE MOON
- In Minnesota, call (612) 291-1970
- We accept VISA, MasterCard, and American Express

ORDER BY MAIL

- Send the full price of your order (MN residents add 7% sales tax) in U.S. funds, plus postage & handling to:

  Llewellyn Worldwide
  P.O. Box 64383, Dept. K696-3
  St. Paul, MN 55164–0383, U.S.A.

POSTAGE & HANDLING

(For the U.S., Canada, and Mexico)

- $4.00 for orders $15.00 and under
- $5.00 for orders over $15.00
- No charge for orders over $100.00

We ship UPS in the continental United States. We ship standard mail to P.O. boxes. Orders shipped to Alaska, Hawaii, The Virgin Islands, and Puerto Rico are sent first-class mail. Orders shipped to Canada and Mexico are sent surface mail.

International orders: Airmail—add freight equal to price of each book to the total price of order, plus $5.00 for each non-book item (audio tapes, etc.).

Surface mail—Add $1.00 per item.

Allow 4–6 weeks for delivery on all orders.
Postage and handling rates subject to change.

DISCOUNTS

We offer a 20% discount to group leaders or agents. You must order a minimum of 5 copies of the same book to get our special quantity price.

FREE CATALOG

Get a free copy of our color catalog, *New Worlds of Mind and Spirit*. Subscribe for just $10.00 in the United States and Canada ($30.00 overseas, airmail). Many bookstores carry *New Worlds*— ask for it!

Visit our web site at www.llewellyn.com for more information.

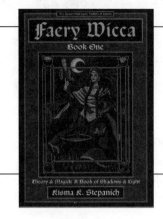

Faery Wicca, Book One

Theory & Magick
A Book of Shadows & Lights

Kisma K. Stepanich

Many books have been written on Wicca, but never until now has there been a book on the tradition of Irish Faery Wicca. If you have been drawn to the kingdom of Faery and want to gain a comprehensive understanding of this old folk faith, *Faery Wicca* offers you a thorough apprenticeship in the beliefs, history and practice of this rich and fulfilling tradition.

First, you'll explore the Irish history of Faery Wicca, its esoteric beliefs and its survival and evolution into its modern form; the Celtic pantheon; the Celtic division of the year; and the fairies of the Tuatha De Danann and their descendants. Each enlightening and informative lesson ends with a journal exercise and list of suggested readings.

The second part of *Faery Wicca* describes in detail magickal applications of the basic material presented in the first half: Faery Wicca ceremonies and rituals; utilizing magickal Faery tools, symbols and alphabets; creating sacred space; contacting and working with Faery allies; and guided visualizations and exercises suitable for beginners.

This fascinating guide will give you a firm foundation in the Faery Wicca tradition, which the companion volume, *Faery Wicca, Book Two: The Shamanic Practices of the Cunning Arts*, builds upon.

1–56718–694–7, 7 x 10, 320 pp., illus., softbound $19.95

To order, call 1–800–THE MOON
Prices subject to change without notice

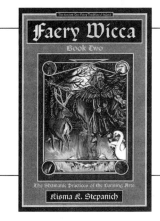

Faery Wicca, Book Two

The Shamanic Practices
of the Cunning Arts

Kisma K. Stepanich

Faery Wicca, Book Two continues the studies undertaken in *Faery Wicca, Book One*, with a deepening focus on the tradition's shamanic practices, including energy work, the Body Temple, healing techniques and developing Second-Sight; meditation techniques; journeys into the Otherworld; contacting Faery Guardians, Allies, Guides and Companions; herbcraft and spellcasting; different forms of Faery divination; rites of passages; the four minor holidays; and a closing statement on the shamanic technique known as "remembering."

The Oral Faery Tradition's teachings are not about little winged creatures. They are about the primal earth and the power therein, the circles of existence, Ancient Gods, the ancestors and the continuum. *Faery Wicca, Book Two* is not a how-to book but a study that provides extensive background information and mystery teachings for both novices and adepts alike.

1-56718-695-5, 352 pp., 7x10, illus., softcover $19.95

To order, call 1–800–THE MOON
Prices subject to change without notice

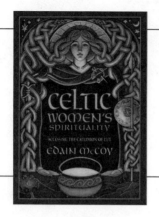

Celtic Women's Spirituality

Accessing the Cauldron of Life

Edain McCoy

Every year, more and more women turn away from orthodox religions, searching for an image of the divine that is more like themselves—feminine, strong and compelling. Likewise, each year the ranks of the Pagan religions swell, with a great many of these newcomers attracted to Celtic traditions.

The Celts provide some of the strongest, most archetypally accessible images of strong women onto which you can focus your spiritual impulses. Warriors and queens, mothers and crones, sovereigns and shapeshifters all have important lessons to teach us about ourselves and the universe.

This book shows how you can successfully create a personalized pathway linking two important aspects of the self—the feminine and the hereditary (or adopted) Celtic—and as a result become a whole, powerful woman, awake to the new realities previously untapped by your subconscious mind.

1-56718-672-6, 7 x 10, 352 pp., illus. $16.95